American Klezmer

American Klezmer

Its Roots and Offshoots

Edited by
Mark Slobin

UNIVERSITY OF CALIFORNIA PRESS
Berkeley · Los Angeles · London

Chapter 6 was originally published in *Ethnomusi-cology* 38:1 (Winter 1994). Copyright 1994 by the Board of Trustees of the University of Illinois. Used with the permission of the University of Illinois Press.

Chapter 8 was adapted from Henry Sapoznik, *Klezmer!: Jewish Music from Old World to Our World* (New York: Schirmer Books, 1999).

University of California Press
Berkeley and Los Angeles, California

University of California Press, Ltd.
London, England

Library of Congress Cataloging-in-Publication Data

American Klezmer : its roots and offshoots / edited by Mark Slobin
       p.   cm.
   Includes bibliographical references and index.
   ISBN 0-520-22717-4 (cloth: alk. paper)—
   ISBN 0-520-22718-2 (pbk. alk. paper)
     1. Klezmer music—Congresses.   2. Jews—Music—Congresses.   I. Slobin, Mark.
II. Klezmer Research Conference (1st : 1996 : Wesleyan University)

ML3528.8 .K54 2002
781.62'924—dc21   00-051168
                                    CIP
                                    MN

Manufactured in the United States of America
10   09   08   07   06   05   04   03   02
10   9   8   7   6   5   4   3   2   1

The paper used in this publication meets the minimum requirements of ANSI/NISO Z39.48-1992 (R 1997) (*Permanence of Paper*). ♾

Contents

Illustrations

Introduction

MARK SLOBIN

What we now routinely call *klezmer* in the United States—"Do you play klezmer?" "There's a new klezmer album out"—is a truly American construct in three ways: the word sidesteps aesthetic and political issues, it standardizes a music system as a brand name, and it overrides history in the cause of contemporary coherence. Record bin marketing and labeling has come to klezmer only very recently; the term was not used in earlier social and commercial contexts. History lurks behind much of contemporary klezmer, even while the past is recreated in the service of present-day interests. The word *klezmer* comes from Yiddish and denoted a professional instrumentalist who earned a living playing for celebrations in the far-flung communities of a multimillion Jewish population that existed in eastern Europe until 1939. *Klezmer music* is a term coined in English around 1980 in the United States to define a bounded repertoire and playing style, mostly based on the 78 rpm recordings of earlier decades. Like many American terms, this adjectival use expanded widely to cover more and more domains, and then broke through to become a convenient, all-encompassing abstract noun.

The aim of this volume is not to offer a history or a thorough survey of klezmer in America, but to suggest the full range and scope of modern klezmer studies by allowing a variety of voices to be heard. The editor has not smoothed out the length or tone of the contributions. The papers echo the backgrounds and standpoints of their authors. Many klezmerologists are practicing, touring musicians who put themselves on the line before audiences, sustain the craft and history of the tradition they represent, and even do fieldwork while on the move. The few academics who have chosen to study the klezmer world come from no unitary disciplinary background or methodological perspective; some are also scholar-practitioners with multiple viewpoints. All, however, share a pragmatic approach that is itself very American. Most of the contributions to this volume began at the first Klezmer Research Conference, held at Wesleyan University in 1996. Our intent is to clarify klezmer as a set of "roots and offshoots," dividing the articles into two overlapping parts.

Like any definable micromusic (a small unit within a large, multi-musical society) klezmer is a distinctive room in the American musical mansion.[1] Many micromusics also reach out to other places, spaces that are left open by the transnational search for novelty and the diasporic quest for identity. Klezmer has spread across virtually all of Jewish and non-Jewish Europe and to Jewish communities elsewhere, from Buenos Aires and Mexico City to Johannesburg and Sydney. Everywhere, including Israel, it is understood to be an American form with distant European origins. Even in eastern Europe, cradle of the music, Americans run workshops for descendants of the original players and audiences of klezmer styles. United States–sponsored "Klezfest" events began in 1998 in Saint Petersburg, from which participants return home eager to reawaken the ghosts of the klezmer past in towns whose walls once echoed to the sounds of courtyard musicians and wedding processions. Diasporic until the destruction of European Jewry, klezmer redefined itself almost magically as Jewish life regrouped after a great catastrophe. It emerged from the shadows of the 1940s, 1950s, and 1960s to bask in the sunlight of renewed public attention of both Jews and non-Jews in the United States, then expanded globally.

Klezmer is a micromusic of the type nowadays called *heritage musics*.[2] To sustain itself, a heritage music relies on a few key factors: a canon; a perceived (if often mythical) history; an appeal to a contemporary audience that responds to the sounds and styles of the music itself; and a social structure of learning, performance, and dissemination that radiates from the work of a set of activists. Klezmer also has a particularly noticeable penumbra, a shading of evocative sensibility. Each of these factors deserves a short review.

A CANON

Klezmer has a concentrated canon because it suffers from an extreme lack of documentation. Before 1939, the eastern European Jews were too preoccupied with pressing issues of political affiliation and cultural survival to research the ways and styles of obscure folk musicians.[3] Waves of Stalinist anti-Semitism forced cultural identity underground for millions of Soviet Jews. After 1939, Hitler's minions destroyed the culture, and with it any possibility of the music scene being available to study. By the 1970s, however, a generation of young American academics and enthusiasts arose who had the detachment and the resources to look at eastern Ashkenazic Jewry afresh, but they could make pilgrimages only to the ruins of the region. I remember vividly the frustration on my first trip to Poland in 1976 of not being able to do fieldwork with Jewish musicians in a country where Jews once formed what was probably the largest percentage ever of the overall population of any country (10 percent).

The canon available to the klezmer activists who started revitalizing the music in the mid 1970s included three parts: a set of master musicians from the immigrant era who could be interviewed, a small but authoritative body of recorded work, and a handful of tattered folios and manuscript versions of tunes. First regarded as the "authentic roots" of klezmer, this canon increasingly looks like offshoots of a musical grafting process that took place principally in New York, headquarters of the recording industry and the Jewish publishing houses. Only in the late 1990s have klezmer studies extended to other venues and other social formations.[4] Slowly, as the picture emerges stroke by stroke, we will see the canon fill out, but past losses determine that it will always be a miniature, never a panorama.

A HISTORY

As the canon expands, so does the history. In this volume, Robert Rothstein's contribution points to the rich, but unwritten history of the life of the klezmers in Europe by suggesting, through their professional argot, the existence of a tightly knit, hereditary group of male musicians. For the United States, the slowly unfolding story of adaptation to an American way of life forces us to go beyond the older sociological model of "assimilation," which suggested that ethnic groups and their music go through a standard process of change, starting with "old world retention" and ending with "ethnicization" in North America. By the mid 1980s, observers noticed that there was no uniform Jewish-European heritage, klezmer being just one manifestation of a long-term habit of eclecticism, a small part of the grand pattern of Jewish musical adaptation to local surroundings.[5] In 1994, Walter Zev Feldman published the first essay on how specific European dance-tune genres evolved into American-styled creations (a revised version of the essay appears in this volume as chapter 6). The generation of immigrant musicians born around 1900 bounced their beats off New York walls, the sounds ricocheting around restaurants and recording studios in subtly shifting patterns of resonance that both echoed and distorted the music of their youth. This was no process of assimilation, but rather a continuation— even a culmination—of centuries of professional strategizing by canny klezmorim.

Jewish American audiences outpaced the musicians in rapid shifts of taste, forcing the music ever further into the background of ethnic consciousness. The end of mass migration (1924) deprived the American scene of the vital influx of new musical energy from Europe. The volatility of North American consumerism combined with the velocity of the Jewish rush from tenements to suburbs, setting off a series of cultural explosions in musical taste. All this was pushed by the accelerant called history, propelled by the Holocaust and the creation of the state of Israel. The musical profile of Jewish American life changed radically decade by decade, from the 1920s through the 1970s. The recent history since the mid 1970s of what we now call "klezmer music" and the klezmer "scene" is marked by ever more rapid waves of taste, invention, and marketing.

I suggest two simultaneous, often conflicting, trends in Jewish American musical history: long-term processes such as the Americanization of style and ongoing redefinition of identity that continue earlier patterns of cultural and musical adaptation, and short-term bursts of innovation, fueled by quick social change. These are processes common to most American micromusics based on a notion of "heritage," especially among groups that arrived in earlier waves of immigration, and have had at least three generations of adjustment under their belts by the year 2000. Newer immigrant groups display similar combinations of canonical columns supporting constantly renovated facades and interiors.

AN APPEAL

Barbara Kirshenblatt-Gimblett, in her contribution, details the recent evolution of klezmer's appeal to American Jews, and Mark Slobin offers an account of the general motivational pattern for klezmer in North America and Europe.[6] A thumbnail sketch would depict an immigrant music and set of musicians who continued European habits on American soil from the 1880s to the 1940s, where the appeal was familiarity. This sense of hominess was part of the larger structure of a feeling usually termed *yidishkayt,* a Yiddish word that literally means "Jewishness," but as used in America implies a tinge of down-home values and recognizable rootsiness. The emergence of a new "ethnic" Jewish identity around 1960 coincided with two important sociological shifts: the movement of the Jews from the column of racialized Other to members of the mainstream majority on the one hand and the ripple effect of the civil rights movement on the other, which propelled Euro-Americans to a new sense of affirmation in response to their changed relationship to African Americans.[7]

This repositioning led to the reevaluation of history and the musical canon described above. In what seemed to be a sudden change, a parade of young musicians caused onlooking "ethnic" Jews to join an identity cavalcade that became only more exuberant and varied as the decades of the 1970s, 1980s, and 1990s stretched ahead like urban avenues to be proudly marched through. In this processional, klezmer became a marching band for the secular wing of the movement of celebratory reaffiliation.

Klezmer's appeal varies across generation, locale, and orientation (political, sexual, cultural . . .). Some of this diversity is mirrored in the essays below. Two general factors can be easily isolated. One is summarized in the subtitle of a newspaper article on the klezmer scene in my corner of the country: "Toe-Tapping Tunes Are Big Hit in Connecticut." Klezmer has the power of animating bodies that all dance musics share across the world, one of the core reasons for its past and continued existence as a culturally valued practice.

A PENUMBRA

There is another factor that is much harder to pin down, which the word *penumbra* helps to evoke, if not explain. The *Oxford English Dictionary* defines *penumbra* this way: "The partially shaded region around the shadow of an opaque body; esp. that surrounding the total shadow of the moon, or the earth, in an eclipse." The word offers an elegant metaphor for the almost magical quality of illumination and mystery around klezmer.

The layered nature of the definition offers openings for multiple metaphors.

The partially shaded region: We have an incomplete view of klezmer's evolution in America, our view being blocked by a set of assumptions deriving from the canon of recordings and a long range of liner notes that offer a chiaroscuro of interpretation.

Around the shadow of an opaque body: Klezmer music and klezmer life themselves present not only a historically shaded, but a culturally opaque core. There is little transparency in the central mystery of klezmer, which combines poignancy with punch in the tunes, spiritual and physical desire in the dance, contemplation and celebration in the occasions where it unites groups—wedding guests from disparate families, concertgoers from dispersed points in town.

Surrounding the total shadow of [a body] in an eclipse: This is a chillingly precise metaphor for the fate of the society that created klezmer. Not only is that body of practice, belief, and daily life in nearly "total shadow" due to scholarly neglect of the culture of eastern European Jewish life, even when it was alive and well, but because of that "total shadow" around a thousand years of history has gone into permanent eclipse. Klezmer is part of a permanent penumbra, a shaded glimpse of a cultural body that will never emerge from the shadows of history.

Even if this metaphor is overstated, the important point is that people actually respond to klezmer as this type of penumbra. Jews, non-Jews, Americans, Canadians, Europeans . . . most patrons of klezmer and many musicians listen and move to the melodies with a sense that they are not just here and now, but somewhere else in time. There is a sensibility around a notion of reflected cultural light coming to us from a shadowed world. This was probably true for dancers and listeners of the postimmigrant age, in the last and crucial phase of klezmer's flowering (1920s–40s). For generations of immigrants arriving after 1900, klezmer was already a system in eclipse as Jews became ever more adapted to modern urban lifestyles in big-city Europe. For those people's children and grandchildren, although they knew some Yiddish and perhaps some traditional dance steps, the older generation was a shadow over their Americanizing lives, as we read in Jewish American fiction. In the

1920s, they would probably have bought "the Yiddishe Charleston" before a Naftule Brandwein record; by the 1940s, they were moving definitively from the bulgar to the mambo. Today, the penumbra offers part of klezmer's appeal, alongside the "toe-tapping" magnetism and the sense of celebration that breaks through the shadows.

A SOCIAL STRUCTURE

Concerts, celebrations, and recordings form the shell around a core of activists. Bands, workshops, and teaching materials emanate from that core. Many of the articles in this collection revolve around the band as central source of power for the music and its meaning, with Marion Jacobson highlighting two influential units. Henry Sapoznik, as founder of the main institutional energy generator, KlezKamp, adds his own story to the mix, while Michael Alpert contributes the life story of one immigrant musician.

Bearing this configuration of concepts in mind, the book is divided into two parts, "roots" and "offshoots," though the two overlap and comment on each other in an antiphonal, if not a call-and-response, way.

"Roots" begins with a short survey of American klezmer history, followed by historical narratives that resonate in the present-day practice of klezmer music and musical life. "Offshoots" starts with an extended consideration of the "revival" period of klezmer, then details the work and attitudes of activists of recent and current times.

The present volume is part of the first wave of publications on klezmer. An enormous amount of historical research and ethnography needs to be done to fully understand the setting and significance of this vital and volatile musical scene. Finally, a need exists for more encompassing surveys of the music culture of the United States and its neighbors to flesh out the partial and often superficial view we generally have of America as a musical space and as a force in the emerging global music system. The editor is grateful to Wesleyan University for hosting the conference on which the book's core is based, to Murray Baumgarten, who published earlier versions of several articles in *Judaism* (Winter 1998), and to Lynne Withey at the University of California Press for her interest in the project.

NOTES

1. See Mark Slobin, *Subcultural Sounds: Micromusics of the West* (Hanover, N.H.: University Press of New England, 1993).

2. See Mark Slobin, *Fiddler on the Move* (New York: Oxford University Press, 2000).

3. There are isolated cases that prove exceptions to this rule; see Beregovski, *Old Jewish Folk Music,* ed. and trans. Mark Slobin (Syracuse: Syracuse University Press, 2001).

4. See Hankus Netsky, chapter 4 in this volume, and James Loeffler, "Di Rusishe Progresiv Muzikal Yunyon No. 1 fun Amerike: The First Klezmer Union in America," *Judaism* 47, no. 1 (1998): 29–39.

5. See Mark Slobin, "Ten Paradoxes and Four Dilemmas of Studying Jewish Music," *World of Music* 11, no. 1 (1995): 18–23; also Kay Shelemay, "Mythologies and Realities in the Study of Jewish Music," *World of Music* 11, no. 1 (1995): 24–38; U. Sharvit, "Jewish Musical Culture," *World of Music* 11, no. 1 (1995): 3–17.

6. Mark Slobin, *Fiddler on the Move* (New York: Oxford University Press, 2000).

7. Regarding Jews' entry into the mainstream majority, see K. Brodkin, *How Jews Became White Folks* (New Brunswick: Rutgers University Press, 1998).

PART ONE

Roots

One definition for *roots* in the *Oxford English Dictionary* is surprisingly apt for klezmer: "the permanent underground stock of a plant from which the stems or leaves are periodically produced."

Culture, too, has its permanent underground stock. Today's American klezmer music grows out of linguistic, social, and musical stock originally transplanted from Europe. The first part of this book examines the common origins from which later offshoots have sprung.

CHAPTER 1

American Klezmer

A Brief History

HANKUS NETSKY

The term *klezmer* (or in Hebrew, *kle zemer,* "vessels of song") has had many incarnations over the years, having been variously used to designate biblical-era Temple musicians, medieval minstrels, and eastern European virtuosi. It was in twentieth-century America, however, that *klezmer* underwent its most radical transformation, from a pejorative used to demean the talents and lifestyles of Jewish wedding musicians, to a catchall phrase for a rapidly evolving contemporary musical culture.[1]

The music now known as *klezmer* took root in the United States during the period of heaviest eastern European Jewish immigration, between 1880 and 1924, although there were traces of it in the Americas before that time. Klezmorim migrated from many parts of the Austro-Hungarian and Russian empires and from Romania and carried with them musical traditions which, while diverse, also share a great deal in common. Some klezmorim traveled extensively, and their resourcefulness in picking up repertoire led to the creation of an extensive tune network throughout the Jewish pale of settlement (for a more thorough look at the music's European period, see chapter 6).[2]

The southern areas of the pale (Moldova, Bessarabia, the Bucovina region of Romania, and the southern Ukraine) were to klezmer almost as New Orleans was to American jazz. Gypsy, Greek, and Romanian elements eventually became so predominant in Jewish dance music traditions that some scholars dismissed klezmer as a separate genre altogether. If one listens closely, however, one can learn to distinguish the sound of a klezmer interpretation from other related performance styles.

Yiddish-speaking Jews routinely use several uniquely descriptive words to identify the sounds found in the Jewish approach to music. The word *krekhts* (Yiddish for "groan") refers to a wailing sound reminiscent of weeping, the term *tshok* might be used to refer to a laugh-like instrumental sound, and a *kneytsh* is a sob-like "catch." These and other typical elements of klezmer music are also found in other forms of Jewish musical expression, including cantorial music and folksong. The cantorial parallel is especially evident in the shape and phrasing of Jewish instrumental improvisations.

The Hasidic movement, which emerged in the latter half of the 1700s, had a profound impact on the klezmer tradition. This populist sect made religion more accessible to the masses by emphasizing dancing and the chanting of wordless melodies known in Yiddish (and Hebrew) as *nigunim*. Hasidim sang these melodies with an intense urgency, hoping to ascend to higher realms through their music.[3] Klezmorim soon became indispensable at Hasidic gatherings, and the spirit of the movement greatly influenced their playing.

Klezmorim brought all of their skills and repertoire with them and re-created the sounds of eastern Europe's cities and towns on this side of the ocean. At first, virtually all of the klezmer orchestra leaders were violinists (many of whom doubled on trumpet to avoid combat during their tenure in the military). Some brought over typical European klezmer instruments such as the *tsimbl* (hammered dulcimer), straw fiddle (folk xylophone), *harmonica* (small accordion), bohemian flute, and rotary valve cornet. By the 1920s, Jewish dance music instrumentation had fallen more in line with typical American vaudeville or concert bands of the time. By then, a large proportion of the European Jewish ritual music repertoire had also been abandoned, along with much of the *badkhones* (wedding jester) tradition, which only lived on in certain Hasidic communities.

Example 1.1 is a transcription of a section of "Lebedik Freylekh" (Lively, Merry), a Yiddish theater song recorded by the Abe Schwartz orchestra in New York in 1927. Schwartz, a Brooklyn-based Yiddish theater bandleader born in Romania, recorded many Jewish dance tunes and theater songs in a career that lasted from the 1910s well into the 1940s.[4] In this arrangement, the melodic line is carried by the cornet, clarinet, and violin, while the rhythmic underpinning is provided by the traditional brass instruments (valve trombone and alto horn) and piano,

Example 1.1 "Lebedik Freylekh" (unpublished, composed by Gilrod and Sandler)

augmented by the more American sounds of slide-trombone, banjo, and drum set. The bass part is played by the left hand of the piano, a contrabass, and a bass saxophone.

Similar arranging techniques were used by many other Jewish American bandleaders of the time, including I. J. Hochman, Abraham Elenkrieg, and Harry Kandel; early commercial recordings of these bands give us a sense of what Jewish immigrant audiences wanted to hear. The brass-laden sounds of these ensembles also reflected the orientation of the popular bandleaders, several of whom functioned as theater orchestra directors or associate conductors for such mainstream American figures as John Philip Sousa and Arthur Pryor.

The Jewish dance tunes reproduced on 78 rpm recordings give us insight into the essential klezmer repertoire of the early immigrant era. Common dances include *bulgars, sirbas, freylekhs, rusishe shers, patsh tantsn, broyges tantsn, zhoks (horas), terkishers,* and *khosidls,* along with a small number of ritual dances and dance arrangements of popular folk and theater tunes. One also finds a variety of tunes for listening, including *doynes, dobrizhens,* and *tishnigunim,* and other Yiddish theater hits. Klezmorim brought regional tunes to their adopted American communities, and soon many American cities had their own instantly recognizable local Jewish repertoire.

Certain aspects of the recorded repertoire of this era are actually quite misleading. The exotic titles of recorded dance tunes were usually thought up in the offices of record companies just prior to their release dates; musicians tended to refer to tunes only by their genre, their key, or the name of whomever they learned the tune from (e.g., "Bulgar from Meyer Swerdlow").[5] Moreover, few private patrons could afford to hire bands as large as those heard on most recordings. Also, the physical limitation of 78 rpm records imposed a three- to four-minute time limit on dance tunes that, when played live, were sometimes sequenced in medleys that went on for fifteen minutes or more.

The clarinet became the predominant instrument in the American bands, and several clarinetists were renowned virtuosi. Naftule Brandwein (1889–1963) was acclaimed for his expressiveness and showed mastery of a tremendous variety of rhythmic and coloristic subtleties. Dave Tarras (1897–1989) was widely considered the technical wizard of the music, with quick trills and finger gymnastics that rivaled any classical soloist (see chapter 6 for details on Tarras's career and repertoire). His career lasted well into the 1980s, and his later recordings show his emotional side to great effect. Shloimke Beckerman (1889–1974) played in a heavily ornamented and rhythmically propulsive style, and Itsikl Kramtweiss (dates unknown) played his E-flat clarinet with a piercing, nasal sound. Max Epstein (1913–2000) synthesized the approaches of Brandwein and Tarras, while drawing on the inspiration of his early Bessarabian mentors. He and his brothers introduced contemporary harmonic ideas to the music.

Accomplished performers also recorded on other instruments. Accordionist Misha Tziganoff (dates unknown) played virtually every eastern European musical style with impeccable authenticity, and tsimblist Josef Moskowitz (1879–1954) held forth at his own Romanian restaurant in New York, performing everything from doynes to ragtime. Percussionist Jake Hoffman (1895–1972) performed with both the Philadelphia Orchestra and the Ballets Russes while honing his skills as an unparalleled klezmer xylophonist.

Few of the performers of this era actually referred to themselves as

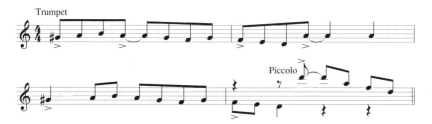

Example 1.2 "Yiddish Blues," second theme

klezmorim, and the term is found nowhere in any Jewish instrumental recording of the time. While the musicians were aware of their continuity in a long line of wedding entertainers (and in some cases, their direct connection to distinguished klezmer families), they tended to think of the term as a vestige of old Europe, and used it only as a derogatory reference to those whom they felt could not adapt to the demands of the contemporary American music scene (an ironic turn of events, since many of these same musicians had been considered pillars of versatility while in Europe). Indeed, such adaptation went both ways, and non-Jewish musicians became very much in demand for work in Jewish orchestras.

The 1910s also gave rise to a new style, which combined traditional eastern European dance melodies with the popular American rhythms of the day. This genre became known as the "oriental fox trot" and inspired not only Jewish musicians but also such important African American artists as Duke Ellington and Fats Waller. The first known recording of this type was "Yiddish Blues," by Lieutenant Joseph Frankel (1885–1953), a Kiev Conservatory–trained bandmaster who led theater orchestras in New York in the early 1910s. In this 1918 composition, Frankel combines the *Mi Shebeyrekh* cantorial mode with typical ragtime rhythms (see example 1.2).[6]

Another well-known selection from this repertoire was Eddie Cantor's 1930s hit "Lena from Palestina," based on a popular Romanian bulgar known as "Nokh a Bisl" (A Little Bit More). In example 1.3, we find a klezmer version of a section of "Nokh a Bisl," while example 1.4 shows us its American transformation as "Lena from Palestina."

In the 1930s, klezmer was beginning to fade, but "Jewish jazz" was all the rage. The biggest of all the hits from this era was "Bay Mir Bistu Sheyn," initially composed for a 1934 Yiddish theater production. When the Andrews Sisters recorded it in November of 1937, their English-language rendition became the top song hit of the year and the most

Example 1.3   "Nokh a Bisl" (traditional)

Example 1.4   "Lena from Palestina" (composed by Conrad and Robinson)

popular record ever released in the United States until that time.[7] The song's success gave the green light for more klezmer and Yiddish fusion attempts. Soon, "Di Greene Kuzine" (a klezmer and folk melody) became "My Little Country Cousin," and "Yossel, Yossel" became "Joseph, Joseph." A 1939 Artie Shaw air-check of a tune entitled "The Chant" goes as far in the direction of fusion as any recording from this era. The tune itself plays on the close, and presumably incidental, relationship between the "St. James Infirmary Blues" and "Khosn Kale, Mazeltov" (Congratulations, Bride and Groom), a popular Jewish wedding recessional (see examples 1.5 and 1.6).

After the initial big band choruses and some fascinating chromatic passages, Shaw switches accents and lets loose with a free-associating jam accompanied only by drums (reminiscent of Benny Goodman's "Sing, Sing, Sing" from the previous year's Carnegie Hall concert), in which he quotes not only "Bay Mir Bistu Sheyn" and "Yossel, Yossel," but also such relatively obscure klezmer tunes as the "Patsh Tants" (Hand-clapping Dance) and the "Ukrainian Kamarinska."

That same year, Benny Goodman cut his classic rendition of "And the Angels Sing." Based on a well-known Romanian dance tune, "Der Shtiler Bulgar" (The Quiet Bulgar), this recording featured a relaxed, swinging vocal by Martha Tilton and a fiery klezmer trumpet chorus by Ziggy Elman, who had previously cut an instrumental version of the same arrangement (entitled "Frailach in Swing") under his own name.

Example 1.5   "St. James Infirmary Blues"

Example 1.6   "Khosn Kale, Mazeltov"

With Goodman's stamp and Johnny Mercer's clever lyrics, the song achieved tremendous popularity. In this recording, we find the perfect expression of the balancing act of the 1930s Jewish musician, now equally at home with two styles. While the swing portion is proudly up-to-date, with contemporary harmonies and voicings, the klezmer interlude seems frozen in time, a nostalgic window into an era that has passed.

In fact, by the late 1930s, the Jewish American public had moved decisively away from its eastern European roots. The younger generation, in pursuit of all things American, sought to distance itself from the Old Country language and ways of its greenhorn parents. Soon, a new type of Jewish bandleader emerged who gave contemporary American couples society-style music with only a hint of Jewishness.

The Nazis' massive destruction of the eastern European Jewish world not only profoundly depleted the source of klezmer music, but tainted the genre with a painful sadness. Then, in 1948, with the creation of the state of Israel, American Jews found a new cultural focus with a positive and modern outlook and plenty of enticing music and dance. Remnants of the past were either carted up to the attic or subjected to various types of parody.

Mickey Katz, a product of the Spike Jones novelty orchestra, used his comedic and musical gifts to invent a uniquely American style of Jewish musical humor that mercilessly lampooned American heroes and icons. His band featured some of the best second-generation American Jewish musicians (including trumpeters Elman and Manny Klein and trombonist Si Zentner), and with the aid of arranger Nat Farber (musical director of the *Dinah Shore Show*), he created a slick but soulful version of klezmer. Farber's three-part harmonic writing gave the melody to the trumpet and the upper harmonies to the violin and clarinet, as in "Mendel's Song" (see example 1.7).

Clarinetist Sam Musiker, son-in-law of klezmer master Dave Tarras,

Example 1.7   "Mendel's Song" (arranged by Nat Farber)

epitomized the dedicated klezmer innovator of this era. A veteran of the
Gene Krupa band, he developed arrangements that incorporated swing
harmonies, rhythms, and instrumentation. He used polyphony and big
band–style *soli* writing, a technique in which an intricate melody is
closely harmonized within an instrumental section. He even based one
of his dance tunes on the chord changes of the swing hit "China Boy."
His album *Tantz,* on the Columbia Epic label, has been a classic for
many years.

By the 1960s, attempts to create new hybrids had become increasingly
unsuccessful. It was the age of rock 'n' roll, and very few of the older musicians were prepared for the new aesthetic. Conversely, hardly any of
the young musicians knew anything about klezmer music. In cities all
over North America, the reigning generation of Jewish instrumentalists edged toward retirement, performing at fewer and fewer exclusively
Jewish engagements for an ever-aging clientele. A different scenario
played itself out in New York, where the burgeoning post–World War II
Hasidic population gave musicians there a new musical outlet within the
Jewish realm.

Meanwhile, unbeknownst to most of the older klezmorim, a new
generation was looking for its roots. Imbued with the aesthetic of 1960s
self-expression, playing in the raw musical styles of blues, bluegrass, old-
time swing, jazz, folk, and soul, and impressed by the African American
roots movement, young Jewish musicians began asking questions about
their musical ancestry. By this time, there were few repercussions for expressing Jewish identity and no need for these grandchildren of immigrants to prove their American credentials. Moreover, the Old World,
brought to their attention by such romanticizations as *Fiddler on the
Roof,* actually looked quite appealing. Down from attic came the klezmer 78s, and a new movement was born (for a thorough look at the

"rupture" that separated the work of the new generation from that of their predecessors, see chapter 7).

Of the four popular klezmer groups that formed in the late seventies, three have retained their status as important role models to this day. The first to record (in 1976) were The Klezmorim of Berkeley, California. Founded by saxophonist Lev Liberman, the group initially took its inspiration from klezmer and Balkan folk music, later drawing from jazz and cartoon-music connections. The group took klezmer to major concert halls in the United States and Europe, and paved the way for many others before finally dissolving in 1996.

Clarinetist/mandolinist Andy Statman, working closely with Dave Tarras and performing with pioneering ethnomusicologist Walter Zev Feldman on the tsimbl, initially played European-style klezmer. Later, Statman took inspiration from his own bluegrass background, forming a group with guitar as rhythmic anchor. Since then, his musical and spiritual path has led him to New York's Hasidic community, where he continues to perform both traditional and innovative Jewish music. Feldman has become a major purveyor of Old World European-style klezmer and an important klezmer scholar.

The Klezmer Conservatory Band and Kapelye (both formed late in 1979) combine klezmer music with a variety of Yiddish vocal styles. The KCB uses a full Yiddish theater orchestra instrumentation to showcase a sound that ranges from big-band hybrid to chamber-orchestral. Starting out with more of a folk sound, Kapelye has evolved into an eclectic ragtime-tinged ensemble.

Argentinean-born Israeli clarinetist Giora Feidman has also had a profound influence on the contemporary klezmer scene, and some of his recordings predate the current American revival. Feidman often cites a more mystical definition of klezmer, pointing out that a traditional Jewish musician does not create music, but is simply a vessel for inspiration that comes from "the Divine source" (a view traditionally used by rabbis to curtail the activities of secular musicians). Although his recordings are not as closely linked to the eastern European–based core repertoire, he is certainly quite familiar with it (his father, Leo Feidman, was highly regarded as a traditional Jewish clarinetist in Buenos Aires).

In the past ten years, several other significant groups and performers have emerged. Brave Old World, a virtuosic "supergroup" with one foot in contemporary Europe and the other in the United States, explores the meaning of postholocaust Yiddish expression. Joel Rubin, an American expatriate, flaunts a scholarly approach and a love of the music's European roots. Since 1995, virtuoso violinist Itzhak Perlman has embraced klezmer, bringing it to the attention of a much larger and more diverse audience than ever before. Don Byron's recordings of the repertoire of Mickey Katz have brought that particular body of work into the popular mainstream.

New types of hybrid klezmer have also emerged. The Klezmatics freely fuse their klezmer with a variety of world and popular music styles while integrating contemporary lyrics that reflect their social consciousness. The New Klezmer Trio (from the San Francisco Bay Area) and Klezmokum (from Amsterdam) both make liberal use of free improvisation (the latter group featuring '60s avant-gardists Burton Greene and Perry Robinson). Toronto's Flying Bulgar Klezmer Band uses both Latin and jazz elements, and one of their founding members, trumpeter David Buchbinder, regularly organizes a cutting-edge klezmer festival known as Ashkenaz. New York's Knitting Factory has also become a patron of the "new" klezmer, encouraging explorations by such important contemporary artists as John Zorn, Frank London, and Anthony Coleman. Klezmer has also spawned a "women's music" branch, including the pioneering Klezmeydlekh and the newer KlezMs, Mikveh, and Isle of Klezbos.

The revitalization of klezmer has become a truly global phenomenon, with bands springing up across Europe and elsewhere (Australia, Mexico, Japan). Klezmer has become a focal point for a general revival of interest in Jewish culture, religion, and history in Germany, Holland, and Poland, countries where klezmer revivalists have closely (and ironically) imitated American models. A revival of many traditional eastern European Jewish dances (spearheaded by Brave Old World member Michael Alpert) has restored relevance to many long-forgotten forms. Previously obscure recordings have now been re-released on CD. Some of the best current klezmer performers are non-Jewish musicians pursuing careers in what they perceive to be an exciting and challenging repertoire. A large number of new compositions have been written, and the style has found its way into prime-time television (*Miami Vice, Rugrats, Saturday Night Live,* and *The David Letterman Show*) and movie soundtracks (including *The Chosen,* the remake of *The Jazz Singer, Enemies: A Love Story,* and *A Stranger Among Us*). Special educational programs, such as Klez-Kamp, Klezkanada, and Buffalo on the Roof, have put younger performers in touch with the older generation and each other. A wave of post–Soviet Russian Jewish immigration has put the young American generation in direct contact with the wellspring of the music and its place within the current regional musical mix. A large number of older performers have come out of retirement to see what all the fuss is about, and the term *klezmer,* out of favor for so long, is finally being worn as a badge of honor.

NOTES

1. The term combines two Hebrew words—*kle,* which means "vessel" or "instrument," and *zemer,* which means "song." In recent years *klezmer music* has gained prominence as the term used to describe the music that *klezmorim* (the plural form of *klezmer;* it refers to the klezmer players) perform.

2. These eclectic tendencies were shared with musicians of many other nationalities, especially Gypsies and Armenians.

3. A. Z. Idelsohn, *Jewish Music in Its Historical Development* (New York: Henry Holt, 1929), 414. Idelsohn examines this process in great detail.

4. Henry Sapoznik, *Klezmer!* (New York: Schirmer, 1999), 90–93.

5. Regarding the exotic titles, see Henry Sapoznik and Pete Sokolov, *The Compleat Klezmer* (Cedarhurst, N.Y.: Tara Publications, 1987), 11–12.

6. The pitches of the Mi Shebeyrekh mode correspond roughly to a Dorian mode with a raised fourth (for example, D, E, F, G♯, A, B, C, D). Beregovski calls this pitch collection "Ukrainian Dorian."

7. See Victoria Secunda, *Bei Mir Bist Du Schön* (New York: Magic Circle Press, 1982), 49.

CHAPTER 2

Klezmer-loshn

The Language of Jewish Folk Musicians

ROBERT A. ROTHSTEIN

In 1888, Sholem Aleichem published *Stempenyu,* a novel about a Berdichev violinist of the same name.[1] In chapter 3, Stempenyu and his klezmer *kapelye* arrive at a wedding, where he notices an attractive young woman. The following conversation ensues (in Joachim Neugroschel's translation):

> "Who's the chick next to the frau-to-be?" asked Stempeniu in musician's lingo, staring at lovely Rachel. "Hey, Rakhmiel!" he said to one of the swollen-cheeked apprentices. "Go and check her out, but snappy man, snappy!"
>
> Rakhmiel quickly came back with a clear answer: "That's no chick, man, she's already hitched. Dig, she's Isaak-Naphtali's daughter-in-law, and she comes from Skvirre. That's her ol' man over there. The one with the velvet cap!"
>
> "You're too much, baby!" said Stempeniu cheerily. "You checked it out that fast? Man, she is really dynamite! A righteous chick! Dig those eyes!"
>
> "If you like," the swollen-cheeked boy asked Stempeniu, "I'll go and rap with her. . . ."
>
> "Go to hell!" replied Stempeniu. "No one asked you to be my go-between, dig! I'll do my own rappin' with her!"[2]

The "musician's lingo" *(klezmer-loshn)* used by Stempenyu and Rakhmiel is represented in this fragment by fourteen words and expressions that Sholem Aleichem (or his editors) felt needed translation into "normal" Yiddish in footnotes.

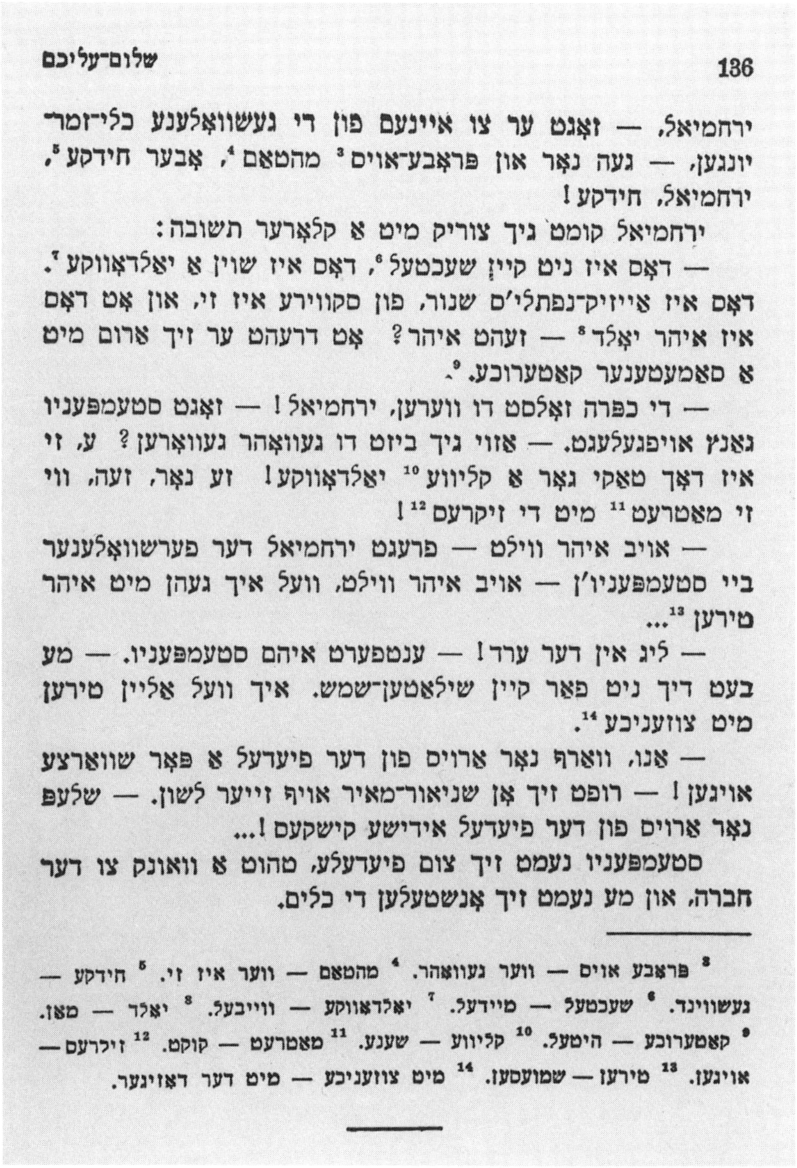

ירחמיאל, — זאָגט ער צו איינעם פון די געשוואָלענע כלי־זמר־יונגען, — גער נאָר און פראָבע־אוים[3] מהטאם[4], אָבער חידקע[5], ירחמיאל, חידקע!

ירחמיאל קומט גיך צוריק מיט אַ קלאָרער תשובה:

— דאָס איז ניט קיין שעכטעל[6], דאָס איז שוין אַ יאַלדאָווקע[7]. דאָס איז אייזיק־נפתלי'ס שנור, פון סקווירע איז זי, און אָט דאָס איז איהר יאָלד[8] — זעהט איהר? אָט דרעהט ער זיך אַרום מיט אַ סאַמעטענער קאַטערוכע.[9]

— די כפרה זאָלסט דו ווערען, ירחמיאל! — זאָגט סטעמפעניו גאַנץ אויפגעלעגט. — אזוי גיך ביזט דו געוואָהר געוואָרען? ע, זי איז דאָך טאַקי גאָר אַ קליווע[10] יאַלדאָווקע! זע נאָר, זעה, ווי זי מאַטרעט[11] מיט די זיקרעם[12]!

— אויב איהר ווילט — פרעגט ירחמיאל דער פערשוואָלענער ביי סטעמפעניו'ן — אויב איהר ווילט, וועל איך געהן מיט איהר טירען[13]...

— ליג אין דער ערד! — ענטפערט איהם סטעמפעניו. — מע בעט דיך ניט פאַר קיין שילאַטען־שמש. איך וועל אַליין טירען מיט צוזעניכע[14].

— אַנו, ווארף נאָר אַרוים פון דער פיעדעל אַ פּאָר שוואַרצע אויגען! — רופט זיך אָן שניאור־מאיר אויף זייער לשון. — שלעפּ נאָר אַרוים פון דער פיעדעל אידישע קישקעס!...

סטעמפעניו נעמט זיך צום פיעדעלע, טהוט אַ וואונק צו דער חברה, און מע נעמט זיך אָנשטעלען די כלים.

[3] פראָבע אוים — ווער געוואהר. [4] מהטאם — ווער איז זי. [5] חידקע — געשווינד. [6] שעכטעל — מיידעל. [7] יאַלדאווקע — ווייבעל. [8] יאָלד — מאַן. [9] קאַטערוכע — היטעל. [10] קליווע — שענע. [11] מאַטרעט — קוקט. [12] זילרעם — אויגען. [13] טירען — שמועסען. [14] מיט צוזעניכע — מיט דער דאַזיגער.

Figure 2.1 Page from Sholem Aleichem's 1888 novel *Stempenyu*. Photo by UMass Photographic Services.

KLEZMER-LOSHN	YIDDISH
shekhte	*nekeyve* (woman)
smisanke	*kale* (bride)
probe oys	*ver gevor* (find out)
mehetam	*ver zi iz* (who she is)
khidke	*geshvind* (quickly)
shekhtl	*meydl* (girl)
yoldovke	*vaybl* (married woman)
yold	*man* (husband)
katerukhe	*hitl* (cap)
klive	*sheyne* (beautiful)
matret	*kukt* (looks)
zikres	*oygn* (eyes)
tirn	*shmuesn* (chat)
mit tsuzenikhe	*mit der doziger* (with her)

Klezmer-loshn is an example of a *professional argot* or *jargon*. Those terms are used to refer to a specialized variety of a language (here, Yiddish) used by members of a particular professional or occupational group. Such an argot differs from slang in the relative size of the group that uses it: typically small and more specialized in the case of the former, larger and more general (e.g., speakers of a certain generation) in the latter. Both concepts are distinguished from that of a *dialect,* which is usually understood to have geographic rather than professional or chronological boundaries. A dialect, moreover, normally differs from the standard language in phonology and grammar as well as in vocabulary, while argots and slangs are typically made up of a body of words and phrases that are not part of the standard language (or not with their specific argot or slang meaning). Argot, slang, and dialects may influence one another and may affect the standard language as well. In American English, for example, the word *cool* moved from musical argot into youth slang; *heist* moved from underworld argot (cant) into relatively general media use.

Professional or occupational jargons fill certain needs. They provide for group solidarity among, say, truck drivers or students. They provide a means for concealment (and/or intimidation of outsiders), as reflected in the popular sense of the term *jargon* (e.g., *medical jargon*). Indeed, the original French meaning of *argot,* according to the Larousse,[3] is *langue des malfaiteurs*—language of criminals.

Probably the most studied of jargons is, in fact, the "language of criminals," known by such terms as *ganovim-loshn* (Yiddish), *Rotwelsch* or *Gaunersprache* (German), *blatnoi iazyk* (Russian), and others. Its first analysts were often police officials, who published dictionaries for internal police use. A number of students of the subject noted the international character of underworld argot in Europe, in the sense of finding common elements in the criminal argot of various countries. Among these common elements are numerous Yiddishisms. Consider, for example, two words cited here in their Polish form: *ksywa,* false papers (cf. Yiddish *ksuve/ksive,* [ornate] writing) and *dintojre,* kangaroo court (cf. Yiddish *din-toyre,* lawsuit in a rabbinical court). The presence of these and other Yiddishisms in European cant has been interpreted variously by Yiddish linguists. Max Weinreich, for example, simply observed that "in creating their secret language, thieves have recourse to those linguistic elements that are unknown to the majority of the population."[4] Ber Borokhov, by contrast, pointed out that "Jews have always constituted a large percentage of thieves' and swindlers' gangs. This explains the fact that a large number of words from Yiddish can be found in the thieves' dialect of the nations of the world. . . ."[5]

The literature on Yiddish klezmer-loshn comes from roughly the first quarter of this century, although there were also some observations published in the late 1950s and early 1960s in the journal *Yidishe shprakh* (by Isaac Rivkind and others). The lists of terms compiled by the several authors add up to over six hundred lexical items, but not all items were used in all areas, and the total just cited includes a considerable number of variants—orthographic (*lash* vs. *lazh,* bad, ugly); phonetic (*svizn* vs. *svidn,* sit; *tentlen* vs. *tintlen,* write); and morphological (*katre* vs. *katerukhe,* hat; *klis* vs. *kliser* vs. *klisalnik,* thief). The authors of these studies and the areas represented are as follows: Samuel Weissenberg (Ukraine); Alfred Landau (Ukraine); Noyekh Prilutski (Poland); Yehude Elzet (Poland); Avrom-Yitskhok Trivaks (Poland); Leon Dushman (Belarus).

What was the function of klezmer-loshn? Earlier, I spoke of the use of argot for purposes of concealment. Indeed, the income of the musicians was largely dependent on the largesse of wedding guests, who had to be encouraged to pay for tunes. This often required the machinations of the musicians. The principle of "paying the piper," so to speak, was summed up in the proverb *Noysn betsimbl, hoylekh betentsl,* roughly,

"When you've paid the musicians, you can go dance." The initial quotation from *Stempenyu* also shows that the musicians sometimes had other matters that they needed to discuss in secret. Since Jewish musicians performed at both gentile and Jewish weddings, ordinary Yiddish often sufficed (although there were non-Jews who understood Yiddish, and patrons' knowledge of German might have made Yiddish insecure), but in the case of a Jewish wedding, a special jargon was clearly needed to ensure secrecy.

It is interesting to note that Jewish musicians and thieves shared a body of vocabulary. In both klezmer-loshn and ganovim-loshn we find such words as *bash* (money), *tokn* (give), *matren* (look), *klift* (coat), *krel* (bread), *shvalyer* (a ruble), and *drizhblen* (sleep; have sex) (only the second meaning is found in ganovim-loshn). Musicians seem also not to have had a much better reputation than thieves. Avrom-Yitskhok Trivaks, for example, characterizes them as *kalim un shtiklekh balaveyre* (debauched fellows and sinners).[6] This reputation is perhaps reflected in the attitude of Leah, Reyzl Spivak's mother, in Sholem Aleichem's novel *Blondzhnde shtern,* who opposes her daughter's planned marriage to the talented violinist Grisha Stelmakh. "The young man is a fine young man; you can't deny it. And he also earns his living. Who says he doesn't? But you can see what comes of that since he's unfortunately a klezmer! . . . He can be a musician thirty times over, but as soon as he plays the fiddle, he's a klezmer. A really fine young man. . . . May God send him his intended, which he deserves. . . . And may the Almighty choose something else for her daughter since her husband, may he rest in peace, didn't play the fiddle, nor did his father or his father's father."[7] Trivaks also observes that "in the Polish provinces almost every barber knows the klezmer argot" since "in the past one and the same person often took up both professions, which were to a certain extent contemptible *(nivzedike).*"[8]

In the lexicon of klezmer-loshn, certain semantic fields are well represented. Surprisingly, musical terminology is not prominent. There are names for some instruments: *foyal* (clarinet), *shoyfer/tshanik* (trumpet), *shtolper* (flute), *tshekal/tshikal* (drum), *varplye/verplye/verfli* (violin), *verbl* (drum; bass), and *vorsht* (clarinet). Note also *leyenen blat* (to read music).[9]

Not surprisingly, given the function of this argot, there are many terms for money and numerals, for example, *baker* (two), *baker baker* (four), *baker baker bakerlekh* (four kopeks), *baker baker detsn* (forty), *baker baker smalyer* (four rubles), *baker baker spen* (nine), *baker baker strom* (seven), and *baker fikslekh detsn* (sixty).[10] Other semantic fields represented by nouns include food, professions, and body parts; there are also miscellaneous adjectives, verbs, and even pronouns. Trivaks points to the layer of obscenity and notes that this is a purely masculine argot.[11]

Numerous words reflect the musicians' sense of humor. A hasid can be called a *botshkar,* from Russian *bochka* (barrel), which alludes to a love of drinking. A promiscuous woman is referred to by the term *borukhe,* from Russian *marukha* (prostitute; thief's mistress), playing on the Hebrew root for "bless," and perhaps also on Hebrew *kedeyshe* (prostitute). A corresponding masculine term, *borukher* (gigolo), apparently derived from the feminine one, also exists. The expression "get married" can be expressed by the verb *fardreyen zikh* (in standard Yiddish: get twisted, tangled); cf. *fardreyung* (wedding). Another humorous or ironic coinage, *kapure* (married woman), is explained with great seriousness by the philologist Alfred Landau. "On the day before the Day of Atonement a rooster is slaughtered for every male family member and a hen for every female family member as a sin offering (Hebrew *kapuru*). Because of the female gender of the Hebrew word, one automatically thinks of a hen, whence the use of that word to designate a woman." [12]

A few other words deserve commentary. There is a term for klezmer-loshn itself, *labushinske,* which is related to several other words: *lábushnik* (musician), *labéshnik* (musician; card-player), *labern* (play [music, cards]), and *labn* (play cards). Compare these to Russian *labát'* (play a musical instrument [deprecatory in musician's argot]) and *lábukh* (musician); German *labbern* (babble); and Russian dialect *lábaidat'* (mutter). Perhaps derived from the root *lab* by metathesis is *baln* (play music), whence also *bálishnik* (klezmer).

Two words that have made their way into "Yinglish" are also part of klezmer-loshn: *yold* and *zhlob.* Uriel Weinreich translated *yold* as "chump, dupe, sucker" and the adjective *yoldish* as "simple-minded." [13] Alexander Harkavy gives three meanings for *yold:* "son of a wealthy man," "dude, fop," and "simpleton, fool." [14] For *yoldish* he has only "foppish," and for *yoldovke* only "fashionable woman." He translates *yoldevn* as "play a trick on; make a fool of." Klezmer-loshn offers different meanings: *yold* is "a Jew (but not a klezmer); husband"; *yóldevke* is "a Jewish woman; wife"; and *yoldish* means "Jewish/Yiddish." In ganovim-loshn, the word *yold* functions in a similar way, meaning "nonthief" (likewise in Russian and Polish thieves' argot, although a 1903 dictionary of cant gives "inexperienced thief" and one from 1907 gives

Jew or merchant." [15] It is sometimes claimed that *yold* is from Hebrew *yeled* (boy), but another possible source is one of the Russian obscene terms for the male sexual organ, *elda*.[16]

As for the word *zhlob*, Harkavy provides "boor, peasant" and U. Weinreich, "yokel, hick, boor." In klezmer-loshn, the word means "a gentile, especially a peasant," and the corresponding feminine term is *zhlóbevke* or *zhlobukhe*. The Yiddish word may well be from Polish *żłób, żłobu* (trough).

In the first quarter of this century, when Yiddish philologists in eastern Europe took an interest in klezmer-loshn, it was already in decline. Samuel Weissenberg, for example, reported that younger musicians frequently did not know all the terms and sometimes had to resort to paraphrases.[17] Today we have only archaeological evidence from Yiddish literature and song. In a song by Shloyme Prizament (1889–1973), "Bin ikh mir a klezmerl," for example, the young fiddler realizes that his beloved Esther is unattainable.

> Zi iz a khsidishe "shekhtele,"
> dos iz nisht azoy gring.
> Vi kum ikh, a "labertshnik,"
> a proster klezmer ying.

> She is a hasidic girl;
> That's not so easy.
> Where do I fit in, a klezmer,
> A simple musician lad.[18]

Another song, "Klezmorim," by Moyshe Broderzon (1890–1956), ends its description of a wedding with the following lines:

> Di telerlekh zey klingen,
> di makhetonim zingen:
> Oy, neskim, neskim, labushnikes,
> Khapt nisht s'fleysh fun tish.

> The plates rattle,
> The bride's and groom's parents sing:
> Oh, no, no, musicians,
> Don't grab the meat off the table.[19]

In an earlier time, when klezmer-loshn was still alive, it was as much of an attraction for Yiddish-speaking youth as the "musician's lingo" used in Neugroschel's translation of *Stempenyu* was in its day for their American counterparts. In Irme Druker's 1940 novel *Klezmer,* whose hero, Ezra Malyarskin, is modeled after the violinist and music educator Petr Solomonovich Stoliarskii (1871–1944), the young Ezra, a klezmer's son, teaches his fellow *kheder* students klezmer-loshn. When the teacher is not in class, the boys test each other's knowledge of vocabulary. The result is:

> Di naye shprakh hot zikh zey azoy farkritst in zikorn, az nit eyn mol bam khumesh fartaytshn flegn zikh bay khevre aroyskhapn a taytsh fun klezmer-loshn:
> —Isho—a yoldevke!
> —Meshumed—flegt zikh Itshe ontsindn un farforn dem khevreman glaykh in ponem,—ver lernt mit dir, ikh tsi Ezra? Isho—a vaybl, a shed zol fun dir vern!

> The new language had embedded itself to such a degree in their memory that during Bible translation one of the boys might come out with a translation from klezmer-loshn:
> "*Isho* ["wife" in Hebrew]—*a yoldevke!*"
> "Apostate!" Itshe [the teacher] would flare up and hit the boy right in the face. "Who is your teacher, I or Ezra? *Isho—a vaybl* ["wife" in Yiddish]; may you turn into a ghost!"[20]

Klezmer-loshn was only one of several documented Yiddish argots. Trivaks, for example, examined it together with ganovim-loshn and the argot of coachmen *(balegole-loshn)*. Leon Dushman adds the argots of butchers *(katsovim-loshn)* and of barbers *(sherer-loshn)*. Yehude Elzet is less systematic, but provides information about the speech of shoemakers, bakers, blacksmiths, turners, watchmakers, tailors, coachmen, and musicians.[21] Of all of these, only ganovim-loshn was as highly developed as klezmer-loshn. Jewish musicians, it turns out, were accomplished wordsmiths as well as tunesmiths.

NOTES

1. The novel was first published in Kiev in the first volume of his annual, *Di yidishe folksbibliotek* (Kiev: Sholem Aleichem, 1888). On 11 January 1889, the author wrote to the historian Simon Dubnow, informing Dubnow that he was sending under separate cover a copy of "my new work *Stempenyu,* my first novel." He added that "the entire fate of my literary activity will depend on its success." Sholem Aleichem, *Sobranie sochinenii v shesti tomakh,* ed. M. Bazhan, et al. (Moscow: Khudozhestvennaia literatura, 1974), 6:678.

2. From *The Shtetl: A Creative Anthology of Jewish Life in Eastern Europe.* Translation © 1979 by Joachim Neugroschel. Published by The Overlook Press,

Woodstock, N.Y. Used by permission. Page 293. In this essay, the hero's name is transliterated from Yiddish in accordance with the YIVO standard as *Stempenyu;* Neugroschel preferred the spelling *Stempeniu.*

The original reads as follows:

> —Ver iz ot di dozike shekhte, vos shteyt nebn der smisanke?—fregt Stempenyu oyf klezmer-loshn, onvayzndik mit di oygn oyf Rokhele der sheyner.— Gey nor, Rakhmiel, —zogt er tsu eynem fun di geshvolene klezmer-yungen,—gey nor un probe oys mehe-tam, ober khidke, Rakhmiel, khidke!
>
> Rakhmiel kumt gikh tsurik mit a klorer tshuve:
>
> —Dos iz nit keyn shekhtl, dos iz shoyn a yoldovke. Dos iz Ayzik-Naftoles shnur, fun Skvire iz zi, un ot dos iz ir yold—zet ir? Ot dreyt er zikh arum mit a sametener katerukhe.
>
> —Di kapore zolstu vern, Rakhmiel!—zogt Stempenyu gants oyfgelegt. Azoy gikh bistu gevor gevorn? E, zi iz dokh taki gor a klive yoldovke! Ze nor, ze, vi zi matret mit di zikres!
>
> — Oyb ir vilt—fregt Rakhmiel der fershvolener bay Stempenyun—oyb ir vilt, vel ikh geyn mit ir tirn. . . .
>
> —Lig in drerd!— entfert im Stempenyu.—Me bet dikh nit far keyn shilatn- shames. Ikh vel aleyn tirn mit tsuzenikhe.

Sholem Aleichem, *Ale verk fun Sholem-Aleykhem* (New York: Sholem-Aleykhem folksfond, 1927), 135–36.

3. *Petit Larousse* (Paris: Librairie Larousse, 1963).

4. Max Weinreich, "Yidish," in *Algemeyne yidishe entsiklopedye* (New York: CYCO, 1940), 77.

5. Ber Borokhov, "Di bibliotek funem yidishn filolog. Fir hundert yor yidisher shprakh-forshung," in *Shprakh-forshung un literatur-geshikhte,* ed. N. Mayzel (Tel Aviv: Farlag I. L. Peretz, 1966), 122.

6. Avrom-Yitskhok Trivaks, "Di yidishe zhargonen," in *Bay undz yidn,* ed. M. Vanvild (Warsaw: Pinkhes Graubard, 1923), 159.

7. "Der bokher iz take a fayner bokher, me ken nisht zogn. Un a fardiner iz er oykh. Ver zogt den, az neyn? Nor vos kumt aroys, az er iz nebekh a klezmer, hostu gezen a bisl! . . . Draysik mol artist, koym shpilt er oyfn fidl, iz er a klez-mer. Take a fayner bokher. . . . Loz im Got tsushikn zayn ziveg, vi er fardint. . . . Un ir tokhter zol der Eybershter bashern epes andersh, vorem ir man olev-asholem hot aleyn nisht geshpilt oyfn fidl, un zayn tate hot nisht geshpilt oyfn fidl, un zayn tatns tate hot nit geshpilt afn fidl." Sholem Aleichem, *Oysgeveylte verk,* vol. 6 (Warsaw: Yidish bukh, 1955), 175.

8. Trivaks, "Di yidishe zhargonen," 159.

9. Cf. *shoyfer* (ram's horn blown on high holidays), Russian/Polish *chainik / czajnik* (teapot), *vorsht* (sausage), *leyenen blat* (read a page of the Talmud).

10. There are also numerous kinship and related terms. Instead of *khosn/ kale* (groom/bride), we find *bsan(ke), msan(ke), shvisán(ke), smasán(ke),* and *smosán(ke).* Others include *tamukh/tamushke* (for *mekhutn/mekhuteyneste* [son- or daughter-in-law's father/mother]); *smarik/smárikhe (smaritshke)* (old man/woman); *fotyashnik/fotyashnitse* (father/mother, especially of the groom) —perhaps from *foter* (father), with Slavic suffixes; and *smarer fotyashnik/smare fotyashnitse* (grandfather/grandmother).

11. Hence nouns denoting women's breasts *(bírgoln, krelikes, spyokhes, ukriles);* male and female sexual organs (respectively: *salép* [cf. Russian *salóp*],

shmurn, sop; ktute, ripke, sakhme, salepnitse); prostitutes or "loose" women (*roshvyalnitshke, tshovalnitse, zi delet di buye*—this may represent macaronic word play: *delet* from Russian *delaet* [makes, does] and *buye* from Hebrew and Yiddish *biye* [sexual intercourse]); and verbs denoting sexual intercourse *(klúnteven* [cf. *kluntevne,* "a brothel"], *róshvinen, tshobn).* Numerous words are derived by metathesis, i.e., by producing anagrams of ordinary Yiddish words. Examples include *geyzer* (watch) < *zeyger; khamen* (make) < *makhn; khat* (eight) < *akht; lakl* (bride) < *kale; loybish* (Polish) < *poylish; lyákike* (cripple) < *kalike; rishkhes* (wages) < *shkhires;* and *zokher* (pork) < *khazer.* Slavic material is also well represented, although reworked rather than simply borrowed, e.g., *batvo/batvikhe* (father/mother, especially of the bride) < Ukrainian *bat'ko* (father); *boytse hobn* (be afraid) < Russian *boiat'sia; kudren/kudreven* (smoke), *kudralnik* (cigarette), perhaps < Russian *kurit'* (smoke); *motren* (see, look), *motrenitse* (mirror), *materyalnik* (eye), perhaps < Russian *smotret'* (look); *tshakhnen* (be sick), *potshakhnen/pritshakhnen* (die) < Russian *chakhnut'* (wither away); *strisilye* (wedding) < Ukrainian *visill'ie,* whence (playing on the Slavic root that means "awful, terrible") *strashil* (idem); *ubirn* (take) < Russian *ubirat'* (take away), and its anagram *uribn* (give); *kliv* (good, beautiful), cf. Polish and Russian slang terms *klevyi/klawy*—whence *klivn* (love), *aynklivn zikh* (fall in love). Trivaks, "Di yidishe zhargonen," 159.

12. Alfred Landau, "Zur russisch-jüdischen 'Klesmer'sprache,'" *Mitteilungen der Anthropologischen Gesellschaft in Wien* 43 (1913): 148. Other examples include *esn links,* "eat non-kosher food" (the root for "left" means "illegal, false, underworld-related" in Yiddish and other criminal jargons); *per(y)ak/perdzhak* (doctor), from the Russian root meaning "fart"; *drapátsh* (scraper), a term of abuse directed at musicians (as in Irme Druker, *Klezmer* [Moscow: Sovetskii pisatel', 1976], 9: "Ir zayt drapatshes!" [You are scrapers!]) < Polish *drapak,* Ukrainian *driapách* (worn-out broom) (< Polish <drapac> [scratch]).

13. Uriel Weinreich, *Modern english-yidish yidish-english verterbukh/Modern English-Yiddish Yiddish-English Dictionary* (New York: YIVO/McGraw-Hill, 1968).

14. Alexander Harkavy, *Yidish-english-hebreisher verterbukh/Yiddish-English-Hebrew Dictionary,* 4th ed. (New York: Hebrew Publishing, 1928).

15. Karol Estreicher, *Szwargot więzienny* (Cracow: Księgarnia D. E. Friedleina, 1903); Antoni Kurka, *Słownik mowy złodziejskiej,* 3d ed. (Lwów: Antoni Kurka, 1907).

16. See, for example, Trivaks, "Di yidishe zhargonen," 163, and see also Tat'iana Vasil'evna Akhmetova, comp., *Russkii mat* (Moscow: Kolokol-press, 1997), 118.

17. Samuel Weissenberg, "Die 'Klesmer'sprache," *Mitteilungen der Anthropologischen Gesellschaft in Wien* 43 (1913): 133.

18. Shloyme Prizament, *Broder zinger* (Buenos Aires: Tsentral-farband fun poylishe yidn in argentine, 1960), 49–50. I am grateful to Jeff Warschauer for this reference.

19. Reprinted in Chane and Yosl Mlotek's column, "Perl fun der yidisher poezye," *Forverts* (22 November 1996): 13.

20. Druker, *Klezmer*, 35.

21. Trivaks, "Di yidishe zhargonen," 159–73; Leon Dushman, "Fakhleshones," *Tsaytshrift far yidisher geshikhte, demografye un ekonomik, literaturforshung, shprakh-visnshaft un etnografye* [Minsk] 2–3 (1928): 875–77; Yehude Elzet, "Melokhes un bale-melokhes," part 4 of *Der vunder-oytser fun der yidisher shprakh* (Warsaw: Bracia Lewin-Epsztein, 1920), 32–42.

CHAPTER 3

Di Rusishe Progresiv Muzikal Yunyon No. 1 fun Amerike

The First Klezmer Union in America

JAMES LOEFFLER

In his 1902 play, *The Kreutzer Sonata,* Yiddish playwright Jacob Gordin presents an intriguing scenario: two klezmorim, Efroym Fidler and son Gregor, emigrate to New York. The son goes on to become a successful classical musician and teacher, while the father struggles to make a living from music and complains bitterly of restrictions on his craft: "I, an old klezmer, must stand for an examination to see whether I'm a decent musician. And if I'm good enough as a musician, I still have to bring in twenty-five dollars in order to be allowed to work as a klezmer. And, worst of all, when I am already a klezmer, I must stand in line until someone officially declares me to be a klezmer. Oy, I've been a klezmer for forty years already. Oy, I need to eat. Oy, I don't have twenty-five dollars. . . ." [1] What makes it so difficult for Efroym Fidler to survive by playing music? It is, of course, the Jewish musicians' union, which labels him a scab for not paying its exorbitant entrance fees. Efroym himself notes the irony, that "*Gevald,* in darkest Russia, anyone who wants to fiddle does so and here in free America you need to ask for permission!" [2] Yet before the play's end, the older klezmer is reinvented again. He reveals that he has quit the union and opened his own music school on Houston Street, joining the ranks of the well-paid capitalists. [3]

What is one to make of this chain of events, especially given that one hears so little from later immigrant klezmorim about the role of the union in their lives? Is Gordin's portrayal an accurate critique or a melodramatic mischaracterization of the union as it existed then? Although

Figure 3.1 Cover to sheet music for a *Trauer-March* played at a 1905 rally.
From Mark Slobin's collection.

there is much speculation as to the activities and experiences of American klezmorim before World War I, short of saying that these musicians found work in the Yiddish theater and at weddings, restaurants,
and cafes on the Lower East Side, historians know little about this pre-
recording community. To some extent this chronological gap stems from
a lack of information; written sources from this period are rare and the

wave of klezmer oral history began too late to catch survivors. But it is also characteristic of a certain trend in American Jewish history, that of canonizing certain cultural epochs and institutions at the expense of others. Few remember, for example, that the *Jewish Daily Forward* (1897) was preceded by twenty years of Yiddish-language journalism, or that before Ellis Island immigrants disembarked in New York at the even more notorious processing center known as Castle Garden. So, too, is it with the first generation of American klezmorim. The interwar recording age of American klezmer music is well documented and heavily promoted as the classical period, the Golden Age, therefore obscuring several decades of earlier activity.[4]

What follows is a brief attempt to rescue another early American Jewish institution from historical oblivion—*di rusishe progresiv muzikal yunyon no. 1 fun amerike* (the Russian Progressive Musical Union No. 1 of America)—the first Jewish musicians' union in the United States and the missing link in the history of the migration of klezmer music and musicians from eastern Europe to the United States.[5] The origins of this union also reveal a great deal about the early effects of social, cultural, and political currents of urban America on this genre of eastern European Jewish music, and about the overall transformation of traditional Yiddish culture in the New World.

While the Jewish labor movement was destined to become the single most important force in the lives of Jewish immigrants within a decade, in the 1880s it was still struggling to gain a foothold in the community. Political organizations such as the Russian Progressive Union, the Central Labor Union, the Knights of Labor, the Socialist Labor Party, and even the Libertarian Socialists (anarchists) each made several unsuccessful attempts to organize Jewish unions throughout the early and mid 1880s. The birth of a Jewish musicians' union owed everything to the establishment of what was to be for decades the foremost institution in New York Jewish politics: the *fareynikte idishe geverkshaftn*, or United Hebrew Trades (UHT). Conceived and initiated in October 1888 as a federation of Jewish unions, the UHT quickly found that it would have to take the lead in creating unions itself or else remain "a mere shell."[6] So in early 1889, the UHT launched an aggressive organizing campaign.[7] Initial successes included the Yiddish theater actors, cloakmakers, tailors, and soda-water makers. Amidst this flurry of labor activism, in March 1889, there appeared a "Jewish musicians' union."[8] A few months later, the UHT delegate to the Socialist International Congress in Paris reported that the "Russian Musical Union, a group of Russian-

and Yiddish-speaking musicians," counted as one of his federation's ten member unions.[9]

The next solid evidence regarding this Jewish musicians' union comes from the Yiddish press for the following year. The *Arbayter Tsaytung* was a newspaper closely linked to the United Hebrew Trades and therefore from its first issue, on 7 March 1890, the editors began to publish union notices and brief minutes from the UHT member unions.[10] The first issue also contains an advertisement for the Russian Progressive Musical Union No. 1 of America (RPMU), which "represented in the United Hebrew Trades, recommend themselves—and their modest prices—for weddings, balls, and parades and suggest that all unions and worker organizations, lodges and associations should contact their office to make arrangements, 412 Grand Street, New York" (*Arbayter Tsaytung,* hereafter cited as *AT,* 7 March 1890).[11]

A survey of the *Arbayter Tsaytung* issues for the next few years conveys a strong sense of both the general role and specific details of the union, making it an invaluable window into this organization of Jewish musicians. The union functioned with a governing board (general secretary, treasurer, UHT delegates), which turned over constantly (*AT,* 25 March 1890). The board held weekly meetings and committees were elected to deal with specific business and administrative matters. Meetings were held first at the local headquarters at 412 Grand Street and then, from 1891, in a variety of locations, including various rented meeting halls as well as the building of the *Arbayter Tsaytung* at 81 Ludlow Street.[12] Occasional special meetings dealt with serious issues, such as reorganization of the group or union-related fraud. From at least October 1890, a constitution existed (*AT,* 24 October 1890). It was eventually published and distributed to other unions in October of the following year (*AT,* 16 October 1891).

The identity and power of the union were inextricably linked to that of its parent organization, the United Hebrew Trades. The union fed a constant stream of communications and petitions to the federation. Much of the exchange involved the enforcement of the UHT's union-only hiring policy, which guaranteed work at all union-sponsored events to UHT-affiliated musicians. The union also turned to the United Hebrew Trades in search of more business for its members. Another method of attracting clients was constant advertising in the pages of the United Hebrew Trades–sponsored *Arbayter Tsaytung.* Ads tended to run in stints of two months and included a basic sales pitch for the union's music and connections to the UHT, along with contact information (*AT*, 24 October and 25 April 1890; 6 February and 10 April 1891).[13]

The fractious politics of the Second Socialist International and the unstable labor market conditions of immigrant New York meant that reorganization was a common fact of life.[14] Writing about the late 1880s and early 1890s United Hebrew Trades unions, labor leader Morris Hillquit reflected on the transience of unions for occupations such as musicians, retail-store clerks, bookbinders, and soda-water makers: "In practically all cases the unions were short-lived. They came and went and had to be reorganized every few years. In the minds of the Jewish workers of that period the unions were associated with strikes and were little more than instruments of strikes."[15]

For the most part lacking an external adversary (i.e., bosses), the Jewish musicians were even less inclined to maintain their union continuously.[16] Indeed, it is easy to imagine a scenario where the musicians were inspired or challenged to organize themselves in the first place because of the aggressive and successful choristers' and actors' unions, fellow performing artists whose paths they crossed in the Yiddish theater and elsewhere.[17] Or perhaps some enterprising musicians saw the potential for tapping into the trade unions' business by joining the labor movement itself. In either case, it comes as little surprise that the musicians —like everyone else—required constant reorganization. Several times over the course of the early 1890s, the union restructured itself, often through the direct intervention of the United Hebrew Trades.[18] Competing Jewish musicians' unions frequently appeared, but they were persistently co-opted or muscled out by the UHT's union.[19] Within the union, the UHT played a definitive role in resolving disputes between individual musicians as well as among larger political factions. Furthermore, the UHT bolstered the authority of the union by officially recognizing the reorganized version and its charter each time.[20]

The periodic administrative reinvention of the union was frequently accompanied by a change of name. Altogether, the constantly evolving names tell a story of shifting cultural identity, from the Russian Progressive Musical Union No. 1 of America (March 1890) to the Progressive Musical Union (December 1890) to the Liberty Musical Union No. 1 of America (1891–92) to the Musical Liberty Protective Union (1893–95) to the American Musical Protective Union No. 1 (1895). The origin of the Russian Progressive Musical Union's name is unclear. While most unions in the United Hebrew Trades had quite mundane names, such as the Cloakmakers' Union or the Knee-Pants Makers' Union, the musicians chose a very distinct and clearly contemporary title. One possibility is that the members proposed a more politicized name to clarify their otherwise ambiguous presence as professionals among trade and industrial workers. The term *progressive* would also have located the union squarely in the mainstream of the social consciousness of the time. The adjective *Russian* might have had multiple connotations, suggesting an affinity with Europe and socialist politics hearkening back to the earlier Russian Progressive Union and Russian Labor Lyceum, or merely articulating the members' country of origin, typical of many trade unions of the day.[21] Whatever the case, over a remarkably short period of time, the Jewish musicians thus moved from an initial Old World point of orientation to more and more generic cultural tropes, from *Russian* to *Liberty* to *American*—a strikingly symbolic evolution.

We cannot draw larger conclusions about the official titles of the union, because variations on each name were also common within each period. Adjectives would switch places and occasionally temporarily disappear, thus in the same issue of the *Arbayter Tsaytung* the union would be referred to as both the *Protective Liberty Musical Union* and the *Musical Liberty Protective Union*. Administrative and professional demands may also have preceded any larger political considerations. Continuities in terms of the union's personnel, place of meeting, and relationship to the United Hebrew Trades nevertheless certify that it is the same union each time. Interestingly enough, in May 1896 the union returned to its original headquarters (412 Grand Street) after a six-year absence (*AT*, 29 May 1896).

The question of cultural identity becomes even more complex regarding the union's membership, the musicians themselves. These musicians were undoubtedly eastern European klezmorim; what else could a "Russian" Jewish immigrant musician in 1890s New York be? In point of fact, however, the term *klezmer* is found nowhere in the writings connected to the union. Yet this absence is not surprising given the extreme pattern of cultural assimilation exhibited by the klezmorim in the United States. The klezmorim themselves took the lead in this process by stripping off their most distinguishing socioprofessional label, the term *klezmer*. In the earliest references to klezmer bands at American Jewish weddings in the 1890s and early 1900s, the use of the term *klezmer* is strikingly absent, even when other Yiddish words are used to describe the proceedings.[22] Among early New York klezmorim, the terms *orchestra* and *professor* likewise predominated.[23] In describing his first piano teacher of 1908, Yiddish theater composer Sholem Secunda recalled, "On the Lower East Side, every hack wedding musician proclaimed himself 'professor.'"[24] The union's advertisements and self-descriptions reveal that this trend began as early as 1890, less than a decade after the start of mass immigration from eastern Europe to the United States; however, they offer no further explanation of its specific origins.

As in the Old World, the bulk of Jewish musicians earned their living from private jobs in the Jewish wedding and *simkhe* (celebration) business. This is clear from the constant newspaper advertisements and exhortations to the union community to hire union members for their *hokhtsayten* (weddings), as well as from the union's attempts to regulate the *privat-dzshob* (private job) industry. There is also a fascinating mention of a union meeting with legendary *badkhn* (wedding jester) Eliakum Zunser at which a "compromise . . . was made over the price of Jewish weddings. In addition, he was inducted into our union as a member" (*AT*, 1 August 1890).[25] Zunser's presence alone suggests the musicians' deep connection to the eastern European milieu and hence their identity as klezmorim. Finally, the best example of a musical description of the union band's performance identifies their repertoire with specific genres associated with klezmer music: "The Russian *kamarinskaya* . . . the Hungarian *tsardas [czardas]*, the Polish *mazurka*, and the Romanian *bolgarka*" (*AT*, 25 July 1890).

Despite these continuities in performance context and repertoire for New York klezmorim, new professional opportunities began to emerge in the form of the Yiddish theater and a large roster of social and political engagements within the New York Jewish community. The early presence of immigrant klezmorim in the Yiddish theater makes sense given later musicians' active involvement. Yet the dynamic role of the union is quite startling. In 1890, in New York, there were only two Yiddish theaters in existence: the Thalia theater and the Romania Opera House.[26] The musicians of both theaters' orchestras were union members, and the union even negotiated an industry wage increase with the management (*AT*, 20 October and 27 October 1891). Negotiations with other theater industry–related groups, such as the choristers' and bill-posters' unions and the Socialist Dramatic League, were also common (*AT*, 5 January, 19 January, and 7 July 1894). At times, the union even struggled to maintain its authority over the theater musicians, who were prone to make their own deals with the theater management (*AT*, 2 March and 18 May 1894). Theater orchestra work emphasized new professional skills and techniques not previously required of klezmorim in eastern Europe, such as the ability to read music, the ability to play in a large ensemble (often twice the size of the largest eastern European klezmer bands), and competency in accompanying singers in full-length dramatic performances.[27]

What really complicates the picture of the early American klezmorim is the other activities of the union, which clearly took the immigrant musicians into wholly new realms of socioprofessional identity, political involvement, and musical performance. The huge mass of Jewish immigrants in New York City, hungry for entertainment and community, naturally gave rise to a large variety of engagements, including worker's association and *landsmanshaft* (an organization of Jews from a specific European city or town) balls, benefit concerts, picnics, and other excursions. With very few exceptions, all of these events had some political sponsorship, because every aspect of the immigrant Jewish community was blatantly politicized. More frequently than not, the Jewish labor movement and its constituent unions were involved.

This was the dawn of the era of mass politics in American society. Parades, rallies, and strikes all took place with incredible frequency, thanks to the interlocking complex of newspapers, political parties, unions, and the commercial halls that were used for large indoor public events.[28] Like the bulk of other Jewish immigrants, klezmorim were in most cases from traditional eastern European Jewish communities and had little exposure to the swirling currents of progressive politics before hitting American shores. Even for the better-traveled and urbanized klezmorim, the union's charge into politics would have been a radical change. To all United Hebrew Trades or *Arbayter Tsaytung*–sponsored events—as well as myriad other benefit concerts, dances, and picnics—the union sent official ensembles to perform.

Dependent on the United Hebrew Trades for its very existence, the musicians' union took its socialist political charge seriously. This conviction meant that in most cases members donated their performances at political events for free. A typical newspaper description reads, "No one can say that the Russian Progressive Musical Union has not voluntarily and wholeheartedly supported the unions with its music during the strikes and boycotts" (*AT*, 31 October 1890). Once the union even went so far as to expel members who performed at an anarchists' meeting in November 1891 (*AT*, 20 November 1891). The union also dealt harshly with its own members who performed with scabs, uniformly suspending them and in most cases expelling them (*AT*, 6 February and 20 November 1891).[29] An interesting case involves one Professor A. Grinberg. In February 1891, Grinberg was kicked out of the union for playing with scab musicians. He promptly retaliated with an impressive and costly one-month advertising campaign in the union's own newspaper, the *Arbayter Tsaytung,* thus turning it into a vehicle for his own capitalist ambitions (*AT,* 6 February 1891). Beginning in 1889, the union also sought to enforce its authority by issuing union cards, which members were supposed to display to prospective customers (*AT,* 9 May and 23 May 1890).[30]

The diversity of events requiring music made the union responsible for fielding groups of varying sizes. While picnics and other outdoor events might typically receive anywhere from seven to thirteen musicians, strikes and concerts could usually get from twelve to twenty men, and mass rallies and parades might get upward of thirty men or from one to three orchestras (*AT,* 1890, passim).[31] Thus the well-known growth in size of klezmer ensembles during this period could have been due as much to the acoustic and logistical demands of a mass rally of thousands of people as to any other factor.[32]

The number and availability of musicians raises the question of membership. In other words, just how large and representative was the union itself? Unfortunately, there are no satisfactory statistics on the New York klezmer community of the 1880s and 1890s. The 1890 Baron de Hirsch survey of three Jewish districts of lower Manhattan reported that out of a total of roughly twenty-two thousand gainfully employed Jews, a mere sixty-seven, or 0.3 percent, were "musicians."[33] A report from the first Congress of Jewish and Canadian Workers, held 4 October 1890, provides a figure of thirty members for the Russian Musical Union, a common shorthand designation for the union (*AT,* 10 October 1890). The next concrete statistic for the size of the union comes from December 1891, a little over a year into its existence, when the Liberty Musical Union declared itself to number one hundred "members in good standing" (*AT,* 4 December 1891). At that time it still constituted one of the smallest unions in the United Hebrew Trades.

The inclusiveness of the musicians' union is also difficult to assess. While their fellow artists in the Hebrew Actors' Union were notoriously closed-shop and elitist, the Jewish musicians appear to have run a rather open, accessible union. Entry into the union did require a *probe* or jury examination of musical skills. But recurrent membership drives allowed musicians to join "without probe" for an entrance fee of one dollar (*AT,* 22 August and 24 October 1890; 8 June 1895). It would appear that Gordin's dramatic vision of the musicians' union was not wholly accurate. Indeed, according to Yiddish actor Muni Weisenfreund (later Paul

Muni), Gordin's union parody was actually a disguised critique of the Hebrew Actors' Union, an organization well known for its coercive and even tyrannical hold on the Yiddish theater.[34]

Of all the holes in the documented historical record, the largest one is regrettably in our knowledge of the music itself. There are apparently no recordings or transcriptions from this earliest era to glimpse the music and the musical change as it occurred. However, there are some clues from which to ascertain the effects of the union experience on the klezmorim and their repertoire. First and foremost, the exposure to and familiarity with labor and socialist songs was the result neither of later union practices nor of the recording-studio experience. The pages of the *Arbayter Tsaytung* overflow with mentions of spirited renditions of the "Marseillaise" at every parade and socialist rally. The musicians also performed other contemporary workers' songs. In every case, the music's effect on the crowds was described as electric (*AT,* 9 May and 11 July 1890; 17 April 1891).[35] Take, for example, this description of a *Shabbat* labor parade of four thousand people: The "music . . . ignited the entire neighborhood with mighty melodies of freedom, equality, and brotherhood. . . . Their inspiring music is the best expression of their brotherly share in the general labor movement of America and of the whole world" (*AT,* 14 March 1890).

Two slightly later mentions provide a bit more detail concerning the repertoire. A report of the 1894 Election Day parade for Jewish Tammany Hall candidates speaks of Jewish musicians playing John Philip Sousa marches, confirming the trend of marching band music. Then, much later at a 1905 strike, an official union band played the "Marseillaise," the wedding dance tune "Khosn kale mazeltov," and the popular Yiddish song, "Lebn zol Kolumbus."[36]

In terms of musical style, the best picture of the genre comes from a description of a July 1890 excursion, at which the union's "good and skillful orchestra" provided "merry music." The rest of the text reads,

> The music was as creative and diverse as the Jewish people themselves. Every single person had the chance to hear the old, beloved songs of his former homeland and to dance his native dances. After the Russian *kamarinskaya* followed the Hungarian *tsardas [czardas],* the Polish *mazurka,* and the Romanian *bolgarka,* and the Jewish representatives from the different countries united as brothers in one international dance. (*AT,* 25 July 1890)

In many ways, this passage raises more questions than it answers. Just what was the "international dance"? And what was the practical distinction between the "old, beloved songs" and the "native dances" mentioned? At the same time, this description does suggest one valuable fact: the musicians possessed a strong knowledge of the different regional repertoires such that they could provide the full variety indicated.[37]

As for instrumentation, two sources from the 1890s confirm the combination of drums and brass as standard for Jewish parades of that time.[38] The loudness (and martial character) of these instruments would have made them ideal for large public rallies, just as it secured a consistent place for them in the klezmer recordings of the 1910s and afterward.[39] The following detailed account of an 1890s parade is probably the most fitting way to close the discussion of the union's structure and performance activities: "The Jewish Musicians' Union turned out in force—brass, drums, and fifes—and they blared forth the 'Marseillaise.' . . . At 10 AM sharp, the band struck up officially. The five policemen, followed by the standard bearers, who were numerous because all organizations represented had their banners in line, headed the march. Following them were the musicians."[40]

The Jewish musicians' union continued throughout the late 1890s and 1900s and officially resurfaced after World War I as the Musical Progressive Benevolent Association.[41] By that time, the union was on its last legs, as New York's Jewish musicians had already begun to integrate themselves into the mainstream locals of the American Federation of Musicians (AFM), the preeminent labor union of American musicians.[42] Following the formation of Local 802 of the AFM in 1921, the union officially changed into a *landsmanschaft,* with its members entering the 802.[43]

The story of klezmorim in New York during the 1880s and 1890s forces a reconsideration of several basic issues of klezmer historiography. Specifically, the activities of this musicians' union challenge the general notion that repertoire diversification occurred primarily in the recording-studio era, which began in the early 1910s.[44] The information about this union's political and economic activities also paints the Jewish musicians of the time in a more complex light with regard to the otherwise swift transition from folk to popular performers. The union appears to have been an ambiguous intermediary stage—both historically and culturally—before the move to mainstream American musicians' unions and work. Like many other traditional or folk institutions from eastern Europe, the practice and profession of the klezmorim underwent a radically new political transformation in the New World. This change could not have occurred without the very new sources of work outside the sphere of traditional Jewish celebrations: the political rallies, parades, and benefit concerts, all connected to the labor movement. On the other hand, the ostensible politicization of the Jewish musicians must be weighed against their growing involvement with the commercial entertainment industry, including the Yiddish theater, the dance hall industry, and even the commercial wedding hall business. Both sets of experiences raised new challenges and fostered new socioprofessional roles for the klezmorim in their quest to succeed in the modern American urban economy. Finally, the overall picture of the union activities suggests an immigrant klezmer community in New York that was just that: a community, with a strongly unified conception of their professionalism and common socioeconomic interests in weddings, Yiddish theater work, and many other engagements. The existence of this strong community only compounds the mystery of what happened to the klezmorim in the two decades following World War I. But perhaps the secret lies precisely in Jacob Gordin's dramatic formulation of the paradox, that is, in the divergence of the two generations. For in response to his father's determination to remain a klezmer and succeed in the New World, Gregor Fidler offers the following brief but telling declaration, "I am not a klezmer, I am an artist."[45]

NOTES

I would like to thank the following individuals for their thoughtful comments and suggestions: Jeremy Eichler, Walter Zev Feldman, Gila Flam, Arthur Aryeh Goren, Barbara Kirshenblatt-Gimblett, Joel Rubin, Henry Sapoznik, Mark Slobin, and Jed Sugarman. In addition, Jane C. Loeffler and William O. Selig provided invaluable editorial assistance in the preparation of this manuscript for publication.

1. Jacob Gordin, *Yakov Gordin's Dramen* (New York: Soyrkel fun Yakov Gordin's fraynt, 1911), vol. 2, 29. See also Jacob Gordin, *The Kreutzer Sonata,* adp. Langdon Mitchell (New York: Harrison Grey and Fiske, 1907). Unless otherwise noted, all translations are mine.

2. Gordin, *Yakov Gordin's Dramen,* vol. 2, 29.

3. Ibid., 60.

4. This phenomenon is easily visible in the catalog of Global Village Records, a company responsible for many of the klezmer re-releases of the 1980s, with its emphasis on such 1920s and 1930s recording artists as Dave Tarras, Abe Schwartz, and Israel J. Hochman, to the exclusion of numerous artists from both the prewar and postwar periods. Lately this trend has begun to be reversed, albeit slightly, with the release of new anthologies, including *Klezmer Pioneers: European and American Recordings, 1905–1952* (Rounder CD 1089, 1993);

Yikhes: Klezmer Recordings from 1907 to 1939, from the collection of Professor Martin Schwartz (Trikont LC 4270, 1991); and *Klezmer Music: Early Yiddish Instrumental Music, The First Recordings: 1908–1927* (Arhoolie Folklyric CD 7034, 1997).

5. The subject of European precedents for a union of Jewish musicians is too far outside the range of the present study for consideration here. The limited scholarship suggests that Jewish musicians did often form guilds in various parts of eastern Europe. However, these organizations were primarily trade associations focused more on regulating local economic competition and providing mutual aid. They lacked the political cast and social network of modern trade unions. For a sampling of research on this subject, see Itsik Shvarts, "Jewish Musicians in Moldavia," http://www.klezmershack.com/articles/1972.moldavia.shvarts.html (28 April 2000); German Zaagsma, "The klezmorim of Prague," http://www.klezmershack.com/articles/zaagsma.prague.html (28 April 2000); Mark Wischnitzer, *A History of Jewish Crafts and Guilds* (New York: Jonathan David, 1965), 237; and Joachim Stutschewsky, *Ha-klezmarim: Toldotehem, oraḥ-hayehem vi-yetsirotehem* (Jerusalem: Mosad Bialik, 1959), 66.

6. Morris Hillquit, *Loose Leaves from a Busy Life* (New York: Macmillan, 1934), 20.

7. Melech Epstein, *Jewish Labor in the U.S.A.* (New York: Trade Union Sponsoring Committee, 1950), 117, 124.

8. Bernard Weinstein, *Idishe yunyons in amerike* (New York: United Hebrew Trades, 1929), 148. There remain faint clues that suggest the existence of earlier, presumably short-lived, musicians' unions. For one, labor historian Melech Epstein's account of the labor movement of July 1886 includes a reference to one Thies, cafe/saloon owner on Fourteenth Street, who was boycotted for the mistreatment of "his union musicians and waiters" (*Jewish Labor in the U.S.A.*, 145). Epstein neglects to provide a source for this incident. In addition, he reproduces an editorial from a private weekly, *Volks Advocate*, from Labor Day 1888, commenting on the Labor Day parade of 1886 in which "the Jewish streets resounded to the merry music of the Jewish unions" (131).

9. International Socialist Congress, *Protokoll des Internationalen Arbeiter-Congresses zu Paris* (Nurnberg: Worlein, 1890), 115–16.

10. On the history of the *Arbayter Tsaytung*, see Hillquit, *Loose Leaves,* 34–37.

11. In many cases, the newspaper's Yiddish was archaic and the spelling irregular. When passages are quoted, they are transliterated in accordance with standard YIVO orthography.

12. Other addresses listed include 274 Grand St., 193 East 2d St., and 80 Clinton St.

13. For a brief time, this practice was supplemented by ads in the *Nyu-York Yidisher Folkstsaytung* until its demise (*AT,* 9 May 1890).

14. For more on the complex relations between trade unions and the international socialist and anarchist organizations and political parties, see James Joll, *The Second International, 1889–1914* (London: Routledge, 1966), 22–55.

15. Hillquit, *Loose Leaves,* 28–29.

16. For more on the identity of musicians as workers, see John R. Commons, *Labor and Administration* (New York: Macmillan, 1913), 297–301, 310–11. See also Wischnitzer, *A History*, 237–40.

17. There remains the little-researched issue of the Yiddish theater orchestra musicians and their professional identity. Beyond mention of their wage negotiations, these musicians are notably absent from accounts of other striking unions of Yiddish theater professionals.

18. For the details on these developments, see *AT*, 14 August 1891; 5 January 1894; 20 January and 8 June 1895.

19. Anarchist Saul Yanovsky recounts a national convention of anarchists in New York on 25 December 1889 at which two musicians' unions from New York were present. No more information about them is provided. Saul Yanovsky, *Ershte yorn fun yidishn frayhaytlekhn sotsializm* (New York: Fraye Arbayter Shtime, 1948), 243. In the pages of the *Arbayter Tsaytung*, there are references to clashes with other musicians' unions, such as the National Music Union (1890) and the Manhattan Protective Union (1894) (*AT*, 24 October 1890; 18 May 1894).

20. On 28 August 1891, the column read, "Liberty Musical Union No. 1 of America / Under this name, the United Hebrew Trades has organized all Yiddish-speaking musicians." There is no indication that this is not the same union as before (*AT*, 28 August 1891; 20 January 1895; 14 October 1895).

21. For an explanation of this euphemism, see Elias Tcherikower, ed., and Anton Antonovsky, trans. and ed., *The Early Jewish Labor Movement in United States* (New York: YIVO Institute for Jewish Research, 1961), 156–57, 363–65. See also Alexander M. Dushkin, "A Statistical Study of the Jewish Population of New York," in *The Jewish Communal Register of New York City, 1917–1918*, 2d ed. (New York: Kehillah [Jewish Community] of New York City, 1918), 82–90.

22. In a 1905 description of a Philadelphia wedding, for instance, the social worker refers to the name of the dance in Yiddish (*shear [sher]*), but calls the klezmer band simply the *orchestra*. See Charlotte Kimball Patten, "Amusements and Social Life: Philadelphia," in *The Russian Jew in the United States*, ed. Charles S. Bernheimer (Philadelphia: John Winston, 1905), 244. See also Abraham Cahan, "A Ghetto Wedding," in *The Imported Bridegroom and Other Stories of the New York Ghetto* (Boston: Houghton, Mifflin, 1898), 27–29.

23. Gordin, *Yakov Gordin's Dramen*, vol. 2, 60. Also, *AT*, 6 February 1891.

24. Quoted in Victoria Secunda, *Bei Mir Bist Du Schön: The Life of Sholem Secunda* (New York: Magic Circle Press, 1982), 64. While the term *professor* also had vaudeville connotations, its use in a Jewish context more likely denoted reference to the liberal professions such as medicine and academia. See Elizabeth G. Stern, *My Mother and I* (New York: Macmillan, 1917), 47.

25. Unfortunately, the numerous, detailed accounts of Zunser and his activities ignore this period in his life almost entirely and come either from his European heyday or his post-badkhn career as a printer. See, for example, Hutchins Hapgood, *The Spirit of the Ghetto* (New York: Funk and Wagnalls, 1902), 91–92; Morris Winchevsky, "Eliakum Zunser: Jester, Printer and Writer of Yiddish

Verses," *New Era* 6, no. 3 (1905): 297–300. See also Eliakum Zunser, *Tsunzers biografye: geshriebn fun im aleyn,* ed. Abraham Hyman Fromenson (New York: Tsunzer yubileum komite, 1905).

26. Elias Tcherikower, *Di geshikhte fun der yidishe arbeter-bavegung in di fareynikte shtatn,* 2 vols. (New York: YIVO Institute for Jewish Studies, 1943–45), 1129.

27. The long-term effects of the Yiddish theater on klezmorim and klezmer music have not been documented in any significant form. For more on this topic, see Victoria Secunda, *Bei Mir Bist Du Schön,* 64–67; Nahma Sandrow, *Vagabond Stars: A World History of the Yiddish Theater* (New York: Harper and Row, 1977), 113–14; Mark Slobin, "Some Intersections of Jews, Music, and Theater," in *From Hester Street to Hollywood: The Jewish-American Stage and Screen,* ed. Sarah Blacher-Cohen (Bloomington: Indiana University Press, 1983), 29–43; Henry Sapoznik, "Dave Tarras: Father of Yiddish-American Klezmer Music, 1926–1956," liner notes for *Dave Tarras: Yiddish-American Klezmer Music, 1925–1956* (Yazoo 7001, 1991).

28. While there is no substitute for the pages of the Yiddish press, two authoritative historical accounts also capture this social phenomenon. See Moses Rischin, *The Promised City: New York's Jews, 1870–1914* (New York: Corinth, 1964), 152–94; also, Irving Howe, *World of Our Fathers* (New York: Harcourt Brace Jovanovich, 1976), 101–5, 287–325.

29. Union solidarity was important enough that the Russian Progressive Musical Union threatened members who bought bread from nonunion bakers with suspension (*AT,* 29 August 1890). Though frequent, suspension was usually a temporary measure (*AT,* 2 May 1890).

30. Cards were common to both Jewish and mainstream American unions during this era. However, this practice became problematic once nonunion musicians acquired old cards and used them to pass as legitimate members (*AT,* 24 October 1890).

31. While a ten-thousand–person rally would usually require at least three orchestras, a two-thousand–person rally might receive only one orchestra. Unfortunately, the range of numbers makes it difficult to gauge what constitutes an *orchestra* or a *double orchestra,* but it seems quite likely that these terms were flexible (*AT,* 8 May 1891).

32. Other possible factors for this development include the influential military and commercial dance bands that many klezmorim had contact with in Europe and the United States. See Mark Slobin, *Tenement Songs: The Popular Music of the Jewish Immigrants* (Urbana: University of Illinois Press, 1982), 21.

33. Tcherikower and Antonovsky, *The Early Jewish Labor Movement,* 154.

34. Jerome Lawrence, *Actor: The Life and Times of Paul Muni* (New York: G. P. Putnam's Sons, 1974), 26. For more on the general history of the Hebrew Actors' Union, see David S. Lifson, *The Yiddish Theatre in America* (New York: Thomas Yoseloff, 1965), 130–34. During an 1895 meeting for reorganization, the musicians' union decided against having multiple "classes" in the union, an established practice of the Hebrew Actors' Union whereby new members were relegated to a lower level of work opportunities in smaller and regional theaters.

See Herman Yablokoff, *Arum der velt mit idish teater: Oytobiografishe iber-lebungen un teater-dertseylungen,* 2 vols. (New York: Herman Yablokoff, 1968–69), vol. 1, 542–59; vol. 2, 155–67.

35. Take, for instance, the following description of a May Day parade, circa 1890, recorded by Abraham Cahan: "Caught up in the music, a Jewish *baleboste* forgot to prepare a red flag to display support. Instead she grabs a red tablecloth and ties it to her broomstick. With that she waves a greeting to the marchers from her window." Abraham Cahan, *Bleter fun mayn lebn,* vol. 3 (New York: Forverts, 1926), 64.

36. Sol Blumenson, "Revolt of the Reefer Makers," *Commentary* 8, no. 1 (February 1949): 65.

37. These dances may also fit into Walter Zev Feldman's four-part model of klezmer music's historical development, which involves a "core repertoire" of eastern European klezmer music—a central, shared body of Jewish tunes common throughout eastern Europe—along with three other categories: localized national dances, such as those in the cited passage; international, "cosmopolitan" dances, known throughout Europe, such as the waltz; and a "transitional" repertoire of melodies that have been partially assimilated into the Jewish from an external source. In terms of this last category, Feldman has specifically analyzed the ways in which one particular national musical genre, the Moldavian *bulgărească,* gradually metamorphosed musically and linguistically into an eastern European Jewish *bulgarish* and eventually into the dominant American Jewish klezmer genre known as the *bulgar.* Thus the "Romanian *bolgarka*" mentioned is significant, for it may very well represent a partially Americanized stage in line with Feldman's model. See Walter Z. Feldman, "Bulgărească/Bulgarish/Bulgar: The Transformation of a Klezmer Dance Genre," chapter 6 of this volume.

38. Epstein, *Jewish Labor in the U.S.A.,* 207; Sol Blumenson, "Utopia on Columbia Street," *Commentary* 6, no. 4 (October 1948), 361.

39. For more on the effects of recording technology on early-twentieth-century klezmer music, see James Loeffler, "A Gilgul fun a Nigun: Jewish Musicians in New York, 1881–1945," Harvard Judaica Collection Student Research Papers, no. 3 (B.A. thesis, Harvard University, 1997), 41–49.

40. Blumenson, "Utopia," 361.

41. The name and presence of this organization in a directory of mutual aid societies might suggest that it had already lost its union status. See Frank Rosenblatt, "Mutual Aid Organizations," in *The Jewish Communal Register of New York City, 1917–1918,* 2d ed. (New York: Kehillah [Jewish Community] of New York, 1918), 849. But, as stressed earlier, organizational names could change frequently and for many reasons. More significantly, as labor historian John Commons points out, many musicians' unions organized themselves legally as unincorporated mutual benefit associations precisely to avoid the legal trap of corporation. Defining itself as an "unincorporated musicians' mutual benefit association" was a common legal trick, for it allowed an organization to freely enforce discipline and claim nonprofit tax status at the same time. See Commons, *Labor and Administration,* 301–7.

42. New York City's Local 310 of the American Federation of Musicians was not formed until 1903, and nativist sentiment usually led to the exclusion of most foreign-born musicians from earlier national musicians' unions and trade guilds. See Commons, *Labor and Administration,* 297–300.

43. Musician Louis Grupp recalled the union as the "Progressive Musicians' Benevolent Society." Grupp also independently suggested that this organization dated from the early 1890s. I am grateful to Henry Sapoznik for this information. Local 802 of the American Federation of Musicians was officially chartered on 21 August 1921. For more on its history in New York, see Commons, *Labor and Administration,* 297–323.

44. Richard Spottswood's monumental work dates the first recording of klezmer music in the United States to 1913, while European recordings date from roughly a decade earlier. See Richard K. Spottswood, *Ethnic Music on Records: A Discography of Ethnic Recordings Produced in the United States, 1893–1942,* vol. 3, *Eastern Europe* (Urbana: University of Illinois Press, 1990), 1323.

45. Gordin, *Yakov Gordin's Dramen,* vol. 2, 30. For more on the history of the early klezmer community in New York, see Loeffler, "A Gilgul," 16–40.

CHAPTER 4

The Klezmer in Jewish Philadelphia, 1915–70

HANKUS NETSKY

In the recently emerging literature on klezmer culture and history, little documentation of the background and repertoire of Jewish dance musicians in "provincial" American communities has been produced. Several major factors have contributed to this neglect: the paucity of studies focusing on Jewish communities outside of New York (a trend that is now finally changing), the general lack of interest in klezmer music from the older generation of Jewish music studies scholars who have routinely dismissed it as lacking in "Jewish content" (i.e., religious content), and the seeming lack of interest on the part of surviving musicians, many of whom regard klezmer as an incidental and inconsequential part of their early careers. Encyclopedia entries on the subject have routinely written klezmer off as an archaic vestige of the distant past, and most recent ethnomusicological klezmer studies have focused on the music's resurgence, paying little attention to its formational performance context, with only a few notable exceptions.[1]

In examining the use of music in such community celebrations, one can gain deep insights into significant aspects of the American immigrant experience, including the evolution of a stylized American Jewish wedding ritual, the longevity of certain forms of European music and dance at American celebrations, the American Jewish wedding musician as heir to the European klezmer legacy, and, perhaps most important, the family celebration as an essential communal expression of American Jewish identity. This article offers an overview of the klezmer tradition as it developed in Philadelphia between 1915 and 1970. My timetable corresponds to the dates of the material available for research: the earliest dance folio in my collection was written in 1915; by 1970, the tradition was generally considered a relic, although vestiges of it remain today.

Charting the history of a local klezmer scene is in no way a straightforward task. I began my research by interviewing elderly members of my own family who had performed klezmer music in Philadelphia. They provided me with sketchy historical information, lists of names, and an assortment of attitudes ranging from enthusiasm to disbelief. They also provided the calling card that I could use in approaching other musicians: my link to a "family," essential in a field where information is routinely kept close to the vest. My frustrated attempts to conduct klezmer research in other locales make me appreciate this link now more than ever.[2]

Still, many of those I contacted were far too bitter to be helpful. They had watched their music (and the culture that produced it) die a slow and painful death and had little faith in its resurrection. It was only after serious evidence of the music's resurgence finally hit the old-timers that meaningful research became possible.

Preparing this project has taught me a great deal about the transmission of cultural heritage. Barbara Kirshenblatt-Gimblett defines heritage as "a mode of cultural production in the present with recourse to the past," which can add value to a commodity. It cannot be lost and found and always remains accessible.[3] Kirshenblatt-Gimblett's definition, quite applicable to the music's revitalization, unfortunately contrasts sharply with the view of klezmer music espoused by many of my informants.

When I found out about klezmer music, I was immediately told that there was no way for me to learn it. My uncle Jerry Adler, generally regarded as the last member of Philadelphia's older generation of Jewish clarinetists, was convinced that the only way to become a klezmer was to be "born into it." Since the music was no longer played, there was no longer a klezmer tradition to be born into. Even though four of my uncles, my grandfather, and my great-grandfather had all grown up playing the music (giving me a legitimate claim to it), it could not be passed on to me. It was part of a culture that had been both abandoned and destroyed, and, as far as he was concerned, it should rest in peace.

From Jerry Adler I learned that an abandoned heritage is really not a heritage at all. Many of the musicians I interviewed saw klezmer music as something eminently discardable, not to be passed on. It fell to me and to several other independently motivated activists (in New York,

Los Angeles, and Berkeley) to create a context in which the klezmer heritage would become available again.[4] I began by organizing jam sessions
and soon realized that I had the raw material for a band. Once my ensemble began to concertize and record, it became obvious to me that the
klezmer tradition did have a future, albeit primarily as a concert music
tradition. My role in creating a new context for the music gave me credibility among members of the older generation, and the presence of an enthusiastic audience at my band's concerts gave the music a reconstituted
sense of legitimacy in the eyes of its former perpetrators. Thus it has become possible for me to reconstruct klezmer communities that had existed in Philadelphia and elsewhere, and to explore their evolution.

PHILADELPHIA'S JEWISH MUSICIANS

Philadelphia's large concentration of Jews from southern Ukraine and
Moldova, long considered the heartlands of klezmer music, actually
makes the city an ideal subject for a regional klezmer study. More than
75 percent of Philadelphia's Jews trace their origins to these two areas,
and more than 50 percent of these come from the single province of
Kiev. Studies of religious customs among Jewish immigrants from various regions of eastern Europe show that Ukrainian Jews were more inclined than Jews from elsewhere toward an ethnic, rather than formally
religious, approach to life.[5] This might explain why Philadelphia's Jews,
generally less observant than their counterparts in other communities,
kept their European dance and music traditions alive long after many
other Jewish American settlements had abandoned theirs.

In the years covered by my study, Philadelphia boasted the third largest
Jewish community in the United States (behind only New York and Chicago).[6] Compared to other North American cities, Philadelphia was unusually hospitable to its Jewish immigrants. Consequently, by the end of
World War I, Jews constituted the city's largest immigrant group.[7]

While little is known about Philadelphia's earliest klezmorim, one
can assume that these musicians began to arrive around 1881, with the
first wave of eastern European Jewish refugees.[8] News of economic opportunities combined with a deterioration of conditions for Jews in Czarist Russia (due to an acceleration of anti-Semitic attacks in the Ukraine
beginning in 1881), prompting a steady flow of Jewish immigrants into
American cities until 1924, when the U.S. government began to impose
strict quotas. Most of Philadelphia's earliest arrivals settled in the South
Philadelphia neighborhood of Port Richmond, which quickly earned

Figure 4.1   A Philadelphia klezmer band playing for Thanksgiving, 1953.
From left: Marvin Katz, Kol Katz, Jack Torchin, and Harold Katz. Courtesy of
Hankus Netsky.

the nicknames of "Jerusalem" among Jews and "Jewtown" among non-Jews.[9] By 1920, Philadelphia was home to 240,000 Jews.

Those who came to the city in this first wave did their best to continue the social affiliations they had brought with them from Europe. Immigrants maintained their European ties through memberships in home region–based religious congregations and burial societies and *landsmanschaften*, social organizations unified entirely by their members' common origins in specific European cities and towns. In many cases, they also maintained allegiances to musicians who came from their towns or regions. A town's musical repertoire (and musical business) would often be passed down within a family. Clarinetist Morris Hoffman, a second-generation klezmer, recalls his early initiation into the music business: "My father [Joseph Hoffman] came from Kriovozer, a small *shtetl* (town) in the Ukraine (approximately two hundred miles north of Odessa). He taught all six of his children to play music, and when anyone from Kriovozer had an affair, there was always a Hoffman in the band." [10]

Other musicians have similar stories. The Lemisch and Swerdlow families controlled the Romanian klezmer business, those from the Buki area (between Kiev and Uman) often hired Berl Friedman, Voliners hired Dave Weinstein, and Teplekers (from another Ukrainian town) stayed loyal to clarinetist Itsikl Kramtweiss and cornetist Nachman Grossman. [11] Other leaders (especially those without large numbers of *landslayt* [townspeople] in the Philadelphia area) staked out their turf by catering to the relatively small Hasidic and Orthodox communities, whose wedding dance and music traditions differed greatly from those found at less observant affairs. [12]

Jewish wedding musicians were among the founding members of Philadelphia's Musicians' Union. [13] It did not take long for them to become a strong presence in the immigrant music scene, playing their repertoire for the Greek and Gypsy communities. [14] Soon, musicians from outside the ancestral klezmer orbit, including many Italian neighbors in the South Philadelphia community, joined the ranks of hereditary klezmer musicians. Many orchestra leaders of this generation had been trained in conservatories or military bands, and they found notation to be the most convenient way to transmit their repertoire to fledgling and substitute musicians; folios from the early 1900s provide some of the earliest evidence for tracing the evolution of local musical preferences. These manuscripts are contemporaneous with the earliest available sources from the music's homeland in Europe.

Catering halls replaced Europe's homes and outdoor gardens as the venues of choice for weddings. Most of these were located in the South Philadelphia neighborhood where the bulk of the community resided. While the bread and butter of the klezmer business was the wedding trade, musicians also found many other occasions to perform their repertoire, including various life-cycle events and landsmanshaft gatherings. [15] Klezmorim also performed in clubs (bars) and alcohol-free gathering places known as "tea houses." Those who could read music found their way into the pit orchestras at one of Philadelphia's three Yiddish theaters and, starting around 1920, began to play on local Yiddish radio.

There were also opportunities for Jewish musicians to record their repertoire. Between 1918 and 1927, bandmaster Harry Kandel cut over ninety klezmer sides for the Victor Talking Machine Company in nearby Camden, New Jersey. Kandel's orchestra employed a variety of Philadelphia's most versatile Jewish musicians, and his recordings provide a valuable glimpse of their music.[16] An assistant band director for John Philip Sousa, Kandel favored a brassy, military-style sound and generally recorded with musicians from the pit orchestra of the Arch Street Yiddish Theater, where he briefly served as musical director.[17] He drew his repertoire from tunes that had been brought to Philadelphia by members of his band, which included musicians from the Hoffman and Friedman families. While his recordings made Philadelphia's repertoire available to the rest of the country, their content seems to have had little impact on most non-Philadelphia musicians, who tended instead to remain immersed in their own traditions or to copy the contemporaneous trends from New York.[18] Recordings by other Philadelphia Jewish bandleaders, including Itsikl Kramtweiss, Abe Neff, and Marty Lahr, also had little national impact.

KLEZMER VS. MUZIKER

In the early 1900s, a key element in the everyday life of Philadelphia's Jewish musicians was the interplay and apparent gulf between the klezmer, the vestige of medieval folklore, and the *muziker,* the versatile mainstream Jewish musician who carried on the klezmer music tradition while distancing himself from klezmorim. While many musicians identified others as klezmorim, none that I spoke with were willing to pin the label on themselves.[19] Cornetist Samuel Katz (whose brother, my grandfather, was identified by many as a klezmer) articulated some of the reasons for this:

> A klezmer could only play the Jewish music. They would have to hire kids like us to play the American repertoire. Itsikl Kramtweiss was typical of the old-timers. He'd point to a page with one flat and say "what key is this?" and I'd tell him, "It's the key of 'F,'" and he'd mimic me, "Key of 'F'! Ha! He thinks he's so smart!" Several times when I worked for him he refused to pay me. I had to get him thrown out of the union.[20]

By the 1920s, the klezmer was already seen as a vestige of the Old World. American musicians took great pains to distance themselves from the term, and *klezmer* never appeared in a title in any recording made by immigrant musicians in the early 1900s.[21]

Klezmorim were commonly thought to be "outside the pale of regular community life."[22] They retained their eastern European reputation as womanizers, gamblers, and swindlers, and because of their tendency to stick together in family dynasties, penetrating their mysterious world could prove difficult. They maintained good relations with their clients, but at the same time kept their distance by speaking in *klezmer-loshn,* the secret argot that they refused to teach outsiders, particularly at times when prices were being negotiated.[23] In Philadelphia, the younger musicians usually referred to the klezmorim by nicknames such as "Old Man Finklestein," "Old Bellow," "Yoina," and "Grossman the *Shiker*" (drunkard). Legends of these figures abound, including Grossman's regular engagement playing the cornet nude in the *shvits* (ritual bathhouse), and old man Lemisch's ability to make dollar bills disappear up the bell of his clarinet. A klezmer named Mr. Morrison was well known both for his ability to play many instruments and for his refusal to distinguish one from another. Morris Hoffman recalls a snowy night when he called Morrison to play bass: "An hour later he showed up with a flute. He said, 'Did you honestly expect me to lug a bass here on a night like this?'"[24]

As in Europe, klezmorim usually needed to hold day jobs to get by and worked as barbers, tailors, upholsterers, and many other professions. In contrast, muzikers were often employed full-time in musical endeavors. Although they were largely conservatory-trained, they seldom passed up the challenge of learning the newest popular styles. Jacob Hoffman, a virtuosic xylophonist, toured on the Keith Vaudeville Circuit and worked with the Philadelphia Orchestra and the touring company of the Ballets Russes. Four members of the Gusikoff family (coming from a long and distinguished line of klezmorim) found their way into the Philadelphia Orchestra, as did two members of the Gorodetzer family.[25] Since the theaters and vaudeville houses where many of these musicians worked were "dark" on Sundays, some of them were still able to stay active on the Jewish circuit, which especially thrived on Sunday weddings.

Klezmorim did not always have the best business sense, and soon "leaders" who knew the intricacies of running an American affair came to the fore. These were often eastern European characters with new "American" names, such as Jack Lewis (Max Essner) and Bernie Berle (Bernard Gorodetzer, brother of the two Philadelphia Orchestra members mentioned above and the grandson of Berl Bas, a popular klezmer from Cherkas, a town near Kiev). The leaders often worked in tandem with caterers, florists, and masters of ceremonies, who performed a role reminiscent of Europe's *badchonim,* the Jewish folk-poets who enlivened celebrations perhaps as far back as the Middle Ages.[26] It was the job of the emcee to announce the arrival of the guests, to run the various ceremonies, and to lead the dancing if necessary.[27]

By the late 1920s, Philadelphia's klezmorim and other Jewish musicians had pooled their resources and synthesized a common core repertoire. Morris Fried's published Russian *sher* formed the basis of a through-composed, twenty-minute composition, profoundly different from the loosely improvised sher medleys performed in other cities. Many of the bulgars and horas recorded by Kandel also became standard fare, but only in Philadelphia. The community also had its share of klezmer-style composers, whose melodies quickly entered the common mainstream.

A sample of the variety of tunes played in the early 1920s appears in a 1927 folio notated by violinist and cornetist Joseph Hoffman. His book featured not only a large variety of dance and concert tunes brought from Kriovozer (from whence he came in 1905), but also many tunes collected later in Philadelphia. The dances include horas, bulgars, khosidls, freylekhs, sirbas, *vengurkas*, doynes, *dobrizhens* (good-morning tunes), *dobranotshes* (good-night tunes), *mazeltovs* (tunes of congratulation), processionals, Russian marches, Cossack dances, *patsh tantsn* (hand-clapping dances), *tatar tantsn* (Tartar dances), concert freylekhs to be played for listening, mazurkas, waltzes, shers, polkas, Greek dances, several *matros tantsn* (sailor's dances, which actually had traveled from the British Isles to Odessa), *tzigayner tantsn* (Gypsy dances), many recent Yiddish theater favorites, a *broyges tants* (dance of anger), a *mezinke* medley (to be played in honor of the mother when the youngest daughter is married off), a *kamarinska* (or *kamarinskaya*), and a *czardas*. According to Morris Hoffman, for whom the book was written, about half of the material was obsolete by the time he received it (in 1927).[28]

AT A WEDDING IN PHILADELPHIA

By the 1930s, Philadelphia had developed a Jewish wedding sequence and ritual that all local Jewish bandleaders knew and that any from a large pool of sidemen could be plugged into. An offspring of the seemingly endless European Jewish wedding, the party was paced in a way that ensured it would build slowly and continue late into the night. Such a format was used by older Philadelphia bandleaders well into the 1950s.

As the guests arrived, the musicians began with quiet background music, American popular standards, and some light classical selections. Usually, the musicians would continue in a similar vein until the ceremony. Here, caterer Bernie Uhr comments on the ceremonies of this era:

> During the ceremony, when the rabbi would make a blessing, the fiddle player would play background music—they would eat this up—they would

Example 4.1   "Toska Po Rodine"

> love that. And as soon as they broke the glass, this was the sign for the music
> to play—"Khosn Kale Mazeltov" (Bride, Groom, Congratulations). To walk
> down the aisle, it was "Here Comes the Bride," there was no other song.
> And, of course, in between, the vocalist with the orchestra sang "Oh, Prom-
> ise Me." There was no such thing as a request.[29]

The ceremony was followed by a receiving line for the bridal party
(while the recessional continued), and then the "Grand March," an institution already noted as early as 1905.[30] The music for this was a popular Russian military march, "Toska Po Rodine" (Homesickness) (see
example 4.1).

Bernie Uhr recalls leading the march at his family's restaurant:

> Before the family went downstairs to eat, they had to clear with us whether
> we were ready for them. If we weren't, the emcee would make what was
> called a "Grand March," where he would zig-zag the couples, and then sepa-
> rate them, and the bride and groom danced. He did it as long as we needed
> time. If we didn't need time, the announcement came and you went right
> downstairs. If we needed time, that march could take forever.[31]

Next, the bride and groom would go to a separate room for *yikhud*
(an old custom, providing the bride and groom with at least eighteen
minutes of intimacy after their wedding ceremony). When they returned,
the bandleader would introduce them and dedicate the "first freylekhs"
to the bride's family (see example 4.2).

Soon afterward, everyone would stand as the orchestra played "The
Star-Spangled Banner" and "Hatikvah." Then the emcee would read
telegrams from the president, or other phony greetings meant to get

Example 4.2   "Pasey's Freylekhs"

laughs.[32] He would also recite a standard wedding toast: "I wish you luck, I wish you joy, I wish you first a baby boy, and when its hair begins to curl, I wish you then a baby girl."[33]

When the waiters brought the food to the tables, it was a clear signal for the musicians to stop playing dance music and switch to background music. In the early 1930s, horas, khosidls, and tatar tantsn were popular as dinner music (after the dances that went with them had become obscure) and doynes (always played as dinner-concert selections) were also common.[34] After the food was served, the musicians would often leave the bandstand and stroll (or "play tables"), a lucrative source for extra tips. By the 1940s, the dinner music repertoire had switched to popular Yiddish theater hits.

It was not until after dinner that the more serious dancing started. This would include medleys of horas, bulgars, and freylekhs, along with a wide variety of requests, depending on the family's geographic roots. A *broyges tants* (dance of anger and reconciliation) might be played for attendees who had been quarreling or as a ritual dance for the mothers of the bride and groom. This dance included thirty-two measures of stalking and threatening gestures, followed by a congenial freylekhs of indeterminate length. Another popular request was the "Dance for the Old Men" (see example 4.3), a slow khosidl that served as a kind of relic through the 1950s. Here, the men would try to recreate the mock (or sometimes real) Hasidic dances they remembered from their own European grandparents, many of whom came from Hasidic background.

One of the most memorable and intricately ritualized parts of any

Example 4.3   "Dance for the Old Men"

Philadelphia Jewish wedding celebration was the *krinsl* (crowning).[35] In Europe, this ceremony had been used to honor the mother of the bride when the young woman was the last daughter in the family to be married. American bandleaders expanded it to include a large number of other family members. Bandleader Bobby Block describes the krinsl ceremony he learned from older leaders:

> I put four chairs out in the center of the floor for the four parents, the two mothers in the center and their spouses on either side. If both mothers are being crowned (if the groom is also the youngest), we call that a double crowning, but even if only one is being crowned we seat both sets of parents out of kuved (respect), and because this is now a brand-new family. If there are grandparents, I seat them as well. Then I get [all the guests] to form a huge circle around these chairs, around the whole perimeter of the ballroom floor, and we start to play the mezinke very slowly, so that everyone can clap their hands on the backbeat. I explain that this is an old Jewish custom, that on the night of her last daughter's marriage, the mother is to be crowned, as a queen is crowned. The crown is made of flowers, the flowers symbolize the sweetness of motherhood. And then we welcome all of the siblings, who come out to congratulate their parents, and if there are grandchildren, they come with them, and they go up and kiss the parents and then stand behind them. After that, I introduce the bride and groom, who bring the crown with them, and when they come out we start to play it half-time, more dramatically, and they kiss their parents and stand directly behind the two mothers. Everyone gives them all a round of applause. Then I tell everyone to join

Example 4.4   "Ot Azoy" and "Sheyne Kale"

hands, and we go into "Ot Azoy" (That's the Way We Dance with the Mother-in-Law), "Sheyne Kale" (Pretty Bride) [see example 4.4],[36] the "Patsh Tants" (Hand-clapping Dance),[37] and "Mekhuteyneste Mayne" (My Dear Mother-in-Law). The family stays in the middle, and everyone dances around them and congratulates them.[38]

Another essential dance that usually took place late in the evening was the "Russian Sher" (see example 4.5), a figure dance for groups of four couples, played at a moderately quick tempo. As noted earlier, Philadelphia had its own sher medley.

Example 4.5   "Russian Sher"

A sher was a "request number" that would require a substantial tip and usually would come with a dedication to its benefactor. After the couples' figures had ended, dancers would form a long "chain," working themselves into a tangled mass and then slowly unraveling. The chain required the guests to become more intimately entwined than some cared to be, and shers often ended in fighting.[39]

As the dancing intensified, the party took on a life of its own:

> When we played for live-wire affairs, we'd play till three, four o'clock in the morning. . . . Let's say the man who ran the affair was short of funds, they'd pass the hat around, make a collection, pay the money up, [and say] "Play another hour!" Sometimes we'd play till four or five o'clock. Now when I'd play for the Kriovozer crowd [families with roots in Kriovozere, in Ukraine], they went to town. After the dinner they got started, and I'd come home and see the milkman delivering the milk.[40]

When the party finally quieted down, the musicians would sign off with a *gute nakht* (good-night tune). In Philadelphia, the tune used for this purpose was "Platsh Yisroel" (Cry, Israel), a slow waltz, well known to Ukrainian klezmorim (see example 4.6).

At this point, the guests would generally say their tearful good-byes and go their separate ways until the next family gathering. In some cases,

Example 4.6   "Platsh Yisroel" ("A Gute Nakht")

the musicians would accompany the bridal party through the streets, back to the bride's parents' house, and return to the family residence for a continuation of the festivities the next day.

LATER YEARS

By examining several volumes notated in the 1940s, and by discussing the repertoire of that era with surviving musicians, one can verify that very few klezmer dance genres were passed on to the next generation. These newer folios contain mostly bulgars and freylekhs, along with more current Yiddish theater hits.[41] Also, by this time, a large variety of Latin music was included, along with "mummers' reels" (a Philadelphia specialty), "Palestinian" (soon to become "Israeli") dances, and a greater sampling of ethnic music outside the Jewish realm. Despite the paring down, standard klezmer volumes published in New York were still useless to Philadelphia's aspiring Jewish dance musicians, who had no choice but to buy hand-copied tune books from local union copyists. New York klezmorim, coming mainly from other European towns and other family dynasties, had synthesized their own klezmer blend, as had musicians in Boston, Milwaukee, and elsewhere.[42]

The contrast between Philadelphia's klezmer repertoire and that of New York in the same period reveals the profound conservatism of Philadelphia. Unlike those in New York, few drummers used sock cymbals, preferring to play mostly on the snare, Russian-army style. While innovative musicians such as Dave Tarras and Sammy Musiker experimented with chromaticism and jazz harmonies in New York, Philadelphia's Jewish musicians tended to rely on old standbys; even the composers stayed completely within traditional boundaries. The genres were the same, but the actual tunes were different. Nevertheless, because of their familiarity with large quantities of "exotic" material, musicians who hailed from Philadelphia (such as trumpeters Max Peters and Mel Davis) were particularly sought after once they moved to New York and mastered that city's repertoire.[43]

The generation that came of age in the 1940s inherited a tradition that was almost entirely obscure and yet often still viable. Most of them were brought into the klezmer world as ringers: they could play the American dance tunes that the old-timers still couldn't cope with. They picked up the tradition on the bandstand or read it from folios. While few had any interest in the origins of the music they played, it did provide an anonymous link to an ancestral musical heritage. New York's klezmer repertoire became known in Philadelphia through secondhand sources; casually transcribed variants of this tradition remain in Philly's vintage klezmer books, mistakes and all.[44]

In the late 1940s, traditional Jewish orchestras began to receive competition from a new breed of Jewish bandleader. These groups were Jewish offspring of the Lester Lanin and Meyer Davis society orchestras, offering such innovations as Latin dance instruction and continuous music. These ensembles discarded most of the older European ethnic repertoire, replacing it with more contemporary Jewish fare.

Musical choices in this new era were a reflection of a larger phenomenon. While assimilation had affected many aspects of Jewish culture (language, business practices, housing choices), weddings and bar mitz-

vahs had always stood out as impenetrable bastions of immigrant identity and expression. Now, the children of immigrants had a choice: they
could have an Old World celebration with an American twist or an
American celebration with a brief nod to their Jewish roots. Indeed,
many musicians attribute the shift that occurred to the increased power
of the contemporary bride, who was no longer willing to allow her parents to dictate the character of her wedding. Morris Hoffman describes
how the tension of this era was played out at one wedding.

> The bride came over to talk to the band. "Please," she said, "I work with
> Gentile girls and my boss is Gentile—no Jewish music!" So we started off with
> "Where or When," "Cocktails for Two," typical popular stuff. So the old
> man comes over and says, in Yiddish, "Why don't you play any Jewish mu-
> sic?" The leader tells him what his daughter said and he becomes furious.
> "How can you listen to that little *pishiker?* Play a freylekhs!" She came back
> over to protest, and he called her every Jewish curse under the sun. And for
> the rest of the night the band played Jewish.[45]

Despite such incidents, by the mid 1960s the older klezmer repertoire was generally displaced by Latin styles, swing, Israeli dance tunes,
and rock 'n' roll.[46] This presented an insurmountable challenge for the
older bandleaders, who could not adapt to the challenging new rhythms.
Bandleader Bobby Block recalls this era: "They thought these new dances
were only a craze. Someone would request a cha-cha, so they'd play a
rhumba. They all thought that after a few months the whole thing would
be over and the freylekhs would be back in style."[47]

The older Jewish leaders eventually found themselves confined to
landsmanshaft and B'nai B'rith functions, or hotels and clubs that catered to the older set. Still, when they played for their traditional audience, Philadelphia's Jewish musicians held on to their repertoire, staying
remarkably faithful to their roots. Unlike New York's musicians, who
phased out their klezmer repertoire when Hasidic work took over (due
to a large local influx of Hasidim after World War II), Philadelphia's
musicians had no choice but to take the klezmer and Yiddish nostalgia
route. Many of them display a strange mix of self-derision and elitism
when discussing their days with the "Jewish" bandleaders. Even so, it is
still possible to find a considerable number of Philadelphia musicians
who continue to play music that dates back to the city's earliest klezmer
generation.

CONCLUSIONS

Philadelphia's unabashedly conservative Jewish wedding music tradition stands in marked contrast to the contemporary klezmer scene, where individuality and glitzy packaging are all the rage. On the other hand, studying older klezmer traditions can teach any neo-klezmer valuable lessons not only about performance practice, tempo, tone quality, and form, but how music can shape a celebration. My recent contact with younger klezmorim from Bessarabia and Ukraine confirms that a surprising number of the traditions I found in Philadelphia's musical past still exist in the dwindling, but surprisingly resilient, Jewish communities of eastern Europe.[48] Indeed, Philadelphia's provinciality had provided an imposing buffer against assimilation for my generation of researchers and players.

By looking at handwritten folios, I discovered a large body of music that enhances the relatively limited material that exists on recordings. I have incorporated many of these tunes into my own band's repertoire, taught them to my students, and disseminated them to other scholars. Conducting research on this side of the ocean has enabled me to reconstruct musical traditions that would otherwise have been obliterated by Nazi and Stalinist repression. I have found these traditions lurking fairly close to the surface despite rampant assimilation in the United States.

My research has also shown me the resilience of the ethnic aspects of Jewish heritage. Religious and mystical contexts really form only the smallest tangent in the Philadelphia klezmer scene, and I believe these aspects of klezmer music are overemphasized in the output of our contemporary klezmer community. Philadelphia's heritage offers another approach for those who balk at assimilationist tendencies: a musical subculture rich in folklore and ritual, populated by colorful outcasts who may well have been the true nonconformists of their day. Its Odessa-style eroticism should resonate well with our contemporary youth culture.

I hope my work in Philadelphia will inspire others around the world to look into the history of klezmer traditions in their own communities. With many older musicians now willing to reveal the secrets of their heritage, a vast social and musical legacy awaits discovery.

NOTES

1. Exceptions include Walter Z. Feldman's chapter 6 in this volume and Joel Rubin, "Rumenishe Shtiklekh: Klezmer Music among the Hasidim in Contem-

porary Israel," *Judaism* 47, no. 1 (1998): 12–22. The following entry, from Macy Nulman's *Concise Dictionary of Jewish Music* (New York: McGraw-Hill, 1975), is typical of what I found. "The *klezmer,* an itinerant musician fulfilling the artistic and cultural needs of the Jewish community, appeared in Central, Western and Eastern Europe toward the end of the Middle Ages and continued to function until about the middle of the nineteenth century." See also James Loeffler, "A Gilgul fun a Nigun: Jewish Musicians in New York, 1881–1945," Harvard Judaica Collection Student Research Papers, no. 3 (B.A. thesis, Harvard University, 1997).

2. I began my research in January 1974.

3. Barbara Kirshenblatt-Gimblett, "Theorizing Heritage," *Ethnomusicology* 39, no. 3 (1995): 367.

4. Ethnomusicologist Moshe Beregovski was spurred on by a similar (albeit Soviet-inspired) feeling when he first published his klezmer research in 1936:

> The forms of music-making among professional and amateur musicians have changed radically, and klezmorim—like many of the old order—are entering the realm of the past. But they are not departing the arena of history without a trace. They have left us a rich and precious legacy that deserves further study. Among the compositions created by klezmorim are many pearls, true works of art that are the fruit of the labors of highly gifted artists. The best of these works, along with the folk compositions of other peoples, will take their place in the international treasure-house as resplendent monuments of their era. We will give thanks to those unassuming folk musicians and composers who graced the lives of the broad masses with their art and whose work was a faithful companion to the people and a medium for their joys and sorrows.

Moshe Beregovski, *Jewish Instrumental Folk Music,* ed. and trans. Mark Slobin, Robert Rothstein, and Michael Alpert (Syracuse, N.Y: Syracuse University Press, 2001), 36.

5. R. P. Tabak, *The Transformation of Jewish Identity: The Philadelphia Experience, 1919–1945* (Ann Arbor: University Microfilms, 1990), 22, 23.

6. Ibid., 9.

7. Philadelphia's tolerance of religious minorities goes back to the city's Quaker origins in 1683; Boston's less tolerant Puritans had sent their first Jewish settlers back to Europe. Philadelphia's Jewish population was also uncharacteristically hospitable when eastern European Jews arrived to join the existing communities of Sephardic (Spanish) and German Jews. In marked contrast to New York's Jews, who conspicuously discouraged eastern European Jewish immigration, Philadelphia's Jewish charities welcomed the new immigrants (in 1881) with the only welcoming celebration ever held for Jews from eastern Europe. See M. Friedman, ed., *Jewish Life in Philadelphia, 1830–1940* (Philadelphia: Ishi Publications, 1983), 5, 6.

8. A notable exception was the Lemisch family, a renowned Romanian klezmer dynasty, which became established in Philadelphia as early as the 1850s. Walter Zev Feldman, personal communication, July 1999.

9. Friedman, *Jewish Life in Philadelphia,* 30.

10. Joseph Hoffman's immigration story is in itself worth noting. The elder Hoffman, a cornetist and violinist seeking to escape the Russian army on the brink of the Russo-Japanese war, bought a ship's ticket to Argentina. Only after

the boat landed did he realize that he had mistakenly gone to Philadelphia. Morris Hoffman, interview with author, 1 August 1996.

11. Samuel Feldsher, interview with author, June 1988. Bandleader Lou Lemisch came from Iaşi, Romania, where his family's klezmer legacy is still remembered by Gypsy and Romanian musicians. In his presentation at the 1996 Wesleyan Klezmer Music Research Conference, Yale Strom mentioned that as recently as 1990 he encountered several musicians in Iaşi who taught him "Lemisch" repertoire.

12. Hasidic and Orthodox weddings usually featured many ritual dances not performed by the less observant. In those celebrations, men and women were not permitted to dance together and were usually separated by a wall.

13. The general union, known as the Philadelphia Musical Society, was chartered on 16 August 1903. Prior to that time, Jewish musicians participated in an exclusively Jewish union. James Loeffler, personal communication, 1999.

14. Klezmer and Greek repertoires have many tunes in common. This may have to do with the presence of a large number of Greeks who lived and worked in important klezmer cities, such as Odessa (Martin Schwartz, presentation at Wesleyan Klezmer Research Conference, October 1996). Gypsies and Jews shared much of their musical heritage in Romania and the Bucovina, and Jewish musicians had no trouble providing dance music for Gypsy affairs.

15. Bernie Uhr, personal communication, 1997. Uhr, a Philadelphia caterer for more than sixty years, has been a particularly helpful informant for this project.

16. While recordings tell us a great deal about repertoire, they also tend to obscure performance practice. Ten-inch 78 rpm recordings, limited to three minutes in length, promote the mistaken notion that dance tunes were played as individual pieces; we know from oral tradition that they were virtually always combined into medleys.

17. Kandel's style was described by Doris Kandel in a personal communication, 1997.

18. The repertoire that Kandel recorded might have been too stodgy for American tastes; certainly New Yorkers such as Naftule Brandwein, Dave Tarras, and Shloimke Beckerman were far more innovative. I am also not certain how many of the ninety-three recordings listed in the Spottswood discography were actually released; certainly many of them are rarities among surviving 78s. See Richard K. Spottswood, *Ethnic Music on Records: A Discography of Ethnic Recordings Produced in the United States, 1893–1942,* vol. 3, *Eastern Europe* (Urbana: University of Illinois Press, 1990).

19. I noticed a change in some attitudes after Itzhak Perlman's klezmer documentary, *In the Fiddler's House,* came out in 1995 (Angel Records A3VE724347782732). Perlman seemed to identify himself with klezmorim, and Jewish musicians sought to identify themselves with Perlman.

20. Samuel Katz, interview with author, June 1981. Here *Jewish* seems to signify a large variety of European genres, including many Polish, Hungarian, Russian, and Greek styles. Within the European community, these musicians had been considered versatile.

21. To understand the double-edged romance and stigma, it is necessary only

to look at Yiddish literature. Quotations from Sholem Aleichem's klezmer novel, *Stempenyu,* portray the essentialized klezmer Other in the most flattering terms: "His father played the bass . . . he danced like a bear . . . [he] comes from ten generations of klezmorim and he's not ashamed of it. He just grabbed the fiddle and made one pass with the bow, no more, and the fiddle began to speak . . . with a voice, like (forgive the comparison) a living person speaking, discussing, singing weepingly in the Jewish manner." Quotations examined in Mark Slobin, *Tenement Songs: The Popular Music of the Jewish Immigrants* (Urbana: University of Illinois Press, 1982), 17.

22. Slobin, *Tenement Songs,* 16.

23. For a full explanation of this phenomenon, see chapter 2 in this volume.

24. Morris Hoffman, interview with author, October 1996.

25. Ibid.

26. The Getzen, Gorodetzer, and Alexander families included musicians and caterers, and at least two leaders, Dave Cantor and Dave Axelrad, doubled as musicians and florists.

27. Philadelphia spawned a particularly intricate bar mitzvah ceremony, replete with several tunes composed by the local emcees.

28. Morris Hoffman, interview with author, June 1997.

29. Bernie Uhr, interview with author, 1997.

30. "All the guests form the wedding march round and round the hall, which terminates in the move toward the supper room." See Charlotte Kimball Patten, "Amusements and Social Life: Philadelphia," in *The Russian Jew in the United States,* ed. Charles S. Bernheimer, 244 (Philadelphia: John Winston and Co., 1905).

31. Bernie Uhr, interview with author, 1997.

32. This practice was also noted in Patten's 1905 account: "Healths are drunk, congratulatory telegrams are read (fakes, say the critics), and the wedded pair is taken to the rabbi's corner for a last word of blessing." See "Amusements and Social Life," 244.

33. Bernie Uhr, interview with author, 1997.

34. Klezmer music scholar Joshua Horowitz points out that the inclusion of these genres as concert music in the klezmer revival has its roots in their context at the traditional wedding. Joshua Horowitz, personal communication, 1999.

35. The "crowning" of the bride, unknown to Lithuanian Jews, Lubavitch Hasidim, or informed observers of Jewish life in Chicago and other cities, is also observed by Ukrainian Christians. See Tabak, *The Transformation of Jewish Identity,* 1990.

36. This tune is still known in Ukraine, but never made it into the New York mezinke ritual. Max Epstein, interview with author, February 1998.

37. The Philadelphia patsh tants melody is played in other communities as a *kozotshok* (cossack dance).

38. Bobby Block, interview with author, 1999. The order that Block describes here was not entirely standardized. Max Mandel, a popular Philadelphia emcee for over fifty years, had another version. He would begin with the introduction of the parents, then would sing "Mekhuteyneste Mayne" (a song which he explained as a wish that the two families would now be as one), then start the

mezinke over and bring in the youngest children in the family to place the krinsls on the heads of the mothers, and next bring in the bride and groom. Then the father of the bride would embrace the mother of the groom, the mother of the bride would embrace the father of the groom, and the band would play the rest of the medley. This information from Elaine Hoffman Watts, personal communication, 2000.

39. Joe Borock has observed that fighting was so common that in his entire fifty-year career he had never seen a sher get to its conclusion. Interview with author, 1996.

40. Morris Hoffman, interview with author, June 1997.

41. In his study of the evolution of the bulgar, Feldman came to a similar conclusion regarding New York's klezmer repertoire. See Walter Z. Feldman, "Bulgărească/Bulgarish/Bulgar: The Transformation of a Klezmer Dance Genre," chapter 6 in this volume.

42. Boston's tradition is traced back to a large number of related families all emanating from the Ukrainian town of Iazaslav. Information from Al Drootin, interview with author, 8 November 1996. Milwaukee's klezmer heritage was brought there from Riga, Latvia. Information from Joe Aaron, interview with author, November 1993.

43. In a personal communication (1999), New York clarinetist Howie Leese recalls that any time he ran out of freylekhs, he would stop and listen to Mel Davis, a trumpeter who hailed from Philadelphia.

44. After going on to a stellar career in New York, trumpeter Mel Davis once got into trouble playing New York repertoire that he had learned in Philadelphia. Figuring he would impress his new employer, legendary bandleader Dave Tarras, he launched into several difficult "Tarras Freylekhs" that he remembered from the Harry Swerdlow book (Swerdlow had seldom transcribed anything from recordings, preferring to take the train up to New York, sit in the back of the wedding hall, and write tunes down as he heard them). Davis was, of course, taken aback when Tarras stared at him instead of joining in. Afterward, the master's only words were "What was that?" Information from Mel Davis, interview with author, October 1997.

45. Morris Hoffman, interview with author, June 1997.

46. Mel Davis put it the following way: "Latin music was the end of klezmer, and rock 'n' roll was the end of the music business altogether." Mel Davis, interview with author, June 1998.

47. Bobby Block, interview with author, 1997.

48. Walter Zev Feldman, Michael Alpert, Jeffrey Wollock, Jeff Warschauer, and others continue to document the work of musicians from these areas who have recently arrived in New York.

CHAPTER 5

"All My Life a Musician"

Ben Bazyler, a European Klezmer in America

MICHAEL ALPERT

The klezmer tradition suffered major discontinuity after World War II, owing to the near destruction of eastern European Jewry in the Holocaust and to the changes wrought by assimilation and acculturation on both sides of the Atlantic, as well as to the increasing importance of Israeli culture in shaping Jewish cultural identity worldwide. As a result, postwar musicians and scholars pursuing the study of klezmer music have mainly been compelled to turn to commercial recordings of the music—in large part, 78 rpm records made during the first four decades of this century—as a primary aural source, rather than to contemporary practitioners. This dearth of opportunities for personal contact and study with master musicians performing a vital, functional repertoire within a broad-based community context has widened the distance between the present musical generation and those who have preceded them, to an extent virtually unparalleled in other Euro-American musical traditions.

In some cases, however, students of the genre in North America, Israel, and eastern Europe have been fortunate to make the acquaintance of both immigrant and native-born exponents of the tradition in various stages of its contemporary development. The repertoire, techniques, lore, and style imparted by clarinetists Dave Tarras (1897–1989), Sid Beckerman, Rudy Tepel, Ray Musiker, and Max Epstein; violinists Leon Schwartz (1901–90), Moyshe Nussbaum (1898–1987), and Aaron Shifrin; saxophonist Howie Leese; trumpeter Ken Gross; pianist/accordionists Sam Beckerman, Pete Sokolow, Leonid Verbitsky, and Isaac Sadigursky; drummers Joe Helfenbein, Louis Grupp, Irving Graetz, and Ben Bazyler (1922–90); and numerous others have helped breathe life into the performance and study of a rich musical tradition from which the present generation was all but cut off.

As a researcher of traditional eastern European Jewish music and dance as well as a professional musician active in the klezmer revitalization, I conducted in-depth interviews with Ben Bazyler between 1984 and 1990, exploring many aspects of his life and work. Our conversations were primarily conducted in Yiddish, with portions in Polish, Russian, and occasionally English, representing the languages in which Bazyler felt comfortable and reflecting the diverse linguistic legacy of his experience. As he succinctly put it, in English, "I speak with an accent, right? Before I came to this country, I didn't have an accent." Bazyler engaged in a great deal of "internal" code switching in conversation, using Yiddish, Polish, Russian, and English, alternately and in combination, even within a single phrase. His subject, as well as the language connected with a given experience, in large part seemed to determine this. While Yiddish was an important vehicle of expression for him, he often turned to Polish in discussing history or to Russian to discuss professional issues like theatricality and stage presentation. While he tended to talk about the personal introspection he undertook in Los Angeles in English, he continued to use Yiddish or Polish to underscore his points and supply proverbial support. His own summation of his behavior illuminated this: "I used to act 'Russian style,' get angry, throw dishes . . ."; later he became more "American . . . contemporary."

The relationship between Bazyler and me was multifaceted and hardly confined by the parameters of traditional ethnography. In addition to time spent in the interview context, he and I performed numerous times together in concert (with other colleagues), traveling at times hundreds of miles, recorded together, taught at festivals and retreats, attended movies and the theater, visited his family, put each other up for days at a time in our respective homes in Los Angeles and New York, spent long hours together on the telephone, and were planning a trip to Poland and the Soviet Union at the time of his death. Even the exchange of information during the interviews themselves, formalized to some extent by the presence of the tape recorder and the attempt to focus on particular topics, was not a one-way street. To a large extent, Bazyler and I "traded material." He shared with me his vast knowledge of the eastern European Jewish milieu, musical and otherwise, as well as his accumulated wisdom, and I offered him not only an appreciation of his expertise and new professional/artistic opportunities, but also songs, tunes, and ideas that enhanced his repertoire and sparked his imagination—just as his songs, tunes, and ideas did mine.

Our relationship was not limited to that of informant/researcher but was also performer/performer, senior/junior, immigrant/native, "uncle/nephew," and more. Indeed, he often characterized his relationship not only with me, but also my musical colleagues, as "a very special relationship: a *maysim toyvim* (good deed) relationship." Far from guarding his knowledge, Bazyler seemed to derive great satisfaction from passing it on to younger musicians. As he himself liked to comment, with a chuckle and customary succinctness, concerning our professional interaction: "*A parnuse larnt men zikh nisht ous, a parnuse dar men tsiganvenen*" ("A livelihood is not learned, a livelihood must be purloined," transliterated here in his dialect of Yiddish).

Space considerations do not allow for a transcript of the interviews here, so the present article covers only Bazyler's life story and its significance. Concerning Bazyler's feeling as to the publication of interviews and biography, upon my cautious, diplomatic broaching of the subject, he replied without hesitation, "*Tsi darf ikh mikh shemen mit mayn fargangenhayt?* (Do I have anything to be ashamed of about my past?) That's the answer!"

Ben (a.k.a. Berl, Beniek, Boris) Bazyler was born in 1922 in Warsaw, Poland, where his parents owned and operated a bar in the predominantly non-Jewish, working-class Staromiejska neighborhood. For generations, his mother's family had formed the backbone of *Di Kalushiner klezmurim* (the Kalushin musicians), an important Jewish folk orchestra centered in the town of Kaluszyn (Yiddish: *Kalushin*), near Warsaw.[1] In the 1920s and 1930s, the then–Warsaw-based Kalushiner klezmurim were led by Bazyler's *Feter Nusn* (Uncle Nusn), the clarinetist Nusn Spiewak. Although discouraged by his father from becoming a musician, from the age of eight, Bazyler played with the band at Jewish and non-Jewish weddings and celebrations throughout central Poland.

His first instrument was the *puk* (standard Yiddish: *poyk*), a large double-headed bass drum with a brass cymbal mounted on top, worn like the bass drum in a contemporary marching band, with two straps passed over the player's shoulders and under the arms. Soon afterward, Bazyler also became proficient on the snare drum and *jazz-band* (the Polish contemporary term for the drum set of jazz and popular music, consisting of a snare drum, bass drum with pedal, and crash cymbal), which he played in a marching and dance band affiliated with Hapoel, the sports organization of the (Right) Poalei Zion political movement. Bazyler had learned to play all of these instruments from other members of the Kalushiner klezmurim. In addition, he taught himself to play the bones after seeing them played by a non-Jewish street musician in Warsaw.[2]

During the 1930s, the repertoire of Di Kalushiner klezmurim consisted of the following traditional Jewish music and dance genres:

freylekhs and *sher:* moderate-tempo to brisk dance tunes played in 2/4 rhythm

khosidl: slow- to moderate-tempo dance tunes played in 2/4 rhythm, also called *pameylekher* (slow) freylekhs

landre: dance and processional tunes played in "limping" 3/8 rhythm, also known as *londre, olyandre, zhok, hora/hoyre,* slow hora, etc.

vulekhl: structured, modally constructed improvisation played in free rhythm, also known as *doyne (doina)*

Hasidic *nigunim:* paraliturgical vocal melodies, particularly those associated with the Gerer and Modzitzer Hasidim, often without words, frequently used as dance or listening tunes and rendered instrumentally

zmires: religious folk songs, generally settings of Hebrew and Aramaic liturgical texts, often sung at home on the Sabbath and holidays

Yiddish folk and popular songs: played for dancing or listening

In addition, the band played the Polish dance genres *krakowiak, oberek, na wesolo, mazur,* and *polonez,* tunes in 2/4, fast 3/8, moderate 3/8, moderate 3/8 and 3/4 time, respectively, as well as the more familiar polka and mazurka. Russian folk and popular dance tunes and songs and popular Polish, continental, and American dance music from the 1930s and earlier, including tangos and waltzes, were also performed, as were famous classical overtures and melodies like the waltz from Gounod's *Faust* or Strauss's "Blue Danube Waltz." This mélange of musical genres remained the mainstay of Bazyler's repertoire for the rest of his life.

At the outbreak of World War II in 1939, Bazyler fled with his parents and sister to Soviet-occupied eastern Poland. After the German invasion of the U.S.S.R. in 1941, the family was deported by the Soviet government to a series of prisons and labor camps in Siberia and central Asia, where all but Bazyler died of starvation. He credits his musical ability, and more importantly his skill as an entertainer, with having saved his life during this period—performing in bands organized in the camps, he was largely able to avoid hard labor. He came into contact at that time with Soviet Jewish musicians, many from traditional klezmer families in the southwestern Ukraine, whose style and repertoire profoundly influenced his own musical development.

Released from a Soviet labor camp in the Uzbek S.S.R. in 1947, Bazyler settled in the city of Tashkent, capital of Uzbekistan. He played in restaurants and at weddings in the ethnically diverse city, particularly for the sizable community of Ashkenazic Jews from the western U.S.S.R. and eastern Europe, earning for himself the nickname *Boris Muzikant* —"Boris the musician." In addition to his musical colleagues from the labor camps, he made the acquaintance of other Ukrainian Jewish musicians, including violinist Mishka Shuster from the town of Bershad', trumpeter/accordionist Petya (Peysye) Izrailevich from Zolotonosha, bassist/trumpeter Dodik Blinder from Gaysin, and a certain Polyakov, also from Gaysin. From them, Bazyler assimilated the "Odessa" or southwestern Ukrainian style of Yiddish dance music, songs, and dancing, which evinces marked Romanian and Russian influence, and added contemporary Russian popular music to his repertoire.

In the 1950s, while also working as a booking agent for the Uzbek State Popular Theater, he helped bring world-renowned performers like Paul Robeson and Dave Brubeck to Tashkent. Returning to Poland in 1957, Bazyler settled with his wife and three children in Lodz, where he worked as a chauffeur, driving a car he had brought from the Soviet Union. In addition, he was the sole Jewish musician in a restaurant and wedding band, which played a repertoire of Polish and some Jewish folk and popular music in cities, towns, and villages throughout the Lodz region.

In 1964, Bazyler and his family emigrated to the United States, spending a year in Minneapolis before settling in Los Angeles. In L.A., which he described as "the most wonderful city in the world," he continued to pursue his career as a professional Jewish musician, adding popular American and Jewish American songs and tunes to his repertoire. Over the years, Bazyler entertained at festivities in the Fairfax neighborhood and through the area, playing at local catering halls such as Palm Terrace and the Star Players Club, as well as in the prestigious ballrooms of the Ambassador and Beverly Wilshire hotels. For the last nineteen years of his life he also worked part-time as a barber. Bazyler's attachment to Fairfax was integral to his sense of well-being in Los Angeles. Though presented at times with the opportunity to move to more luxurious accommodations in more "prestigious" neighborhoods, he was reluctant to even consider leaving. This sense of locale—rare for Los Angeles—was one of the main themes of the "Treasures of Fairfax" festival and made Bazyler an ideal participant.

In spite of the diversity and continued reshaping of his musical persona, Bazyler continued to perform and hold in high esteem the old-time Jewish music of his younger years. It was of paramount importance to him that he was the last surviving member of Di Kalushiner klezmurim, the sole heir to a long and proud tradition that met a tragic end. In addition to the "trap set" favored by contemporary percussionists, which remained permanently set up in his living room, he kept his old-style *puk* ever at hand and could be heard making music late into the night with friends and colleagues or playing along with recordings from his voluminous collection of Jewish and international music.[3]

Nonetheless, his professional sensibilities as musician and entertainer allowed him to adapt to a variety of musical styles and contexts, merging these diverse strains into a harmonious whole without sacrificing the integrity of any one repertoire. His desire and ability to move, entertain, and find favor with his audience by creating an exciting and heartfelt musical moment is a hallmark of Jewish professional musicians and constituted one of the most consistent threads running through his musical career.

Examining Ben Bazyler's life history and diverse professional experience, and hearing him insightfully and articulately discuss his past and present, enriches our picture of twentieth-century eastern European Jewish traditional musical behavior in all of its complexity. Gifted with the arts of memory and orality, naturally inquisitive and constantly seeking to analyze and understand his diverse experience, Bazyler himself delineated the various periods of his musical development, with their distinctive blends of the Jewish and non-Jewish, the traditional and contemporary, even giving them names: *Feter Nusn, Shuster, Fairfax,* etc. He was a "native ethnographer," who, from the beginning of our acquaintance, displayed a sometimes uncanny affinity for the ethnographic process. On numerous occasions, I arrived at his home to find him waiting with a list of themes, episodes, and questions to discuss with me, compiled in the course of his daily life, ideas or reminiscences jotted down as they occurred to him, whether at the barbershop or in the middle of the night in bed. Often he anticipated the issues I intended to raise or intuitively spoke to the very question I was about to pose in a particular session.

His ethnographic sensibilities, combined with his enjoyment of audio and video technology, made him partially self-documenting, prompting me to jokingly dub him the "self-service informant." He began to keep his own cassette recorder at hand, even in settings as untraditional as a long freeway trip to a musical engagement, in order to generate his personal document of our conversations, or, in my absence, to record long soliloquies focusing on specific aspects of his experience. The messages he left on my telephone answering machine were themselves often noteworthy, containing songs or stories appropriate to the occasion, and flowery Yiddish and Polish salutations.[4]

Bazyler's expertise and his eloquence in recounting his musical experience attracted the attention of other Jewish American performer-researchers active in the revitalization of klezmer music, including multi-instrumentalist Stuart Brotman and clarinetist Joel Rubin, both of California, who also recognized him as an invaluable resource: a source of tunes, songs, information, and attitudes, and a link to older levels of professional Jewish music making.[5] Bazyler taught on the staff of the YIVO Institute's Yiddish Folk Arts Program (KlezKamp) in 1989 and was featured in concerts and workshop presentations at several California festivals featuring Jewish traditional music. Between 1984 and 1990, he worked frequently at affairs and in concert with Los Angeles's Ellis Island Band, and with the Euro-American klezmer ensemble, Brave Old World. Bazyler can be heard singing, playing, and holding forth in a suite of Jewish wedding tunes from prewar Warsaw, which he arranged, on Brave Old World's 1991 recording, *Klezmer Music* (Flying Fish Records, FF 70560/FF 90560).

The contours of Bazyler's life history are not uncommon among Polish Jews of his generation, many of whom survived World War II in the Soviet Union and emigrated to "the West" shortly after the war. However, Bazyler's unusually long stay in the Soviet Union and his relatively recent arrival in the United States do not place him neatly into any of the three postwar waves of eastern European Jewish emigration: the immediate postwar refugees, known colloquially as *DPs* or *survivors;* the numerically small Jewish exodus from Poland in 1967–68 in response to government anti-Semitism there; and the constant but fluctuating stream of Soviet Jews leaving that country since 1972.

In fact, Bazyler exhibited characteristics of all three of these groups and evinced an American identity as well. Walking through his Fairfax neighborhood or talking on the phone, he was as likely to speak Yiddish with his Jewish contemporaries as he was Polish with the recently arrived, non-Jewish family from Lodz who rented half of his duplex; Russian with the Soviet Jewish next-door neighbors; English at the Iranian Jewish–owned dry cleaner's; or a mixture of all four languages with his daughter. For many years he belonged to an Orthodox synagogue whose congregation included a large number of Polish and Soviet Jews. The large Reform temple he later joined boasted a largely American-born membership, yet has also been frequented by other European-born survivors like him, comfortably established after several decades in the United States. His choice of colorful household decor was unmistakably Soviet, yet his kitchen was stocked not only with smoked meat and fish from the Amerikanskii Gastronom market, but also with bread and pastries from one of the Israeli-owned Jewish bakeries on Fairfax Avenue, and with imported Polish jam and chocolate. This cultural versatility was evident in his social life and choice of entertainment as well. In a given week, Bazyler might have attended the opera, seen the latest from Broadway, dined at a central European or kosher restaurant, and celebrated with friends at Black Sea, a Russian Jewish nightclub on Fairfax, comfortably in his social and ethnic element the entire time.

For eastern European Jewish immigrants who have suffered the violent destruction of the eastern European Jewish world and the resultant displacement and discontinuity, reconciling the contemporary American present with the tragically vanished environment of their younger years takes diverse forms. In Bazyler's case, his experiences in prewar Poland, the U.S.S.R. of the 1940s and '50s, postwar Lodz, and Los Angeles between 1965 and 1990 seemed to have had an almost simultaneous immediacy (this may, however, have manifested itself disproportionately in our relationship, which was originally predicated on his sense of continuity with the past).

Though vibrantly connected to the present through an active professional, social, and family life, Bazyler seemed to live in all of the places and eras of his life at once. The patchwork, free-associative style of his thoughts in the course of our conversations exemplifies this. The complex linguistic and social identity described above was paralleled by Bazyler's mosaic of musical styles and repertoires. In all areas of his life, memory and the evocation of the past played a significant role.

The importance of memory and remembrance in Jewish life and ritual has been much noted. That which is remembered lives on, while the forgotten dies. One need only contrast the blessing inserted into Yiddish speech and narrative at the mention of a particularly virtuous member of the deceased, *zikhroyne levrokhe* (may his or her memory be for a blessing), with the curse invoked against an evildoer, *yimakh shmoy* (may her or his name be erased). By remembering and recounting, Bazyler breathed continued life into the past for himself, his community, and subsequent generations.

In negotiating the distance between past and present, reminiscence, anecdote, proverb, and other verbal devices served as the vehicle through which Bazyler gained, and provided others with, access to his vast store of experience. Yet the past, as he evoked it, was not a seamless whole. There are contradictions in his accounts and a bifurcation of attitudes. In one interview, he speaks of not having played the tune genre landre in prewar Poland, but later he remembered that he probably did. He described the bass drum technology that he uses in Los Angeles as a "primitive" version of that which he used in Poland, yet he concluded the same account with a comment on the "primitiveness" of the Polish set-up. On several occasions he described prewar klezmorim as shabby dressers, yet often proudly recalled his uncle Nusn and others dressed to the nines in black suits.[6] In fact, Bazyler seemed to possess a kind of "pluralistic" memory, in which a variety of contradictory attitudes or even "facts" coexisted simultaneously. While one must always subject oral histories to close scrutiny, I tend (cautiously, to be sure) to see these contradictions as complementary rather than antagonistic, sometimes indicative of ambivalence toward the persons and phenomena of his life. In fact, the "pluralism" of his reminiscences is strikingly analogous to his variegated ethnicity and chameleon-like linguistic identity.

Like many immigrants, Bazyler's attitudes toward the past were often ambivalent. On one hand, as noted above, he deplored the difficulty of life in prewar Poland, saying in the interview, "Life was somehow so primitive that you had to suffer." At the same time, in his recounting, that era often seemed imbued with almost holy significance, though not necessarily romanticized. He speaks in the interview of the "primitiveness" of standing up wearing a bass drum all night, but revels in his still-vivid recollections and his expertise in the almost-forgotten techniques he was describing. Hardships are not forgotten, the scene is not sanitized, but the fact that he experienced it and is able to tell the tale seems to hold enhanced meaning for him.

One of Bazyler's most important routes to reconciling past and present was through his musicianship, in particular his attachment to traditional Jewish klezmer music. His was both the duty and the honor, as he stated, "*untsihaltn di haylike traditsye fin klezmeray*" (to maintain the sacred tradition of klezmer music), as he said at KlezKamp in 1989.

Although klezmer music per se has little if any sacred status in eastern European Jewish life—the opposite is far more the case—for Bazyler it was elevated to an exalted position, embodying a multifaceted eastern European Jewish ethos: simultaneously celebratory and contemplative, worldly and sacred, fortunate and tragic. Music in general played a powerful, even decisive, role in his life. "Music is magic . . . the most beautiful thing in the world," says Bazyler. Without it, he "would have been in *yene velt* [the next world] long ago."

For Bazyler, not only did klezmer music and its milieu become a holy tradition, but one that he strove to maintain in part through his remembrance of the past. It is as if he was compelled to bear witness to a vanished way of life by remembering, by being "the last living member of the Kalushiner klezmurim," by recounting and recreating not only the music, but also the setting, the characters, and the episodes of all the milieux of his life—prewar Warsaw in particular—which were the context for his experience as musician and human being. The klezmer revitalization and the interest of younger Jewish musicians provided him a particularly receptive venue for his reminiscence, greatly validating both his unbroken connection with the past and his continued activity in the present.

Finally, Bazyler was most conscious of, though at times puzzled by, his role as chronicler. It was a gift that, while it enriched his life and brought him joy, often caused him great pain. "Sometimes you just can't knock something out of your head, no matter which way you turn. . . . I've been through a great deal in my life: I was seven years in the Siberian camps," he says, adding, on more than one occasion, "Why do I remember, Moyshe? Some people can't even remember their names. Why do I remember all of this?"

Indeed, pain was a companion to Bazyler to the end. The veritable life of the party, a man who saw no higher purpose than *misameyakh tsu makhn di velt* (to make the world rejoice), he was at the same time deeply scarred by his personal encounter with both Nazism and Stalinism. It was a legacy that clouded even the brightness of his remarkable optimism, energy, and warmth. On 22 September 1990, in excellent physical health, closely connected to his family, and with years of professional and artistic endeavor likely still ahead, Ben Bazyler took his own life by leaping from an eleventh-story window in Hollywood. As with many of his generation, a world died with him. His departure—as determined as was his approach to life—is an immeasurable loss to both the art and the study of eastern European Jewish traditional music. This article is dedicated to his memory.

Zol er hobn a likhtikn gan-eydn.

NOTES

I would like to express my gratitude to Stuart Brotman, Chane Mlotek, Roberta Newman, and Marek Web for their generous and invaluable assistance in preparing this article, and to Deborah Dash Moore for her continual support and encouragement.

1. Standard Yiddish for *klezmurim* is *klezmorim.*

2. Bazyler referred to this instrument by the Yiddish name *humenklaper,* literally, "Haman-beater," a reference to the use of simple percussion instruments during the late winter holiday of Purim. Such instruments are used to drown out the name of the villain Haman (Yiddish: *Homen/Humen*) whenever it is pronounced during the reading of the Megillah—the biblical Book of Esther—as part of the Purim liturgy. Until recently, Bazyler's version of this instrument consisted of two wooden rulers that he shortened to a length of about seven inches, rather than the commercially available bone, wooden, or plastic models. Bazyler made a distinction in nomenclature between this instrument and the more common *grager,* another Purim noisemaker traditionally made of wood.

3. When Bazyler began performing in concert with the author and other musical colleagues involved in the klezmer revitalization, he generally dispensed with the snare-drum stand employed by most percussionists nowadays, and insisted on the self-consciously folkloristic touch of tying the snare drum at a 45-degree angle between the back and the seat of a straight-backed wooden chair, a technique he claimed to have used as a boy in Warsaw.

4. Interestingly, in this regard, the outgoing message on Bazyler's own answering machine began with an instrumental version of the Yiddish song and international hit "Bay Mir Bistu Sheyn," a song he credited with having saved his life in a Soviet labor camp.

5. The fact that Bazyler was Stuart Brotman's father's barber provided the first link that brought him into contact with musicians involved in the klezmer revitalization.

6. In fact, Bazyler was intrigued by the stage dress of many younger musicians in the klezmer revitalization, which has often affected a loose "vintage" (1920s–30s) style featuring suspenders or vests, or, of late, a 1980s–90s "hip," contemporary look. By contrast, he would often recall the three-piece suits worn by Feter Nusn and his contemporaries.

CHAPTER 6

Bulgărească/ Bulgarish/Bulgar

The Transformation of a Klezmer Dance Genre

WALTER ZEV FELDMAN

Like Jews in many parts of the world, the Jews of eastern Europe had families whose hereditary occupation was the performance of music. However, unlike any Jewish group that has been documented in the twentieth century, the hereditary Jewish musicians of eastern Europe, called *klezmorim* (singular, *klezmer*) performed an instrumental repertoire that included musical genres not shared by the co-territorial musicians. The klezmer repertoire included both dance and nondance genres. The dance genres as they appear in both the European and American notated documents and recordings display a remarkable uniformity over a very wide geographical area. While there probably was considerable variation in the nondance genres, the dance genres, especially those secular genres that were considered to be Jewish, were basically uniform over most of the areas of Jewish settlement within the Russian Empire, including eastern Ukraine, Belorussia (Belarus), Lithuania, eastern Poland, and Bessarabia (Moldavia, Moldova).[1] Significant amounts of material remain for the Jews under czarist rule, for the Kingdom of Romania, and for Austrian Bucovina and Galicia, which together constituted the large majority of eastern Europe's Jews during the nineteenth and early twentieth centuries.

Within the repertoire of klezmer music in eastern Europe, the *bulgarish* was a regional phenomenon, originating in Bessarabia as the *bulgărească,* and then spreading as the klezmer bulgarish to parts of Eastern Ukraine. In America between 1881 and 1920, however, the bulgarish

Figure 6.1   Wedding celebration, c. 1950. From left: Irving Gratz, Dave Tarras, Mrs. Gratz, and Sammy Musiker. Courtesy of the Center for Traditional Music and Dance.

became increasingly identified as a major genre of klezmer dance music for Jews of various regional backgrounds. The "klezmerization" of the bulgarish, then known as the bulgar, attained its final shape in New York City between 1920 and 1950. The European-born klezmorim who dominated the professional Jewish dance music of this city together created the new form of the bulgar. Among these musicians, the most influential was the Podolian clarinetist Dave Tarras (Dovid Tarrasiuk, 1897–1989). His influence took two forms: he composed a vast repertoire of bulgars that exemplified the new bulgar structure and that came to replace most of the Jewish bulgarish repertoire that had been brought from eastern Europe, and he composed tunes that combined the rhythmic and melodic features of the American Jewish bulgar with various Jewish musical genres.[2]

After World War II, the American conception of Jewish dance music centered around the bulgars (mostly of American vintage) and the new bulgar-hybrid melodies. The older core klezmer dance repertoire, which had been somewhat current in America until the 1940s and in eastern Europe until the contemporaneous Holocaust, was replaced almost entirely by the new American klezmer genres, the bulgar and the bulgar-hybrids.

In this article, I trace the development of a single klezmer dance genre, from the bulgărească of the Moldavian *lăutari* (professional musicians), to the bulgarish of the Moldavian and Ukrainian klezmorim, and then to the bulgar of the klezmorim in the United States. I interpret the significance of this transformation, contrasting the situation in the Old World with the adaptation of this dance genre to suit the needs of the largely proletarianized Jewish immigrants in America during the first half of the twentieth century. In order to explain the significance of the bulgarish within American klezmer music, I introduce several points about the nature of klezmer professionalism and the composition of the klezmer repertoire, which may be summarized as follows.

It appears that the repertoire of klezmer music had been created in both eastern Europe and America by full-time professional musicians who formed a hereditary caste. The amateur and part-time artisan-musicians do not seem to have taken an active role in the creation of the repertoire. In several regions, this caste of klezmorim had intimate contact with Gypsy professional musicians. The close professional contact of this klezmer caste with low-status non-Jews, plus the function of instrumental music as a means of exciting and releasing passionate emotions without any devotional context, put the klezmer and his music in a marginal position within Jewish society. When eastern European Jews emigrated in large numbers to the United States and Canada, the dance element within the klezmer repertoire became a ubiquitous feature of life in the larger cities, especially New York. Nevertheless, klezmer music was never supported by Jewish communal institutions and was never used as a positive symbol of Jewish musical culture until 1980, a century after the initial immigration; by that time the genre itself had become largely defunct. The American situation of klezmer music differs fundamentally from the situation of several peasant and semiprofessional instrumental genres that had been successfully maintained in the New World, but agrees with several Gypsy professional genres that were never widespread here.

In eastern Europe, the professional klezmer repertoire had been heterogeneous but not eclectic. Some genres were local in origin and performed for Jews and non-Jews; other genres were part of a cosmopolitan European repertoire that klezmorim performed but rarely composed. There was also a repertoire of secular dance tunes, wedding ritual tunes, and paraliturgical melodies that were composed and performed by klezmorim and performed exclusively for Jews. This repertoire differed in many respects from the co-territorial non-Jewish repertoire, but parts of it were occasionally played by non-Jewish musicians as Jewish music. In addition to this, there was yet another klezmer repertoire that was inspired by the music of Gypsies from Moldavia, the Balkans, and the Crimea. This repertoire did not remain locally based but diffused over a wide geographical area and mixed structurally with the core Jewish repertoire. It was this transitional, or "orientalized," repertoire that gave rise to the bulgarish dance form.

I contend that in America the distinction between the orientalized and the core klezmer repertoire collapsed between 1930 and 1950. During this period, the bulgarish (bulgar) became the dominant genre within the entire repertoire and absorbed many elements from both the core klezmer repertoire and several Near East and Balkan musics. While this process was in part a continuation of Old World patterns, its cultural significance became rather different in the American environment.[3]

KLEZMER MUSIC

Finding a conceptual framework for this analysis was not an easy task, because klezmer music in America was not studied when it was still a vital musical form, roughly from 1881 until 1950. In the Soviet Union, Beregovski was able to accomplish considerable collection of repertoire, but his well-conceived program to interview klezmorim and their audiences was never carried out.[4] Although klezmer music was a major musical factor within the lives of the large Jewish community of New York and other cities for two generations, it attracted virtually no scholarly or even literary attention. By the late 1970s, when the fieldwork for the present study was undertaken, only one major klezmer musician (Dave Tarras) was still alive in the entire northeastern United States. However, this apparent lack of scholarly or institutional interest in klezmer music, inconvenient though it is for us today, is not anomalous. Rather, it is consistent with the role this music has played in both Europe and America.

The castelike structure of the klezmer families has been noted in several literary and scholarly sources, but recent discussions of klezmer music have not stressed this point sufficiently.[5] The position of the klezmorim as a rather low-status caste explains much of the obscurity of klezmer music in studies of Yiddish culture. It appears that klezmer families sometimes intermarried with the families of wedding jesters (badkhonim); this was the case of Dave Tarras, whose grandfather was a *badkhn.* However, the badkhonim were not as closed a caste as the klez-morim, because many of the best badkhonim had been yeshivah stu-dents; they were sometimes "spoiled" rabbis.[6] There may well have been higher *yikhes* (lineage status) for those klezmer families whose badkhn members had rabbinic connections. On the other hand, there is some evidence that Gypsy professional musicians had been assimilated into the Jewish community via the klezmorim, representing the lowest rung on the yikhes scale.[7]

In addition to these groups, there were also semiprofessional and amateur instrumentalists. Beregovski's and Stutschewsky's evidence sug-gests that barbers may have functioned as part-time klezmorim, in con-junction with other semiprofessionals. This seems to have been the case in very small settlements, which had no professional klezmer *kapelye* (ensemble). We do not know whether the full-time or part-time klez-morim were the more numerous. It appears, however, that the most fa-mous and skilled klezmorim came almost exclusively from the full-time professional caste rather than from the part-time artisans.

The role of the klezmorim in the Jewish shtetl communities of eastern Europe was partly similar to the role of Gypsy musicians there and in the Balkans.[8] They performed a repertoire that differed from any non-professional "folk" repertoire and that was performed on instruments, often played in a virtuoso fashion. Although the klezmorim were far more integrated into the majority community than the Gypsies were, the klezmer was a special kind of Jew. While the mobility and business acu-men of many klezmorim fit into accepted patterns of Jewish profession-alism, most Jews regarded the klezmorim as irresponsible, sexually over-active, and violent. These attitudes appear in literary sources and were common among immigrants in America. As Mark Slobin noted, "Dis-trusted and even feared for his unorthodox ways, the klezmer was of-ten contemptuously called 'gypsy.'"[9] Isaac Bashevis Singer gave voice to these folk attitudes in his story "The Dead Fiddler," in which a young woman becomes possessed by the soul of a dead klezmer who is the epit-ome of licentiousness, drunkenness, and blasphemy. While the klezmer hero of Sholem Aleichem's novel *Stempenyu* is not violent or uncouth, he is portrayed as a seducer. A document survives dated 1805 from the *kehile* (official Jewish community) of Minsk, Belorussia, which describes the beating of a local badkhn by the members of a klezmer kapelye.[10]

In our interviews, Dave Tarras took much trouble to distinguish him-self and his family from this commonly held view of the klezmorim, em-phasizing his family's religiosity, sobriety, and contacts with the local

Polish nobility. On the other hand, according to many informants, Naftule Brandwein, Tarras's great rival, was a drinker and a womanizer and had a violent temper. The existing sources provide sufficient material for both conceptions of klezmer life and reflect a complex social reality; a wide variety of social attitudes were possible within the economic conditions of the fully professional klezmorim.

In America, a greater range of social opportunities became open to the Jewish musicians and relatively few of the American-born children of klezmorim retained their professional involvement in this music. Most of them seem to have branched out into classical music, popular entertainment music, or jazz. In some cases, this branching out had already begun in Europe, but it accelerated greatly in the New World.[11]

For most of the twentieth century (until the early 1980s), klezmer music was not viewed by American Jews, whether immigrants or American-born, as a cultural model or "icon." Jewish institutions, whether of the establishment, religious, left-wing, or Zionist varieties, had no interest in using klezmer music to augment or to symbolize ethnic or religious cohesion. This situation contrasts with several Old World folk and professional music repertoires that were the objects of some institutional patronage by churches or national associations in America, such as the Bečar music sponsored by Serbian Orthodox churches, Irish dance music sponsored by the American branch of the Comhaltas Ceoltoiri Eireann, or the Anatolian Armenian dances and songs sponsored by the Armenian Gregorian churches.[12] These three ethnic societies had developed a significant degree of amateurism, and the first two had begun to use certain instrumental or instrumentally accompanied vocal genres as symbols of an ethnic or national identity (particularly the Irish).[13]

The generic and genetic connections between klezmer music and Romanian Gypsy music can lead to a heuristically useful comparison of the former with other professional instrumental repertoires within eastern Europe, which will be more relevant than comparison with any peasant instrumental repertoire. While it is not my intention now to develop such a comparison in detail, this general scheme is essential to understanding the fundamental difference between klezmer music and other European instrumental repertoires that have been transplanted to America. In general, peasant instrumental repertoires were brought to the New World with their amateur or semiprofessional peasant performers. In many (although by no means all) cases, these repertoires received support by the community in general, by its official organizations, and by ethnic/religious institutions. Examples of such rather well-supported genres are

Irish fiddling, Polish fiddling, Ruthenian fiddling and cymbal playing, the Pontic Greek lyra, and the Serbian tamburitza. In some cases, original instruments were retained; in others they were supplemented or replaced by other instruments. Nevertheless, the genres and much of the older repertoire survived for many decades. Exposure to these genres was considered an important element in ethnic identification among these immigrant groups. By way of contrast, in many cases the professional, usually Gypsy, instrumental repertoire of these groups (where it had existed) was not transported successfully to America. The contact between local, usually peasant, groups and Gypsy musicians was often not maintained in the New World. Several of these Gypsy repertoires, such as Romanian *musicá lăutarească*, Macedonian/Albanian *zurla tapan*, Macedonian *čalgija*, and so on, have not played a significant role among the immigrant groups and their children, as they had in the Old Country. Among eastern European immigrants, the most widely accepted Gypsy repertoire appears to be the tamburitza among Serbs. Although this genre had originated among Hungarian Gypsies in the nineteenth century, it developed along two tracks; one remained Gypsy and professional, while the other became largely amateur and urban, thereby shedding its Gypsy, outsider associations and becoming a symbol of ethnicity for Serbs.[14]

Our poor knowledge of the interrelationships between Jewish repertoires and genres in eastern Europe is true as well for America. Slobin's valuable studies of the music of the Yiddish theater (1983) and of the synagogue (1989) cannot make up for the absence of studies conducted when these forms were flourishing and influential in American Jewish life, during the first half of the twentieth century.[15] There is still a great need for an integrative study of music among American Jews, including both the "traditional" repertoires and the roles of Jewish musicians in various forms of music in America. In the absence of such a study, the research done on other "immigrant" or "ethnic" musical styles cannot be duplicated for any area of Jewish music, least of all for klezmer music.

CLASSIFICATION OF THE KLEZMER GENRES

While the notated and recorded documents of klezmer music do not predate the early twentieth century, this repertoire can be divided into new pieces by known klezmorim and older anonymous items. Judging by the ages of the performers, much of the anonymous, commonly shared repertoire dates from roughly the middle of the nineteenth century. Beregovski had noted the uneven temporal depth of the existing repertoire and thought that analysis might help to determine its relative age.[16] While the entrance of the bulgarish or the *zhok* into the repertoire can be dated with some precision, the relative antiquity of other genres is much less clear.

Written and visual documents from the first half of the seventeenth century onward show a preference among Jewish musicians for ensembles of fairly fixed character, usually featuring one or two fiddles, a bass, and a *cimbal* (the portable hammer dulcimer), and sometimes also a flute. A document from Lemberg dated 1629 mentions a harp and a zither, but these were apparently solo instruments, and by the end of the century they are no longer mentioned in connection with Jewish musicians.[17] As Sarosi notes for seventeenth-century Hungary, non-Jewish dance music of northeastern Europe featured no fixed ensemble—a single fiddler or piper could suffice, or a variety of instruments might be added.[18] The sources depict a fairly stable three- to five-man klezmer ensemble—two fiddles, with cimbal and/or bass, occasionally also flute (and no bagpipe) for Poland, Galicia, and Belarus until the last third of the nineteenth century. While the cimbal may have been in use also among Christians in the western part of the Polish state, it was Jewish in the eastern territories of the Polish-Lithuanian state and in the Danubian principalities, where it remained part of the typically Jewish ensemble for a period of roughly two centuries. In Hungary, it was adopted by Gypsies after the second half of the eighteenth century, while in Wallachia and Moldavia it remained Jewish until the middle of the nineteenth century.[19]

The distinctive nature of the klezmer ensemble and performance style in Poland is noted by Anna Czekanowska: "The dulcimer and violin were clearly instruments of highly skilled Jewish musicians, well described already in the sixteenth century," and "The dulcimer has a special position as an instrument which is still preserved in folk practice. Though played today by Polish peasants, it is clearly connected with Jewish musicians." On general performance style: "The old Jewish tradition is thoroughly documented, and although mainly of urban character it had developed some peculiarities of performance style that can be detected even in the folk tradition. These related especially to dulcimer playing and to some kinds of violin music."[20]

The role of klezmorim both in developing the distinctive chromatic tuning for the dulcimer and in diffusing the instrument throughout northeastern Europe and the Balkans, as far as western Anatolia, is note-worthy. The ubiquity among klezmorim of the cimbal/dulcimer with its chromatic tuning suggests that their repertoire already contained a significant proportion of melodies in scales using the augmented second degree and that the klezmer technique included some form of broken-chord playing. Thus the probable antiquity of chords and arpeggios in klezmer performance helps explain the presence of these elements in much of the oldest repertoire played exclusively or primarily for Jews.

The musical and social environment of the klezmorim east of the Elbe was vastly different from that of the more westerly *spielleute* (Jewish professional instrumentalists of late medieval and early modern Germany, Bohemia, and Austria). Whereas the latter had to play largely for a non-Jewish audience in order to survive economically, the klezmorim of the Polish-Lithuanian state were supported by a very large Jewish population. In the eastern territories of that state (which would become the czarist Pale of Settlement), the Jews also assumed the dominant role of professional musicians for society at large.[21] In the northern parts of the eastern territories, there was no other numerous class of professional musicians, such as they would encounter in Galicia, in the Danubian principalities, and in Hungary in the form of the Gypsies. While the Polish-Lithuanian klezmorim still played partly for Gentiles, their dominant role in the musical profession plus the much larger size of the Jewish population constituted two important factors in the emergence of a distinctively Jewish instrumental repertoire.

In order to clarify the generic context of the bulgarish prior to its transplantation to America, I present a classificatory scheme of the entire klezmer repertoire.[22] For our present purposes, the repertoire of klezmer music can be divided into four categories, which I term *core; transitional* or *orientalized; co-territorial;* and *cosmopolitan.*

The existing documentation is sufficient to represent the dance repertoire and the performance style of klezmorim who had been trained toward the end of the nineteenth century and in the first two decades of the twentieth century in Ukraine, Bucovina, Bessarabia, and Belorussia. The American documentation also allows a view of the main developments within the klezmer repertoire in New York (the most important American Jewish population center) from World War I until the decline of the klezmer genres in the 1960s.[23]

The *core repertoire* principally featured freylekhs with a large number of equivalent names, such as *skochne, sher,* and *khosidl.* These names implied structures that differed choreographically, but not musically.

Beregovski stated that the freylekhs and sher were "the most popular dances." He considered all four names to have a pan-regional distribution. He devotes particular attention to the origin of the dance sher, which was a group couple (or contra) dance.[24] He notes that the sher had been adopted into Moldavian and Ukrainian folklore from the Jews. He also states that "from the music and its character it is very difficult to distinguish the sher from the freylekhs, if the latter is in a moderate tempo."[25] The name *skochne* referred to a freylekhs, sometimes not in a dance context.[26] There were a large number of linguistic variants for the freylekhs (such as *hopke, dreydl, rikudl*), but these had no musical significance. Judging by commercial recordings from Europe and the United States, some khosidls had the same structure as freylekhs (such as "Behusher Khosid," recorded in New York by Max Leibowitz, and "Sedugurer Khosid," recorded by Josef Moskowitz; see Folklyric Records 9034). Others resembled the vocal dance tune *(nign)*. We are led to the conclusion that the three names—*freylekhs* (with its variants), *sher, skochne* (and at times also *khosidl*)—referred to a single musical entity.

Nondance metrical genres included wedding ritual tunes such as *dobraden', dobranoch,* some of the *mazeltov* tunes, *kale bazetsen* (in Belorussia), and *opfiren di makhetonim.* There also were nonmetrical wedding melodies, such as *kale beveynen* (known as *kale bazetsn* in Ukraine) and various tunes played before the *khupe* (wedding canopy), as well as metrical and nonmetrical paraliturgical melodies for such holidays as Chanukah and Purim.[27]

The *transitional* or *orientalized repertoire* consisted of the dance genres named *volekhl, hora, sîrba, ange,* and *bulgarish.* In the nondance category, the most important genre was the *doina (doyne)*. In addition, there were a number of nondance genres (such as *mazltov far di makhetonim*) that were related to the zhok—the latter having either a dance or nondance function. Thus, while cosmopolitan and co-territorial repertoires were exclusively dance music, the transitional repertoire had both a dance and a nondance component. The history of the tunes called *volekhl, zhok, hora, gas-nign,* and *mazltov far di makhetonim* is roughly parallel to that of the bulgar, in that it consists of the adaptation of a rhythmic structure (in this case, in 3/8 time) from Moldavian music and its gradual integration into the older Jewish melodic and rhythmic types. This process began somewhat earlier than the bulgar, because by the mid-nineteenth century there were already volekhl and mazl-tov tunes whose Moldavian element was confined to the rhythm, and so should be

classified with the core repertoire above, while others (usually termed
zhok or *hora*) were still almost identical to the Moldavian prototype.

These names and their musical substance point in the direction of Bessarabian musicá lăutarească (professional musicians' music) of the later
nineteenth century. Nevertheless, there are four reasons why this repertoire cannot be subsumed with the co-territorial repertoire: the tunes
were performed far from their original geographical home; they were
frequently composed by klezmorim; they displayed clear interaction
with the older Jewish repertoire, which resulted in the creation of new
hybrid genres; and their foreign provenance was still remembered
among klezmorim in this century. For example, Beregovski states that
the oldest klezmorim in his time remembered that the doina had been
only recently introduced from Romania, replacing an older genre named
taksim.[28] The taksim, in its turn, was probably derived from the improvised instrumental sections of the Romanian epical ballads *(cîntece
batrînești)*.[29]

Early researchers sensed that these genres were somehow transitional
between the core Jewish repertoire and the co-territorial non-Jewish repertoires performed by Jews. As early as 1904, the Chuvash/Russian musicologist Ivan Lipaev noted the Romanian influence on the music of the
klezmorim.[30] Beregovski had observed that the street tunes *(gas nigunim)*, related to the zhok, appeared alien to the klezmer repertoire, but
could find no explanation for this phenomenon.[31] Joachim Stutschewsky, on the other hand, knew that this genre had entered Jewish music
from Moldavia and concluded that "even though the musical environment of these creations was influenced by the melodies of the klezmorim,
and lost somewhat the Moldavian-Romanian musical content, it is best
not to join this music to the treasury of klezmer music."[32] The use of
zhok-like melodies for street tunes seems to have developed in the later
nineteenth century—in Palestine, the local klezmorim knew some of the
same tunes but did not use them as gas nigunim.[33] Some mid-nineteenth-
century Hasidic nigunim are termed *volekhl* or *nign gaguyim* (tunes of
longing) but have no association with the *gas-nign*. Hasidic lore con-
nects them directly with music of Romanian shepherds and not with either klezmer or lăutar music.[34]

More recently, the Latvian Jewish musicologist Max Goldin has
brought up the question of Moldavian Jewish musical contacts.

> The question of the common elements and connections between the music of
> the Jewish and Moldavian peoples is among the unstudied questions of com-
> parative folkloristics. . . . While preparing for publication Beregovski's *Jewish*

Instrumental Folk Music,[35] the author of these lines came to the conclusion that the most important non-Jewish source for klezmer music was Moldavian music.[36]

Considering the great importance of this repertoire within the Ukraine, Bucovina, Bessarabia, and Belorussia, as well as in the United States, one can understand the nature of the entire klezmer repertoire of these regions only by viewing the transitional genres as a separate repertoire within klezmer music.

The development of the transitional/orientalized repertoire in eastern Europe and in America constitutes two related, but nevertheless distinct, problems. Within eastern Europe, the transitional repertoire discussed here was a feature of the more easterly regions of Ashkenazic settlement —the Ukraine, Belorussia, Bucovina, and Bessarabia.[37] From the little evidence remaining, it is not clear to what extent the other regions participated in this development, but it would seem that Galicia and parts of Poland were involved as well.[38] Within this large area, the transitional repertoire was a documented fact of the klezmer repertoire by the later nineteenth century. There is also evidence within the klezmer repertoire to demonstrate the penetration of Greco-Moldavian and Crimean Tatar elements even in the early nineteenth century.[39] Beregovski also suggests this in his discussion of the taksim genre, which had preceded the doina. It is probable that this movement of musical features from the southern to the northern areas of Jewish settlement is at least as old as the identical process that took place in cantorial singing at the end of the eighteenth century, culminating in the triumph of the Volhynian over the Lithuanian school. Although many of A. Z. Idelsohn's arguments are dated today, his explanation for this phenomenon is not unconvincing: "Southeastern Europe brought forth infinitely more creative Jewish musicians than did the northern part, apparently because of the inspiration drawn from the Near East which borders the southeastern districts. Volhynia, Ukraine, Podolia, and Bessarabia were the cradle of the great Jewish singers and composers."[40] Despite the rejection by the Jews of many specific *makam* features, common approaches to "free" and "loose" rhythm and ornamentation, as well as some common musical scales, linked both the *khazzanic* (cantorial) and klezmer musical styles more to Greco-Moldavian and Crimean music than to the co-territorial musics of Belorussia, Lithuania, and so on.

The immediate impetus for this musical movement from south to north was the Russian colonization of the Pontic steppe, now southern Ukraine, which began with the annexation of the Crimean Khanate in

1783 and continued with the annexation of Bessarabia in 1812. The Crimean instrumental repertoire shows an important link mediating between the Balkans, the Caucasus, and the Ashkenazic Jews. The tragic dispersal of the Crimean population by Stalin has made it impossible to fully document the musical role formerly played by this ethnic group in the development of the klezmer genres.[41] Earlier musical contacts had been occasioned by the Ottoman annexation of Podolia (1672–99), the region from which the Hasidic movement diffused. Still earlier contacts had existed, but, of course, they cannot be connected with existing repertoire.

The *co-territorial repertoire* consisted of local dances of non-Jewish origin, played by klezmorim for non-Jews, and also at times for Jews within a limited geographical region (such as the Polish mazurka, Ruthenian *kolomeyka,* and Ukrainian *kozachok*).

The *cosmopolitan repertoire* consisted of couple dances of western and central European origin—*lances, pa de span, padekater,* quadrille, polka, waltz, and so on, played for both Jews and non-Jews.

BULGĂREASCĂ, BULGARISH, BULGAR

As I will explain below, the dance bulgarish is much more in evidence in the American than in the European klezmer documents. Therefore, I will begin the story at the end, in post–World War II New York.

At this time (late 1940s–50s), klezmer music of all genres rapidly lost commercial viability in the United States. The klezmer families, formerly a caste among the Jews, had made heavy inroads into several genres of mainstream American music, including jazz, nightclub popular music, and Western classical music. Only a minority of the American-born children of these families continued to earn their livings as performers of Jewish dance and wedding music. Even the name *klezmer* was avoided, having become synonymous with "musically illiterate folk musician." Among these professional musicians the older klezmer repertoire had been reduced almost entirely to dance music, which was referred to as *the bulgars. Bulgar* was the American Jewish name for a dance genre that had come to epitomize the entire klezmer dance repertoire. The discography of American klezmer music, beginning with the 1913 recording of "Shulem's Bulgarish," is saturated with this dance. In addition, the earliest substantial American printed collection of klezmer music, Kostakowsky's *International Hebrew Wedding Music,* published in 1916, features the bulgar as the dominant genre. The largest single section of the book is taken up by bulgars (pages 23 through 64), and the bulgar is frequently used elsewhere in the book as the fast part of a two-part suite, beginning with a hora (zhok). Andy Logan inadvertently referred to the tenacity of the bulgar in outliving all other klezmer genres in the course of her description of that great klezmer survivor, the ninety-eight-year-old Isaac Fishberg: "Mothers of Fishberg brides are schooled in the necessity of leaving ample space in one corner of the living room for Fishberg and his flute, and he has plenty of opportunity at these gatherings to play the strenuous *bulgar,* a form of dance music he thinks so highly of that he himself has composed twenty-seven in his considerable time." [42]

On the other hand, Beregovski's published collection of over two hundred klezmer tunes (collected in the 1930s) contains only five items called *bulgarish.* In his 1937 article, he does not mention the name of this dance at all. The Israeli scholar Joachim Stutschewsky, originally from the Ukraine, does not mention the name *bulgarish,* nor was the name (or music) known to the indigenous klezmorim of Safed.[43] How can we explain that the dance genre that dominated American Jewish music for a period of over forty years appears to be virtually unknown in the eastern European regions from which the Jews originated?

THE BULGĂREASCĂ/BULGARISH IN EASTERN EUROPE

Although several stages in the development of the bulgarish are undocumented, historical and musical facts can be adduced to reconstruct its history.

The annexation of the Ottoman Moldavian province of Bessarabia by Russia in 1812 had a significant effect on the development of klezmer music, and on the composition of professional musicianship in northeastern Europe. The Russian annexation of 1812 resulted in several demographic movements. Yiddish-speaking Jews from Ukraine began to settle in Bessarabia in increasingly large numbers, because the Russian government was less oppressive toward the Jews in its newly acquired southern territories than in the older Pale of Settlement. Conversely, Bessarabian Gypsies were able to move more freely into the Russian territories. In addition, Christian Bulgarians and Turkic Gagauz migrated from Ottoman Bulgaria to Russian Bessarabia. While there had been a Jewish population of Ashkenazic, Sephardic, and other (probably Crimean) origins in pre-nineteenth-century Moldavia, the Russian annexation of Bessarabia caused a significant increase in the number of Jews living in that province, which became significantly higher than the number resident in the Turkish (later Romanian) portion of Moldavia. By 1839, Jews accounted for 10 percent of the population of Bessarabia and the majority of the population of several major towns.[44] During the same period, Jews appear prominently as musicians in Bessarabia and the West Moldavian capital, Iaşi.[45]

There is evidence to suggest that, due to the increasing Jewish settlement in the towns and to the glut in professional musicians, Jews and Gypsies sometimes created combined ensembles. In one case, the leader of an ostensibly Jewish band was a Gypsy, who was apparently the main repository of the older klezmer repertoire of the region.[46] The professional contacts between Jewish klezmorim and Gypsy lăutari resulted in the creation of a repertoire that had some of the features of both musics, thus adding a Jewish element that was not present in the musicá lăutarească of the Kingdom of Romania. These demographic movements were crucial in the creation of both the Moldavian dance genre bulgărească and the Jewish bulgarish.

The dance bulgărească (in the Bulgarian manner) was documented in the first half of the nineteenth century in Bessarabia; the dance, with its characteristic music, is known primarily in Bessarabia.[47] It is therefore doubtful that the dance existed prior to the migration of Bulgarians after 1812, or it would have appeared more prominently in other regions of Bulgaro/Romanian contact. Choreographically, the bulgărească is related to the sîrba, the chain dance that is ubiquitous in every region of Moldavia and Wallachia. The sîrba is based on a six-beat measure, consisting of cross to the right, kick to the right, kick to the left. This dance pattern was alien to Ashkenazic dance, which followed symmetrical patterns.[48]

Apart from modal and melodic differences, both the sîrba and the bulgărească were rhythmically differentiated from the core klezmer dance genres due to the presence of triplets. The core klezmer dance repertoire almost never allows triplets (as compared to the freylekhs, skochnes, and shers in Beregovski's collections).[49] The sîrba features running triplets throughout its 2/4 measures, while the bulgărească alternates triplets with syncopated phrases frequently using eighth-note/quarter-note/eighth-note patterns, with frequent held notes of a half-note duration or longer. Example 6.1 shows typical rhythmic patterns that appear in both the bulgărească and the bulgarish.

It is likely that the bulgărească adopted some of these rhythmic patterns from the Northern Bulgarian *pravo* dance genre, but, in any case, they were exotic in Jewish dance music. Like its choreographic form, the

Example 6.1   Rhythmic patterns of the *bulgărească* and the *bulgarish*

Example 6.2   *Sîrba* "Haiducilor" from Susleni, Orhei

Example 6.3   *Bulgărească* from Şeleste, Orhei

music of the Moldavian bulgărească is a subspecies of sîrba; P. Stoianov groups his bulgăreascăs with the sîrba. The slight rhythmic difference between these two dances in Moldavian music is illustrated by the opening measures of a sîrba and a bulgărească (examples 6.2 and 6.3), both collected in villages in the region of Orhei.[50]

Although there were Moldavian sîrbas that employed some of the syncopations of the bulgărească, in general the repetitive triplet patterns seen in examples 6.2 and 6.3 were more typical of sîrba. Evidently, the Jews were quite sensitive to this rhythmic differentiation, because they adopted and developed the bulgărească, while the sîrba remained marginal within the klezmer repertoire. For example, Moshe Bik's material, which was collected in Orhei, contains examples of the freylekhs, sher, and bulgarish, but no sîrba.[51] In Bucovina, tunes related to the bulgar were called *sîrba* by the Jews.[52] By the post–World War I period, *bulgar* was known to the klezmorim of Western Galicia.[53]

In the course of the nineteenth century, the bulgărească expanded beyond its original location in southern Bessarabia and became one of the major dance forms in all of Bessarabia. Its music combined the "West European, Turkish and Romanian peasant elements" that are present in the regional dance music of other parts of Moldavia and Wallachia.[54] The development of the klezmer bulgarish reveals rapid changes in the nature of the genre, so that each set of musical documents must be analyzed virtually as a distinct subgenre. The Jewish bulgarish, as documented outside of Bessarabia, reveals its musical identity as a genre within the broader klezmer repertoire both positively and negatively, by agreeing with that repertoire in several features and by rejecting those same elements that were rejected by the broader repertoire. The development of a distinctive klezmer bulgarish genre did not prevent the klezmorim from borrowing individual items from the non-Jewish parent genre, the bulgărească.

Unfortunately, the existing documentation is not equally complete for all phases of the development of the Moldavian bulgărească and the Jewish bulgarish. The bulgărească can be studied thanks to the collection of Stoianov, which includes a substantial selection of bulgărəascăs and sîrbas from many regions of the Moldavian SSR.[55] However, the bulgarish tunes that were notated from klezmorim in Bessarabia or elsewhere in eastern Europe are not sufficient in numbers to serve as a basis for comparison with the Moldavian material. Non-Jewish Moldavians (and Moldavian Gypsies) did not emigrate to America in significant numbers, so there is no Moldavian American bulgărească to compare with the bulgarish.

The earliest substantial record of the klezmer bulgarish is the Kostakowsky collection of 1916. This corpus displays a structure of sections and modulation that is significantly different from the Stoianov collection. Therefore, it can be posited that by 1916, in New York, the bulgarish was becoming differentiated from the Moldavian bulgărească. We cannot be sure whether this difference already existed in Bessarabia, whether it was developed by klezmorim elsewhere (such as in Ukraine), or whether it appeared first in New York.

Example 6.4   "Shulem's Bulgarish," played by Max Yenkovitz, accordion, New York City

Two bulgarish tunes were notated from klezmorim in Bessarabia it-self. These appear in Bik's Hebrew article (24–26) and were apparently transcribed by him from klezmorim in Orhei and Dubosari in the 1920s. Both tunes were called "Der Dubosarer Bulgarish." Dubosari is located almost one hundred miles due east of Iaşi, while Orhei is approximately twenty-five miles north of Chişinau (Kishinev), the Bessarabian capital. The second bulgarish tune is still well-known in Bessarabia (where it has appeared on commercial recordings), but does not appear in any other klezmer source. It was played by the Jewish mandolinist Martin Kalisky (born in Bessarabia, resident in Brooklyn since the 1920s) as a Molda-vian, not a Jewish, tune. The first bulgarish is in three parts, all of them using a minor scale with a raised fourth degree (g-a-bb-c♯-d-e-f-g).[56] Its third part is identical to the second part of the bulgarish recorded by the clarinetist Philip Greenberg under the Yiddish title "Biz in vaysen tog arayn" in New York during the early 1920s. Therefore, this first "Dubosarer Bulgarish" is probably a document of a Jewish bulgarish tune created by klezmorim in Bessarabia.

The earliest notated and recorded documents of the klezmer bulgarish are both of American provenance: Herman Shapiro's "Korohod," which uses the cadences and several rhythmic structures of the bulgar, and "Shulem's Bulgarish," recorded in New York in 1913 by the accordion-ist Max Yenkovitz and a cimbalist named Goldberg (see example 6.4).[57]

Example 6.5   "Arcanul" played by Sidor Andronicescu

"Shulem" is the Bessarabian pronunciation of the name *Sholem* (Sha-
lom), which suggests that the originator of the work had been a Bessarabian klezmer, probably of the generation before Yenkovitz. While its
rhythmic structure seems identical to many of the bulgăreascăs and bul-
garishes, the fact that all three parts never modulate from the minor
scale with raised fourth is atypical for the klezmer bulgărească as seen
in Kostakowsky and in the American commercial recordings. The clos-
est connection I have been able to establish is with the West Moldavian
dance *arcanul* (see example 6.5).[58]

Although the name *bulgărească* does not appear in the Cîmpalung region, the source of example 6.5, the dance type *arcanul* (known as *arkan*
in Ruthenia) is related to the sîrba and the bulgărească. Cîmpalung is
almost one hundred miles west of the Prut River, which forms the border
with Bessarabia. Considering that the musical folklore of this mountain-
ous region near Maramureş differs considerably from that of the Bessarabian plains, the stylistic relationship between these two tunes is clear
enough, although they are certainly not variants of one tune. Both are
three-part tunes in the minor scale with raised fourth, featuring prominent pedaling on the tonic (D). "Arcanul" (example 6.5) modulates into
minor in its third part, while the bulgarish remains in the raised-fourth
minor scale throughout. The identical cadential formula ends part II of

"Shulem's Bulgarish" and parts I and II of "Arcanul." This formula is not part of the later style of bulgarish in America, nor is it typical of the bulgǎreascǎ melodies in the Stoianov collection. Cadential formulas are important features in the identification of genres of dance music in many musical cultures, so this concurrence suggests a generic affinity between the two melodies. Rhythmically, however, they are somewhat divergent. Triplets are even more prominent in "Arcanul" than in "Shulem's Bulgarish," and the rhythmic pattern found in part III of "Arcanul" is absent from the bulgarish and does not appear in any Jewish bulgarish, to my knowledge. The modulation in "Arcanul" from a minor scale with raised fourth into standard minor is typical of several genres of both Moldavian and Ukrainian music, but is rare in the bulgarish.

THE BULGARISH IN AMERICA

The bulgarish underwent a rapid structural development in America and continued to develop until the decline of klezmer music in the late 1950s. So many new bulgarish tunes were created that by the 1920s much of the functioning bulgarish repertoire had been written recently in America. Very likely, the Americanization of the name from *bulgarish* to *bulgar* (which had already occurred by Kostakowsky's 1916 publication) testifies to the great currency of this dance among American Jews. In New York, klezmorim from all over the czarist empire, Romania, and Galicia suddenly had direct access to all varieties of bulgarish tunes. The result was an unprecedented transformation of the klezmer dance repertoire.

In America, this expansion of the bulgar seems to have occurred at the expense of the freylekhs, sher, and khosidl. In Kostakowsky's book, the bulgar is seen already to be outstripping these core dance genres. While some new compositions in the older genres appeared in the 1920s, the vast majority of freylekhs and shers that were recorded in New York studios were anonymous, older pieces that many klezmorim already knew. They were usually performed in an ensemble; by contrast, the bulgars were usually performed by soloists who were frequently also the composers. It is in accordance with this pattern that the 1913 recording by the accordionist Max Yenkowitz mentions the name of the composer of the tune, an otherwise unknown klezmer named Shulem.

Stylistically, the bulgars of Kostakowsky differ both from the Moldavian bulgǎreascǎs collected by Stoianov and from the bulgar as it was to develop in succeeding decades. By 1916, when Kostakowsky's book was published, the name *bulgar* had become broad enough to include also a number of Near Eastern and Romanian (non-bulgărească) items, but at the same time, the more exotic Turkish and Romanian melodic structures were eliminated from the bulgar repertoire. Apparently, for the Ukrainian, Belorussian, and other Jews in America, elements of other Near Eastern repertoires were being subsumed under the rubric *bulgar*.

Several examples exist. The "bulgar" on page 24 of Kostakowsky is apparently derived from the dance *jumatate joc* (not a bulgărească) from Bacau in southern Moldavia.[59] The specific version in Kostakowsky is closer to the one recorded by André Hajdu among Hasidic klezmorim in Israel (Hajdu and Mazor, part I, band 1), among whom the name *bulgarish* is not known. Part I of the "bulgar" on page 28 of Kostakowsky is a well-known Greek *hassapiko*, which had been recorded several times in New York by both Greeks and Jews. In 1923, Naftule Brandwein recorded it as "Heisser Bulgar" in four parts. Part I is similar to Kostakowsky, part II is in the style of a freylekhs, and parts III and IV are in the style of bulgarish in the raised-fourth minor scale. His parts II through IV do not resemble the parts of the Kostakowsky tune.

The first part of the "bulgar" on page 23 of Kostakowsky (example 6.6) is identical to a čalgija (Turkish instrumental ensemble) dance recorded during the 1960s by the Macedonian clarinetist Tale Ogenovski (see example 6.7).[60] This melody is in the augmented-second scale (here like the Turkish makam Uzzâl/Hicâz), easily assimilated to similar patterns existing in klezmer music, despite certain differences in melodic construction. The first parts of both tunes are identical, except that the Jewish version has introduced a bulgarish cadence with the eighth-note–quarter-note–eighth-note pattern and triplets. By the second part, the tunes are totally divergent. The melodic movement and the triplet pattern in the klezmer tune have no echo in the čalgija melody, which introduces the major ascending and minor descending sixth of the Turkish makam Hicâz (and Uzzâl) in part II.

In general, the bulgars in Kostakowsky's collection feature augmented-second scales, of either the "Hicâz" type or the "Nikrîz/Altered Dorian," and sometimes transpositions of these to the fourth or fifth scale degrees. This modality is typical of the core repertoire of klezmer music far more than of the Moldavian bulgărească (as seen in Stoianov). In addition, there is often one part of the bulgar tune that modulates into major. Although two-part tunes were more common, the three-part structure, often with modulation in the second and/or third part, was

Example 6.6   "Bulgar"

Example 6.7   "Deverevo Oro," played by Tale Ogenovski, clarinet

well known in klezmer dance tunes.[61] Example 6.8 is a typical example of the "bulgars" in the Kostakowsky collection.[62]

In this example, we see a raised-fourth minor scale melody on "d," composed almost entirely of short ascents and descents with a triplet structure. The second and third bars use motives that are common in

Example 6.8   "Rumanian Bulgar"

Jewish tunes of several genres in this scale, which forms the tonal basis
for the *Mishebarakh shteyger* of synagogue song.[63] Other than the triplets, nothing in this first part is unfamiliar in Jewish music; the melodic
material could have been used in several instrumental and vocal genres.
At the same time, these motives would not be out of place in several genres of Moldavian Gypsy music. We can conclude that the klezmer who
created this tune knew what he was about; using the rhythm of the bulgărească, he constructed a melody that gave his Jewish audience familiar melodic material, but which was not so Jewish as to be beyond the
stylistic boundaries of the bulgărească. In his second part, which modulates into major (still on "d"), however, he seems to be following older
klezmer practice.

   During the 1920s, several of the bulgars recorded in New York were
in three parts, with parts I and II in the minor scale with raised fourth
and part III in major, similar to the Kostakowsky example above (cf. "Biz
in vaysen tog arayn," by clarinetist Philip Greenberg, 1923).[64] Other bulgars recorded at that time display three separate scales in parts I, II, and
III, similar in this respect to both the three-part freylekhs and the mazltov genres in the core klezmer repertoire, such as the "Volyner Bulgar-

ish" recorded by Abe Schwartz's studio ensemble.[65] Judging by the name, it is possible that this tune had already been created in Volhynia (Wolyn). In general, the New York bulgars do not show this pattern of modulation, which is closely related to the core repertoire. I might surmise that the bulgarish tunes with this modulation pattern sounded "too Jewish" for the American bulgar; that is, they were not sufficiently differentiated from the core klezmer repertoire.

One of the three bulgarish tunes recorded by Beregovski in 1937 from a klezmer in Tiraspol (at that time within the Moldavian Republic, but separated from Bessarabia proper, which was Romanian) displays a structure very similar to the bulgars in Kostakowsky's book, including the modulation from the augmented second to major (number 205).[66] His two other bulgarish tunes (numbers 206 and 207) are essentially Jewish, with only slight suggestions of bulgărească in the rhythmic structure (part II of number 207). While it is not impossible that Beregovski's example was influenced by American sources, it is more likely that the affinity between Kostakowsky's bulgars and Beregovski's bulgar from Tiraspol, east of the Prut River (number 205), is explained by the fact that the Jewish bulgarish was taking shape among klezmorim both inside and outside of Bessarabia in the early decades of the twentieth century. By 1937, the klezmorim of Tiraspol had been cut off from Romanian Bessarabia for twenty years and so were in contact with the bulgarish in the form it had taken in Ukraine.

At the same time, the bulgar underwent yet another development in New York, consisting of a stylization of the modulatory schemes and cadential formulas of the genre. During the 1920s, the New York bulgars often employed the cadential rhythmic formulas seen in example 6.9.

A common structural pattern predominates in the influential recordings of the Galician-born virtuoso Naftule Brandwein and the slightly later recordings of Dave Tarras. In this pattern, the first part of the tune is usually in a major scale, which immediately distinguishes these bulgar melodies from the core klezmer dance repertoire, whose first part is almost never in a major scale (cf. the freylekhs, skochnes, and shers in Beregovski's collections). Naftule followed this by two parts either in minor or in the raised-fourth minor scale (as in, for example, the nameless bulgars following Naftule's recordings of "Vie tsvei is Naftule der driter," 1922, and "Doina," 1923).

At first, Tarras kept to this formula (see example 6.9), but later modified it by staying in major for the greater part of the tune. Tarras was extremely prolific in composing bulgars, which he sometimes named for

Example 6.9   Cadential rhythmic formulas of the
New York bulgar, 1920s

Example 6.10   "Bulgar," played by Dave Tarras, clarinet, 1925

the landsmanshaft associations for whom he played, such as "Yedinitser
Bulgar" (1941). There can be no doubt that these numerous tunes (and
recordings) of Tarras's became the dominant influence in the perpetua-
tion of the bulgar as the major klezmer genre in America after 1930. Examples 6.10 and 6.11 represent typical Tarras creations from the 1920s

Example 6.11   "Der Heisser Bulgar," played by Dave Tarras, clarinet, 1941, New York City

and 1940s.[67] The first and second parts of example 6.10 use "bulgar cadences," which became very common in the American bulgar compositions of the 1920s and afterward and which employ the cadential formulas seen above.

Despite the length of time separating the creation of these two tunes, the stylistic differences between them are not great. The first modulates from major into the raised-fourth minor scale after the first part, while the second remains in major until the third part. The melodic direction of the first parts of both tunes is divergent, and the ascending pattern of the second seems to be more characteristic of Tarras's middle period. In addition, the held notes are more prevalent in the 1940s tune than in the 1925 tune.

Even in 1925, Tarras gave evidence of the direction in which he would

move twenty years later. On the reverse side of the "bulgar," he recorded
a composition named "Der Monastrishtsher [*sic*] Rebin's Chosidl," dedicated to the Hasidic rebbe of Monastyrishcha (in Podolia) with whom
his family was affiliated. This three-part tune shows the influence of
the bulgarish even in the first part, which closes with the same cadential
formula that Tarras would later use in part II of "Der Heisser Bulgar."
Part III is entirely in the style of the bulgarish; it features nothing to link
it to the khosidl dance genre.

The final stage in the "bulgarization" of American klezmer music is
represented by several Tarras compositions of the 1940s, in which the
melodic structures of Jewish tunes of various genres are mixed with
the rhythmical structure of the bulgar. These tunes never were called
bulgar, but rather *sher, freylekhs,* or idiosyncratic names (such as "Mein
einikle's bar mitzvah" [My grandson's bar mitzvah], "A khasene in
shtetl" [A wedding in town], and so on). By the end of World War II,
almost the entire core klezmer dance repertoire had disappeared; thus
for the American-born generation after this time, these new freylekhs-
bulgar hybrids, along with the "bulgar," came to represent Jewish dance
music.

Example 6.12 ("Ternovker Sher") was composed by Dave Tarras in
the 1940s and was named after the small Podolian town of his birth,
Ternovka, in the region of Heisin (Uman). Melodies of this type had
never been heard in Ternovka, however, but only in New York. In part I
of the tune, one can recognize the rhythmic pattern of part I of the bulgars that Tarras had composed around the same time (see example 6.10);
it has no analogue in the existing corpus of European sher melodies.
The rhythmic and melodic patterns of part III are reminiscent of many
American bulgar tunes. Part II, however, uses augmented-second ("Aha-
vah Rabbah") melodies, which might be found in several genres of eastern European Jewish music, less commonly in the bulgarish. The unusually high note density seems to indicate the placement of originally
slower melodies into the tempo of the bulgar. The skochne appearing
as number 78 in Beregovski's collection (see example 6.13) serves as a
model of the type of Jewish dance melody that Tarras may have used for
part II.[68]

Tarras's many tunes of this type were so differentiated from the traditional genres, whether Jewish or Moldavian, that they constituted a
genre of their own. The businessmen who issued these recordings were
not unaware of this musical fact, and were therefore able to package the
same tunes to both Jews and Greeks (in the absence of non-Jewish Mol-

Example 6.12   "Ternovker Sher," played by Dave Tarras, clarinet, 1940s

davians). A certain Dimitriades, who owned Colonial Records in New York at this period, issued Tarras's "Ternovker Sher" first on a Jewish LP ("Dave Tarras Plays Again—Jewish Dances"),[69] then later as a hassapiko (without Tarras's name) on one of his Greek LPs, side by side with pirated recordings of *kalamatiano* and *tsamiko* melodies by the Greek clarinetist Karakosta.

CONCLUSION

The process described above represents the continuation of the same process that had created the transitional repertoire during the nineteenth century in eastern Europe. Notable is the absence of significant input from any musical genre that was current among non-Jews in Amer-

Example 6.13   "Skochne," 1928

ica. The Western musical features of the new bulgars and their deriva-
tives are related to some of those that appear in the Moldavian bulgărească. What is new in the American klezmer development is the almost
total abandonment of the older core dance repertoire. In eastern Europe,
the adoption of the transitional repertoire had not been accompanied by
the loss of the core repertoire prior to World War II.

My own interviews with Tarras in 1978 suggest that he was anxious
to achieve this result. He repeatedly characterized the core Jewish dance
repertoire as "simple" and viewed Romanian (that is, Moldavian) music as a higher musical culture. He was able to dismiss his principal klezmer rival, Naftule Brandwein, by saying that the latter "played beautiful Jewish music," and that he had a "small" repertoire. While this may
explain the intentions of one highly talented and influential klezmer musician, it does not account for the change in musical taste among a great
many European-born American Jews. In dance, this change was not in
the direction of any form of American popular dance music, but was to
a large extent in the direction of Moldavian Gypsy (lăutar) dance music.
It has been possible to describe the musical shape of the bulgarish and
the transitional repertoire, but it is more difficult to adduce an explanation for the development of this repertoire.[70]

The development in America of the bulgarish, as part of the transitional repertoire, must be viewed as a continuation of earlier musical movements, but in a radically different cultural environment that attributed some new meanings to the older patterns. Two points seem to have been most important in America: the secular associations of the transitional klezmer repertoire and the reputation of Romania, Bessarabia, and southern Ukraine as areas that had a lively secular proletarian Jewish culture.[71]

In America, the paraliturgical and Hasidic klezmer repertoires began to atrophy quite early. Even the secular core repertoire (freylekhs, sher) was little developed. The co-territorial repertoire changed its character as the Jews acquired different non-Jewish neighbors. This change is seen in Kostakowsky, where the co-territorial repertoire is represented by the *tarantella,* in addition to the kolomeyka and kozachok. It appears that the Hungarian *czardas* (in the collection) represents a New World rather than an Old World co-territorial repertoire. The Old World cosmopolitan repertoire is still represented in Kostakowsky, but it appears that, with the passage of time, it was mainly the waltz that remained productive.

While the freylekhs and sher were secular dances (indeed, in some regions pious Jews would not dance the sher), it is probable that in America the entire core klezmer repertoire was felt to be part of an increasingly obsolete, religion-centered lifestyle. The major cause of this was the association of this core repertoire with the orthodox Jewish wedding, because, in Beregovski's words: "Klezmer music used to be played almost exclusively at weddings."[72] While the zhok had already been transformed into several wedding genres (such as mazltov and opfihren di makhetonim), this process had not been completed in the case of the bulgarish, which had been employed occasionally to replace the older *freylekhs fun der khupe* genre. It appears that in Odessa (and probably elsewhere), the bulgarish, along with other Moldavian genres, had been played by klezmorim in taverns, outside of the wedding context. In Odessa and Kishinev, the bulgarish, zhok, and doyne were ethnically neutral genres. It is for this reason that they are played even today by Jewish musicians of Odessa, who have virtually no other "Jewish" repertoire (such as the fiddler Sasha Feldman, resident in New York since the late 1970s).

The major facts confronting the Jewish immigrants to America were proletarianization and secularization of many areas of life. While these factors had operated in several large centers of Jewish population (such as Warsaw), they were especially characteristic of the frontier area of "the Jewish South," that is, southern Ukraine, Bessarabia, and the Kingdom of Romania. The Moldavianized transitional repertoire had diffused from these southern areas and already in the later nineteenth century constituted a musical icon of a transformed Jewish lifestyle. While the Jews of Bessarabia and Romania were regarded by other Jews as lacking either a religious or a secular Jewish (Yiddish) culture, Yiddish popular music in America idealized Bessarabia and Romania as lands of plenty and of freedom from religious restrictions (see, for example, the theater repertoire of Aaron Lebedeff, "Rumania, Rumania," "Gib mir Bessarabia," "Kishinev," and so on).[73] In eastern Europe, Jews from Bessarabia, Romania, and (to some extent) Odessa had been stigmatized as un-Jewish. The founder of the Yiddish theater, Abraham Goldfaden, had described the young Romanian Jews in the following way: "These grew up in ignorance, without Jewish or general education, and were employed as laborers and artisans. For entertainment they frequented saloons where Jewish singers, badchonim, delighted their public with trivial jingles and jests."[74]

However, in America, it was precisely their proletarian and marginally Jewish cultural traits that seemed more relevant to the New World situation. The adoption of the bulgarish as *the* Jewish dance in New York suggests that the Jews were using this genre as a symbol of both proletarianization and secularization, in order to shield them from totally surrendering to these same factors in a completely American environment.

It is tempting to link the development of the Romanian element in American klezmer music with similar shifts in the Yiddish theater. The Ukrainian Abraham Goldfaden began his experiments in Yiddish theater in the Moldavian city of Iaşi in 1875 and established a permanent theater in Odessa in 1878. In America, the Bessarabian and South Ukrainian dialects of Yiddish dominated the theater, and Romanian elements are common in the repertoire of Yiddish theater singers such as Aaron Lebedeff or Moishe Oysher, among others. Nevertheless, the musical forms of these Romanian influences were rather different from klezmer music, largely because they had separate historical antecedents. The introduction of Moldavian elements into the transitional klezmer repertoire began to occur at least two generations prior to the birth of the Yiddish theater. It must be at least as old as the creation of the Volhynian school of cantorial singing in the early nineteenth century.[75]

However, the frequent appearance of these Moldavian song and dance elements must have helped create an atmosphere among the Jewish im-

migrant public in which the klezmorim were encouraged to further develop the existing Moldavian features of their repertoire, in particular
the bulgarish and the doina. Although the Yiddish theater and klezmer
music appealed to the same immigrant stratum in America, the musicians employed in both areas were not usually the same. While the musicians working for the theater were probably predominantly of klezmer
origin, very few of them were practicing klezmorim. Most European-
born klezmorim did not have the playing technique or reading ability to
be able to succeed as theater musicians, nor did they have the knowledge
of Western music to succeed as theater composers. Tarras was one of the
few klezmorim who did work in the theater as a musician, and he supplemented his income and increased his prestige by performing there frequently. Current knowledge indicates that the Romanian/Moldavian
elements in the Yiddish theater repertoire and in klezmer music were addressed to the same audience, but were derived from different sources
and were created by musicians who moved in different musical spheres.
The preliminary cataloguing of the Yiddish theater sheet music at the
YIVO collection indicates that klezmer material played a small part in
this repertoire, in which the introduction of western European "light
classical" and popular genres was a major concern.[76] Furthermore, the
sentiments of Goldfaden, who claimed that the musical taste of eastern
European Jews was "contaminated" by non-Western elements that were
an obstacle to the cultural uplifting of the Jewish masses, suggest that
the motivating spirit of the Yiddish theater and that of klezmer music
were in many ways not complementary, but antithetical.[77] In both Europe and America, klezmer music was persistently introducing those
same "oriental" musical features that prevented the Jews from fully accepting the "higher"musical culture of the West.[78]

During the 1930s and 1940s in America, klezmer music experienced
an overall decline in the variety of dance and nondance genres performed,
in the creation of new tunes in the core repertoire, and in its ability to ensure its transmission to the American-born generation of musicians who
were frequently drawn to more mainstream American styles. American-
born Jews of non-klezmer origin rarely participated in the music during
this period. American klezmer music displayed vitality and creativity
mainly in a single area—the development of the bulgarish dance genre
that led to the creation of bulgarish-freylekhs–hybrid dance melodies.
The immigrant generation (which could not be replaced after more stringent immigration laws were adopted in 1924) was no longer young, and
memories of the Old World coexisted with lifetime experiences in Amer-

ica. The bulgarish could no longer serve its cultural function as Odessa, Kishinev, and Iaşi faded further into the horizon of the past. By the 1940s, the "pure" bulgarish was of less interest than a hybrid form in which the Moldavian and Jewish elements were combined. In the transitional repertoire as a whole, most of what was structurally foreign in the Moldavian genres had already been eliminated in Europe, leaving a number of exotic rhythmic structures (principally triplets for the bulgarish, a 3/8 pattern for the zhok) and some novel combinations of melodic and modulatory patterns. The transition from the core klezmer genres, freylekhs and sher, to the newer bulgarish was neither radical change nor "flexible non-change," but something intermediate.[79]

From a purely commercial aspect, both for the professional klezmorim and later for record producers, the Moldavianized repertoire possessed a value that other repertoires did not. The concentration of the majority of eastern European Jewish immigrants in one city (New York) certainly aided in the propagation of these new genres of klezmer music. Between World War I and the 1950s, this new repertoire evolved principally in New York and came to constitute the American repertoire of klezmer music. For the American-born generations, especially after World War II, the bulgarish and the bulgarish-freylekhs hybrids were the only genres of klezmer music that had any currency, and hence they have retroactively shaped the American conception of the nature of klezmer dance music.

In America, for a period of more than eighty years (1881–1960s), klezmer music remained in the hands of musicians from the klezmer families. Unlike other eastern European immigrant groups (such as Serbs or Ukrainians), the Jews developed no acculturated style, apart from brief experiments that never grew into a coherent style (for example, nothing comparable to the "orquesta" style that developed among Mexican Americans during roughly the same period).[80] The professional European-born klezmorim continued to expand only the transitional or orientalized repertoire of klezmer music. Due to the physical proximity in New York (and possibly other cities) of both north- and southeastern European Jews, as well as various Balkan ethnic groups, especially Greeks, the orientalized klezmer repertoire was able to draw upon fresh sources for its Gypsy and/or Balkan material. For a period of two generations it was this orientalized repertoire, rather than the core klezmer repertoire or a more acculturated style of dance music, that dominated American klezmer music. Within this repertoire, the bulgarish/

bulgar became the focus of considerable stylistic development and new composition.

During this entire period, klezmer music retained some function in familial celebrations (weddings, bar mitzvahs) and regional (landsman-shaft) festivities, but it was never supported by Jewish cultural, educa-tional, or religious institutions. As a result, for the post–World War II generation, who were usually the grandchildren of immigrants, klezmer music, by then predominantly an American development of the orien-talized repertoire, had no cultural relevance and was usually viewed by them with incomprehension. It was not closely related to other known Jewish repertoires, such as that of the synagogue, Hasidism, or Yiddish folk or theater song, and it was even more remote from the new Israeli popular music that was coming to play an increasingly large role in American Jewish life. The period from 1950 to 1970 saw the passing away of almost all the klezmorim who had been born in Europe and who had shaped the development of the repertoire in America. This twenty-year hiatus, in which klezmer music was rarely performed, was the cause of the fundamental discontinuity between American klezmer music, as it had developed from 1880 until 1950, and the klezmer revival of the late 1970s.

The so-called klezmer revival has ensured that some elements of the klezmer repertoire and style will continue during the lives of the post–World War II generation.[81] A rather similar revival has also begun more recently in the Russian, Ukrainian, and Lithuanian republics of the for-mer Soviet Union. Whether the musical elements within these revivals of klezmer music will be productive enough to generate a new repertoire, as they did in the 1920s, 1930s, and 1940s, is at present a moot point. However, it appears that the dominance of the bulgar as the preeminent American klezmer genre, and with it the stylistic continuity of American klezmer music, ended in the 1960s.

NOTES

1. The breakup of the Soviet Union has added further complexity to the al-ready complicated nomenclature of eastern European geography. One of the two medieval Danubian principalities of the Romanian-speaking peoples called itself *Moldova*, which usually appears in English in the Russianized form *Moldavia*. The capital of this principality was located on the west side of the Prut River. During the fifteenth century, Romanian speakers from Moldova began to colo-nize the Slavic and Turkic area to the east of the Prut, which acquired the name

Bessarabia, after the Bessarab family of boyars. Beginning in 1511, Moldova on both sides of the Prut was under Ottoman rule. In 1812, Russia wrested Bessarabia from Turkey. In 1920, the area was annexed by the Kingdom of Romania. In 1924, the Soviet Union established a small Moldavian republic east of the Prut. Bessarabia changed hands twice during World War II. At the end of the war, the Soviets established the Moldavian Soviet Socialist Republic, which comprised most of the territory between the Prut and the Dniester Rivers as well as some land to the east (Tiraspol), but excluded the northernmost and southernmost regions (Hotin and Ismail), which were awarded to the Ukraine. In 1992, the Moldavian republic declared itself independent and reverted to its Romanian name, *Moldova.* The *New York Times* seems to have coined the adjective *Moldovan* to replace the more usual *Moldavian,* but this usage has not been generally accepted as yet. A useful source in English is C. U. Clark, *Bessarabia* (New York: Dodd and Mead, 1927).

2. Much of the material for this article was collected in 1978–79, when I codirected an NEA project entitled "Jewish Instrumental Folkmusic," sponsored by the Ethnic Folk Arts Center (New York City), which focused on Dave Tarras and his accompanist, Sam Beckerman. The clarinetist Andy Statman and I spent those years studying with and interviewing Tarras. In 1978, Statman and I formed the first klezmer revival group on the East Coast. I had come from a family in which klezmer music and in particular the bulgarish were still appreciated. My father, Max (Meshilem) Feldman (1898–1970), was born into a family of furriers in the Bessarabian town of Yedinits (Edinti), Hotin province, and emigrated to the United States in 1922. For him, in the 1950s, the dominant dances were still the sher and the bulgar, which he often called the bulgărească.

3. I would like to thank Professors Judit Frigyesi, Marina Roseman, and Jane Sugarman for their contributions to this paper. I am also indebted to Kurt Bjorling (Chicago Klezmer Ensemble) for reviewing the bulgar transcriptions.

4. See Mark Slobin, "A Fresh Look at Beregovski's Folk Music Research," *Ethnomusicology* 30, no. 1 (1986): 253–60.

5. For example, Mark Slobin, "Klezmer Music: An American Ethnic Genre," *Yearbook for Traditional Music* 16 (1984): 34–41.

6. E. Lifschutz, "Merrymakers and Jesters among Jews," *YIVO Annual of Jewish Social Sciences* 7 (1952): 49.

7. Moshe Bik, *Klezmorim be-Orgeev* (Haifa: Publications of the Haifa Music Museum and Library, 1964), 7.

8. Mark Slobin, *Tenement Songs: The Popular Music of the Jewish Immigrants* (Urbana: University of Illinois Press, 1982), 16.

9. Ibid.

10. Lifschutz, "Merrymakers," 62.

11. See Andy Logan, "Profiles: Five Generations," *New Yorker* (29 Oct. 1949): 32–51.

12. Regarding the tamburitza, see M. Forry, "Bečar Music in the Serbian Community of Los Angeles: Evolution and Transformation," *Selected Reports in Ethnomusicology* 3, no. 1 (1978): 173–209.

13. See E. O. Henry, "Institutions for the Promotion of Indigenous Music:

The Case of Ireland's Comhaltas Ceoltoiri Eireann," *Ethnomusicology* 35, no. 1 (1989): 69.

14. Forry, "Bečar Music," 189.

15. See Mark Slobin's works: "Some Intersections of Jews, Music, and Theater," in *From Hester Street to Hollywood: The Jewish-American Stage and Screen,* ed. Sarah Blacher-Cohen, 29–43 (Bloomington: Indiana University Press, 1983); "The Music of the Yiddish Theater: Manuscript Sources at YIVO," *YIVO Annual of Jewish Social Sciences* 18 (1983): 372–90; and *Chosen Voices: The Story of the American Cantorate* (Urbana: University of Illinois Press, 1989).

16. Moshe Beregovski, *Evreiskaia narodnaia instrumental'naia muzyka,* ed. Max Goldin (Moscow: Sovetskii kompozitor, 1987), 532.

17. Majer Balaban, *Zyda Lwowsey na przelomic XVI^{go} XVII^{go} wieku* (Lwow, 1906), 533.

18. Balint Sarosi, *Gypsy Music* (Budapest: Corvina Press, 1970), 54.

19. Regarding Hungary, see A. Borgo, "Pharao barna ivadekai es a klezmorim: A cigany es jiddis zenekultura magyarorszagi kapcsolatai," *Muszika* 36, no. 9 (1993): 32–40.

20. Anna Czekanowska, *Polish Folk Music: Slavonic Heritage, Polish Tradition, Contemporary Trends* (Cambridge: Cambridge University Press, 1990), 155, 172, 204.

21. Beregovski, *Evreiskaia,* 1987.

22. I have expanded on this scheme from my paper, "The Repertoire of Klezmer Music," which was presented at the Folklore Department Colloquium of the University of Pennsylvania in November 1987.

23. The major source for the klezmer dance repertoire is the collection of Moshe Beregovski (1892–1961), which was collected in the Soviet Ukraine, Bessarabia, Belorussia, and Lithuania during the 1930s. Beregovski's sound and notated collection had been voluminous. However, the entire sound archive was apparently destroyed just after World War II, before most of it could be transcribed. Part of what had been notated was prepared for publication in his multivolume *Jewish Musical Folklore.* The recent Soviet edition titled *Jewish Instrumental Folkmusic* (Beregovski, *Evreiskaia*) contains 217 dance tunes. An earlier edition, published in the United States (Moshe Beregovski, *Old Jewish Folk Music: The Collections and Writings of Moshe Beregovski,* ed. and trans. Mark Slobin [Philadephia: University of Pennsylvania, 1982]), contains 79 dance tunes. A new edition of the Beregovski material, including the klezmer material, appeared in 2001 (see Sources).

During the interwar period there had been several small-scale publications of klezmer material in Austrian and Russian journals. After War World II, the Ukrainian/Israeli Joachim Stutschewsky published a significant collection of klezmer repertoire that had been collected by other researchers in various places (Joachim Stutschewsky, *Ha-klezmarim: Toldotehem, oraḥ-hayehem viyetsirotehem* [Jerusalem: Mosad Bialik, 1959]). In Europe, there had been a few commercial recordings of klezmer music, in such cities as Warsaw and Bucharest, as well as others. The earliest recordings date from c. 1910 (such as several records of "Belf's Rumanian Orchestra"), and the latest are a group of pre-Holocaust Soviet recordings.

In America, klezmer material had been issued exclusively for commercial reasons. Commercial recording commenced in the second decade of the twentieth century. After the 1920s, American recordings became less numerous and were dominated by a small group of musicians. Nevertheless, some commercial recordings of klezmer music were issued in America through the 1960s. The numerous American commercial recordings can be located in Richard K. Spottswood (*Ethnic Music on Records: A Discography of Ethnic Recordings Produced in the United States, 1893–1942*, vol. 3, *Eastern Europe* [Urbana: University of Illinois Press, 1990]). Several of these recordings have been reissued recently.

A single major printed collection of klezmer material was issued in America —Wolff Kostakowsky's *International Hebrew Wedding Music* (Brooklyn, N.Y.: Kostakowsky, 1916).

In Palestine, the resident Ashkenazic community had lived a pious life that forbade instrumental music in almost all situations. Klezmer music in Palestine has been studied in connection with the pilgrimage to Meron (near Safed), which features an instrumental repertoire (see André Hajdu, "Niggun Meron," *Yuval* 2 [1971]: 73–113; Hajdu and Mazor, *Hassidic Tunes* [New York: Folkways Records, LPFE 4209, 1976]).

There is very little evidence concerning the instrumental dance repertoire of several Jewish communities within the Habsburg domains of central Hungary, Transylvania, Maramureş, Slovakia, and Bohemia. It may be that these Jews (or some of them) had formerly possessed instrumental genres similar to those of the more easterly Jews, they may have developed independent Jewish instrumental genres that were lost during the nineteenth century, or they may never have had such genres. According to the documents mentioned by A. Z. Idelsohn (*Jewish Music in Its Historical Development* [New York: Henry Holt, 1929], 455–60), it would appear that the German, Austrian, and Bohemian Jews did not have such repertoires. Since the nineteenth century, Jews in Hungarian-speaking areas usually employed Gypsy musicians to play their usual repertoire at Jewish celebrations, although the Gypsy repertoire might also have been performed by klezmorim. Recent research with Gypsy musicians from Transylvania (Romania) has shown that these musicians had performed a specific repertoire for Hungarian- and Yiddish-speaking Jews consisting of core repertoire dances of the freylekhs types (called there *husid* or *khosid*), Hungarian dances not or no longer current among non-Jews, popular Yiddish songs, and instrumental rubato melodies that seem to display a confluence of Jewish, Hungarian, and Romanian melodic elements (Judit Frigyesi, personal communication with author, 1992).

There has also been some documentation of klezmer or other Jewish repertoire performed by non-Jewish musicians in Romania and Ukraine (1970s to 1990), such as the recordings by the late Harry Brauner in Maramureş in the 1960s and by Izalii Zemtsovsky in Vinnitsa (Ukraine) in the 1980s.

24. Moshe Beregovski, "Yidishe instrumentalishe folksmuzik," in Beregovski, *Old Jewish Folk Music*, 533–34.

25. Beregovski, *Old Jewish Folk Music*, 502.

26. Ibid., 535.

27. Nikolai Fedorovich Findeisen, "Evreiskie tsimbaly i tsimbalisty Lepian-

skie" (The Jewish Cimbal and the Lepianski Family of Cimbalists), in *Muzykal'-naia etnografiia*, ed. N. F. Findeisen, 37–44 (Leningrad: Izdatel'stvo Komissii Po Izucheniiu Narodnoi Musyki Pri Etnograficheskom Otdelenii Russkogo Geograficheskoko Obshchestna, 1926).

28. Beregovski, *Old Jewish Folk Music*, 539.

29. A taksim from the Beregovski collection was published by Joachim Braun ("The Unpublished Volumes of Moshe Beregovski's Jewish Musical Folklore," *Israel Studies in Musicology* 4 [1987]: 133–36). Although Braun states that "the intrinsic features of the Arab taksim . . . are preserved in Beregovski's Jewish-Ukrainian klezmer-taksim . . ." (132), his musical example does not bear this out. Beregovski had observed that the distinction between taksim and doina was known only to klezmorim then in their seventies to nineties. Max Goldin, who has compared the Jewish and Moldavian doinas on the basis of extensive materials of both cultures, has concluded that "Jewish doinas do not have any distinctive structural features" (*On Musical Connections between Jews and the Neighboring Peoples of Eastern and Western Europe*, ed. and trans. Robert A. Rothstein [Amherst: University of Massachusetts, 1989], 27). A variant of the dance following the taksim (Braun, "Unpublished Volumes," 136) was recorded by Dave Tarras in the 1940s as "A Heimisher Sher." An example of the Romanian taksim may be heard on record no. 6 of *Antologia de muzicii populare romaneşti*, vol. 2, ed. Tiberiu Alexandru (Electrechord, EPD-1017).

30. Ivan Lipaev, "Evreiskie orkestry," *Russkaia muzykal'naia gazeta* 6 (1904): 170.

31. Beregovski, *Old Jewish Folk Music*, 501.

32. Stutschewsky, *Ha-klezmarim*, 216.

33. According to Y. Mazor, of National Sound Archives, Jerusalem, personal communication, 1997.

34. S. Zalmanoff, *Sefer haniggunim*, vol. 3 (Kvar Chabad, n.d.), 61.

35. Refers to Beregovski, *Jewish Instrumental Folk Music*.

36. Goldin, *On Musical Connections*, 22–23.

37. A remark by the Yiddish folksinger Bronya Sakina (1910–88), born in the Podolian region of the Ukraine, points to the importance of the transitional Romanian-influenced repertoire there: "The more Romanian it was, the more our klezmorim liked it, and the more we liked it." From an unpublished interview by Michael Alpert; see Goldin, *On Musical Connections*, 22–23.

38. Several Polish recordings attest to the popularity of the orientalized repertoire, for example, the recordings of the fiddler Jozef Solinksi, recorded in Warsaw in the 1920s, and the flute doinas of S. Kosch, recorded in Lwow in 1910, mentioned by Slobin ("Klezmer Music: An American Ethnic Genre," 36–38). Not only does Solinski perform Moldavian material, but also a klezmer version of a late-nineteenth-century *longa* dance tune from Istanbul (in makam Nihavend). All these pieces were labeled on the discs "Rumeynisher Fantazi." Lipaev ("Evreiskie orkestry") referred to Romanian repertoire among the klezmorim of Russia. A variety of Romanian repertoire was also performed by the klezmorim of Galicia in the early twentieth century (Yeremiah Hescheles, personal communication, 1998).

39. See Walter Zev Feldman, "Modulation in Jewish Instrumental Folkmu-

sic," paper presented at the meeting of the Mid-Atlantic Chapter of the Society for Ethnomusicology, Baltimore, Md., 1988.

40. Idelsohn, *Jewish Music in Its Historical Development,* 311.

41. My interviews with Jacques Press (1978) of Tbilisi, whose father had been a klezmer in Feodossia (Kafa), suggest the lively two-way musical contacts between Tatars and Ashkenazic Jews at the end of the nineteenth and the beginning of the twentieth centuries.

42. Logan, "Profiles: Five Generations," 34.

43. Beregovski's 1937 article was published in Beregovski, *Old Jewish Folk Music,* 530–48. For Stutschewsky, see *Ha-klezmarim.* However, the so-called "Shir La-Halikha" (no. 8a) in Stutschewsky's work is a well-known bulgarish, recorded in New York as "Odessa Bulgar" (Abe Schwartz Orchestra, Columbia E4322).

44. *Evreiskaia entsiklopediia* (St. Petersburg: Brockhaus-Efron, 1908–13), 739.

45. Georgii Fedosievich Bogach, *Pushkin i moldavskii fol'klor* (Kishinev: Kartia Moldoveniaske, 1963), 230.

46. Bik, *Klezmorim be-Orgeev,* 7. My father told me that in his north Bessarabian town the resident klezmer kapelye was led by a Jewish fiddler and a Gypsy clarinetist. He felt that this was not an unusual situation.

47. This first documentation appears in the memoirs of A.F. Velt'man (1831), which can be found in Bogach, *Pushkin,* 232. A dance named *bulgărească* is apparently known in Oltenia, but its music is unrelated to the sîrba or to the Bessarabian bulgărească; an example can be found in Corneliu Dan Georgescu, *Melodii de joc din Oltenia* (Bucharest: Editura Muzicala a Uniunii Compozitorilor, 1968), 78.

48. The bulgar dance pattern, facing the opposite direction, appears to have been adopted by Israelis of Polish and other eastern European origin as the hora. The origin of the name in Israel is obscure. It is not unlikely that in parts of Poland, the Romanian names for dance genres were confused. On the other hand, the same dance is termed *hora* (without the velar *kh* of Greek *khoron* or Romanian dialect *khora*) in Aegean Turkey, and this Turkish usage may have been current in Palestine. There also seems to be a form of this dance in Lebanon called *hawra,* the name of which is perhaps derived from the Turkish. According to Michael Alpert, some Jews in Ukraine performed a couples' dance to the music of the bulgarish (personal communication, 1989).

49. This may be compared to the freylekhs, skochnes, and shers in Beregovski, *Old Jewish Folk Music* and *Evreiskaia.*

50. Petr Fedorovich Stoianov, *500 melodii de jocuri din Moldova* (Kishinev: Kartia moldoveniaske, 1972). The sîrba comes from page 55 and the bulgărească from page 36.

51. The only published klezmer source featuring a substantial number of sîrbas is Kostakowsky, *International Hebrew Wedding Music.* Moldavian sîrbas appear on a few klezmer recordings, but only in Europe and only in conjunction with doinas—never as dance music. In the Ukraine, the name *sîrba* was employed for a totally different dance form, which in Bessarabia had been called *hora.* Dave Tarras used *sîrba* in the latter meaning.

52. Leon Schwartz, personal communication, 1984.

53. Hescheles, personal communication, 1998.

54. R. Garfias, "Survivals of Turkish Characteristics in Romanian Musica Lăutareasca," *Yearbook for Traditional Music* 13 (1981): 99.

55. Unfortunately, I have not had access to the earlier Moldavian collection of V. Korchinski (*Moldavskie naigrysh i pesni* [Moscow: Muzgiz, 1937]) or of Boris Iakovlevich Kotliarov (*O skripichnoi kul'ture v Moldavii* [Kishinev: Gos. izd-vo Moldavii, 1955]).

56. There is no convenient name for this scale, which is predominant in the klezmer bulgarish and doina (doyne). Throughout his 1929 book, *Jewish Music in Its Historical Development,* Idelsohn had called it the "Ukrainian Dorian Scale," while in all of his Russian- and Yiddish-language articles Beregovski had called it the "Altered Dorian Scale." Garfias noted its scalar (but not modal) identity with the Turkish makam Nikrîz (Garfias, "Survivals," 100–104). Jewish sources frequently identify it with the so-called Mishebarakh Shteyger of synagogue chant. Slobin discussed it as well (Beregovski, *Old Jewish Folk Music,* 184). The distribution of this scale and certain specific melodic movements (that are not related to the Turkish makam Nikrîz) from Aegean Turkey to Ukraine requires special investigation.

57. Herman S. Shapiro, *The European-Jewish Wedding,* no. 2, "Zmiros" (New York: Hebrew Publishing, 1905), no. 16.

58. The arcanul comes from Vasile D. Nicolescu and Constantin Gh. Prichici, eds., *Cîntece şi jocuri populare din Moldova* (Bucharest: Editura muzicala a Uniunii compozitorilor din R.P.R., 1963).

59. Orchestra "Plaiurile Bistritei" din Bacau, *Jocuri din Moldova* (Electrechord EPC 10.018).

60. PGP, Radio-Televizje Beograd, EP 14711.

61. Beregovski, *Evreiskaia,* 31.

62. Kostakowsky, *International Hebrew Wedding Music,* 14.

63. See Idelsohn, *Jewish Music in Its Historical Development,* 185.

64. Columbia 9037, 1923.

65. Regarding the similarities, see Feldman, "Modulation."

66. Tunes being compared here are from Beregovski, *Old Jewish Folk Music.*

67. These two transcriptions are based on ones done by David August for my course in klezmer music, given in the music department of Princeton University in 1985.

68. Beregovski, *Old Jewish Folk Music,* 431.

69. Colonial LP-218.

70. This issue (in relation to the doyne) was brought up by Mark Slobin without his, however, attempting to find a cause: "Ultimately, I do not feel there can, nor need there always be a concrete reason for such aesthetic choices on the part of an ethnic community" (Slobin, "Klezmer Music," 37).

71. A recent study of the culture of the Jews of nineteenth-century Odessa, focusing mainly on the intelligentsia, however, is Steven J. Zipperstein (*The Jews of Odessa: A Cultural History, 1794–1881* [Stanford: Stanford University Press, 1986]). Jewish life in Bessarabia has attracted little scholarly attention, the main sources remaining the Holocaust Memorial Books published in Israel by the

community organizations founded by survivors, such as Yitzkhak Spivak, et al. (*Orheyov be-vinyanah uve-hurbana* [Tel Aviv: Vaad yotse Orheyov, 1959]), Yitshak Korn (Yitshak Korn, ed., *Yahadut Besarabyah*, in *Entsiklopedyah shel galuyot*, vol. 11 [Jerusalem: Hevrat entsiklopedyah shel galuyot, 1971]), and Shelomoh Shitnovitzer (*Sefer kehilat hotin [Besarabyah]* [Tel Aviv: Irgun Yotse Hotin (Besarabyah) be-Yisrael, 1974]).

72. Beregovski, *Old Jewish Folk Music*, 531.

73. See Slobin, "Klezmer Music," 37.

74. Idelsohn, *Jewish Music in Its Historical Development*, 448.

75. In an earlier paper, I traced a specific modulatory pattern in the core repertoire of klezmer music to Moldavian sources of the early nineteenth century (Feldman, "Modulation"). The Romanian elements in the songs of Lebedeff or Oysher are not derived from the klezmer transitional repertoire, but more directly from Moldavian sources. For example, "Rumania, Rumania," the Lebedeff song that has become an icon of the entire Yiddish theater repertoire, begins with a section of doina employing a major scale (Slobin, "Klezmer Music," 37). However, this type of doina, while familiar from Romanian sources, is not found in any klezmer recording or transcription. Among all the performances and lessons (in the 1970s) and his earlier commercial recordings, in which Tarras had played doina, he never once used this pattern as the opening phrase—he employed it only as a reference to a performance of Lebedeff's song. A thorough analysis of the Romanian elements within the Yiddish theater repertoire can reveal many such divergences from klezmer usage.

76. Slobin, "The Music of the Yiddish Theater."

77. Goldfaden's remarks are found in Slobin, *Tenement Songs*, 187.

78. In his interviews, Tarras was proud to have accompanied such famous Yiddish theater stars as Molly Picon and Moishe Oysher, but he was resentful of the subordinate and often parodic role into which his music was cast.

79. John Blacking, "Some Problems of Theory and Method in the Study of Musical Change," *Yearbook of the International Folkmusic Council* 9 (1977): 15.

80. See M. Peña, "From Ranchero to Jaiton: Ethnicity and Class in Texas-Mexican Music (Two Styles in the Form of a Pair)," *Ethnomusicology* 29, no. 1 (1985): 29–55.

81. Mark Slobin avoids the term *revival* and sees a deep cultural continuity between the pre-1970s klezmer music and its current phase ("Klezmer Music," 38). This is a debatable point, and for the present I prefer the word *revival*.

Offshoots

One definition in the *Random House Webster's College Dictionary* tells us that offshoot once meant "anything conceived of as springing or proceeding from a main stock."

In this section of the book, we take "anything" seriously as a category, since the surprising offshoots of klezmer roots that have sprung up in recent decades vary vigorously. To give a sense of that diversity, we look at broad trends of revivalism, the evolution of an institutional base, and the work of individual bands, at the same time listening to the voices of some major activists.

CHAPTER 7

Sounds of Sensibility

BARBARA KIRSHENBLATT-GIMBLETT

Today's klezmer scene, while it affirms a degree of musical continuity with the past, is in fact the result of an experience of rupture. Reviewing The Klezmorim's first album, *East Side Wedding,* which appeared in 1977, Nat Hentoff commented, "For years now, I had thought the *klezmorim* to be nearly extinct. Oh, some old players must still be boldly wailing in some dwindling Orthodox Jewish neighborhoods, but surely they are the last of their line." When he heard them, he recalled, "I would close my eyes and grin at the ghosts of my clan in Minsk and Pinsk." Now, he continued, a new generation has "taken up and merrily revivified this heritage."[1] At the time, Hentoff heard the past. Years later, Lev Liberman, who cofounded The Klezmorim in 1975, would look back and see harbingers of the future: "I'd like to think that the current klezmer revival had its origins in our early experiments with tight ensemble playing, improvisation, klezmer/jazz fusions, neo-klezmer composition, street music, world beat, and New Vaudeville."[2]

In the hiatus between the old and the new players can be found keys to changes of sensibility that have made today's scene possible. Whatever their ostensible subject, the contributors to this book sound the sensibilities specific to the klezmer phenomenon of the last twenty-five years. They show "klezmer music" to be a powerful index of what Raymond Williams has called "changing structures of feeling." Williams distinguishes feeling ("meanings and values as they are actively lived and felt") from ideology ("formally held and systematic beliefs"), noting that they

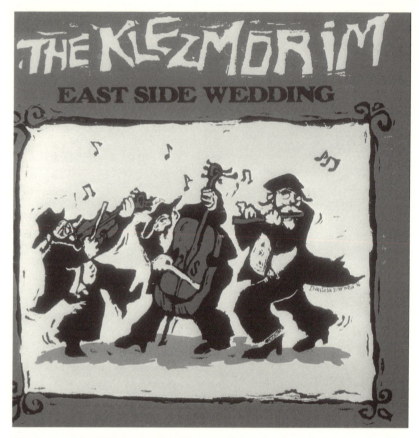

Figure 7.1   The Klezmorim's *East Side Wedding* (1977), acknowledged as the first revival album. Used with permission of Arhoolie Records.

are of course interrelated in practice. "Methodologically, then, a 'structure of feeling' is a cultural hypothesis, actually derived from attempts to understand such elements [affective elements of consciousness and relationships] and their connection in a generation or period, and needing always to be returned, interactively, to such evidence."[3] This book provides rich evidence of just such "affective elements of consciousness" and their historical location.

Here I explore the historical formation of the klezmer phenomenon in terms of changing structures of feeling. I begin by considering arguments over terminology—not only the term *klezmer,* but also the word *revival*—and how these debates situate klezmer music within a larger musical landscape. I then relate the klezmer phenomenon to what Haym

Soloveitchik has called the end of self-evident Jewishness.[4] While stringent orthodoxy is one outcome of the tension between tradition and ideology, the klezmer revival is another. There follows an analysis of the fault lines of sensibility in the period immediately preceding the klezmer revival. While the popularity of old-time Jewish wedding music declined and an incipient heritage orientation to it can be detected within the Jewish music world of the time, this music was notably absent from the folk song and music revivals of the fifties and sixties. To better understand this absence, I contrast the musical sensibilities of Theodore Bikel, an international folk singer who specialized in Yiddish, Hebrew, and Russian songs, and those of Mickey Katz, who performed English-Yiddish comedy and musical parodies for largely Jewish audiences. Seen not as a musical wasteland, but as a plenum of shifting sensibilities, the fifties and sixties hold clues to the emergence of the klezmer revival in the seventies, its efflorescence in the nineties, and its changing character in the United States and in the "Jewish space" of Europe today.[5]

THE KLEZMER PHENOMENON

What to call this scene and how to characterize the music are matters of ongoing debate. As Williams writes of keywords more generally, the term *klezmer* is tangled up with the phenomenon it is being used to discuss.[6] While *klezmer music, klezmer musicians,* and *klezmer revival* are commonly heard terms, Andy Statman recently said that the music he plays is not klezmer but Hasidic, and Giora Feidman has declared that "Klezmer is not Jewish music."[7] Some take issue with the term *revival.* Members of a young Swedish band, Vurma Klezmer Orkester, insist on two revivals, not one, and see themselves as part of the "second renaissance" of the music, the first one having occurred in the late seventies.[8] Others reject the term *revival.* Either they argue that Jewish instrumental music never "died," or they insist that what today's musicians are doing is not revival, but something utterly contemporary.

Most would agree with Frank London (chapter 10 in this volume) that *klezmer* "has gone from an underused term to being overgeneralized." In 1981, before klezmer music was an established category, the jacket for The Klezmorim's *Metropolis* carried the following instruction: "File under: Folk or Jazz."[9] Since then, klezmer music has become not only an identifiable genre, but also a highly differentiated phenomenon. It is no longer possible to speak generally of a klezmer revival, a klezmer scene, or a Jewish music scene as if there were a single entity. Klezmer or "klez" (it is not even necessary to specify "music") circulates within a vast musical landscape. Part of the success of the music in today's popular music market stems from the strategic placement of the music. As Joel Lewis notes in his review of a Klezmatics concert in 1995, they play "the Ashkenazic Jewish folk music known as klezmer" but "have a broad enough appeal to fit equally into the programs of folk, jazz and world music festivals."[10] They aren't "trapped inside a musical 'shtetl,'" according to journalist Seth Rogovoy.[11]

Not only is klezmer one of several kinds of Jewish music on a Sunday morning music show that features "Israeli/Jewish/Klezmer/Yiddish" music, but it has also become a kind of "world music."[12] The Klezmatics describe themselves as "the planet's radical Jewish roots band," Klezmos plays "world klez music," and Rubinchik's Orkestyr features "Old-World Beat" (a pun on Old World and world beat).[13] The music of Brave Old World has been described as "world-Jewish." Ben Brussell identifies the format of Klezmania! (San Francisco) as "definitive world music." In order to tell the many klezmer bands apart, musicians and critics identify ever more eclectic and specific musical alignments and orientations. The Cayuga Klezmer Revival band characterizes its style variously as "folk/roots/electric/acoustic" and "jazz, rock, swing, folk, ska, and reggae (yes, really!)," and identifies its repertoire as "a mixture of traditional Eastern-European tunes, Ladino, Israeli, and original tunes."[14] The British group Souls of Fire performs "klezmer-roots-worldbeat-dance." HaLaila calls its music "tribal Jewish funk, or depending on our mood, 'acid klez.'"

Objections to the term notwithstanding, *revival* speaks to a rupture of cultural transmission in postwar America. During the early fifties, while playing in Las Vegas, comedian and bandleader Mickey Katz was approached by a Texan who asked him to play some "Jew music": "I haven't heard me a good *frailach* since my bar mitzvah down in Waco," the Texan explained. Katz complied and "played him some Jewish jazz."[15] By the seventies, the "Texan Hebrew" would have been able to hear those "frailachs" again and then some. During the intervening years, however, many stellar performers of the music he remembers from his bar mitzvah party were no longer active or had passed away. Nor had the music been enshrined as heritage in the way that many other musics were.[16] Indeed, performers like Henry Sapoznik came to the Jewish instrumental tradition through other heritage musics, in his case Appalachian, while others started from Balkan heritage music. As Robert Cantwell has argued, "Many kinds of music that at other periods had been commercially performed and recorded, such as blues, old-time, and bluegrass music—music of chiefly southern or southeastern rural origin—came to be regarded as folk music and enjoyed a revival on that basis, to be followed in the next decade by Irish ceili, Klezmer, and other ethnic musics." [17] It was only a matter of time, in Hankus Netsky's view, before Jewish instrumental music would reemerge: "Archaic things come back. . . . The blues came back. . . . And the same thing eventually happened when our generation came of age and said, 'Wait a minute. What happened? Where's our folk music?'" [18]

Sapoznik's now legendary account of his career is a vivid case in point. While the Texan Jew would fondly remember the "Jew music" of his bar mitzvah in the thirties, Sapoznik remembers hating the music at his bar mitzvah in the sixties:

> My parents had hired one of the top New York City klezmer clarinetists to play at the reception. So there he was on the bandstand blowing some of the best *bulgars* in the business and all I wanted to do was to crawl into the nearest, deepest hole.
> "Can't this guy play anything modern?" the bar mitzvah kvetshed. At that point all my life had been spent in the presence of this music. I made no distinction between the hasidic *nigunim* we sang on the schoolbus going to Lubavitch yeshiva or the klezmer and Yiddish music ubiquitously heard at the Catskill hotels where we sang during Passover. I thought everybody had a cantor father who wandered around the house softly humming the High Holidays liturgy to himself.[19]

Sapoznik's parents had paid for klezmer, but he wanted rock 'n' roll. His sense of rupture pointed not to the music but to interest in it: "The music was patiently waiting for us to hear it again." [20] Meanwhile, Sapoznik played rock 'n' roll, made his way through the folk song revival (Woody Guthrie, Cisco Houston, Bob Dylan), and "soon found myself getting into more traditional kinds of music: Irish, New England Contradances, but mainly Appalachian string band music." In the mid-seventies, Sapoznik was visiting Tommy Jarrell, a Southern senior string musician, when Jarrell, observing that many Jews were interested in old-time music, asked Sapoznik: "Hank, don't your people got none of your own music?" Sapoznik was stunned. He headed back to New York, consulted with his grandfather, who was the same age as Jarrell, and began the search for his "own music." [21]

I use the term *heritage music* to distinguish between music that is part and parcel of a way of life and music that has been singled out for preservation, protection, enshrinement, and revival—that is, heritage music.

Heritage music, as it emerges from Hentoff's account of hearing The Klezmorim for the first time, verges on necromancy—a conjuring up of the dead. Heritage, as I have argued elsewhere, is a mode of cultural production that gives the disappearing and gone a second life as an exhibit of itself.[22] In 1978, Hentoff wrote of a new generation of musicians revivifying—literally, giving new life to—a nearly extinct musical "heritage." At the same time, he distanced himself from "heritage" when he conceded that, although Liberman was "director of music and arts at the Judah Magnes Museum in Berkeley, California, . . . he and his colleagues do not play as if they are in a museum."[23]

It is significant, however, that two pioneering klezmer figures, Liberman and Sapoznik, found support for their early efforts in the context of Jewish arts institutions—Sapoznik directed the Jewish music research project at the Martin Steinberg Center for Jewish Arts of the American Jewish Congress from 1977 to 1979, thanks to government support in the form of CETA grants. This is the period during which folk arts became recognized as a division or funding category or priority within government agencies such as the National Endowment for the Arts (1974), the New York State Council for the Arts (1980), and the American Folklife Center at the Library of Congress (1976). The Smithsonian Institution, which had established the American Folklife Festival in 1967, featured Jews at their bicentennial festival in 1976.[24] Situated in these agencies and in state arts councils, professionally trained folklorists and ethnomusicologists curated, evaluated, and otherwise guided increasingly sophisticated heritage programs in the public sector. The Klezmer Conservatory Band was incubated at the New England Conservatory of Music in Boston, where Hankus Netsky taught and eventually chaired the Jazz Studies department.

Almost twenty years later, Seth Rogovoy would praise the "downtown jazz artists who don't approach it [klezmer music] as a fossilized object of ethnomusicological interest but as a living form worthy of updating and experimentation."[25] The formulation *living form* is less an affirmation of continuity than a statement of aesthetic orientation. It suggests a musical point of departure rather than an historical destination.

The klezmer revival accommodates not only historical and aesthetic orientations, but also religious ones. Describing a concert by the David Krakauer Trio, Rogovoy wrote in 1996 that a "standing-room-only crowd jammed the pews and aisles of St. James Church on Tuesday night to worship at the altar of klezmer."[26] As a metaphor for the enthusiasm of fans, "worship at the altar of klezmer" suggests that listening to the

music is (or is like) a religious experience. Such metaphors are remind-
ers that the term *revival* has historically been associated with religious
revivals.[27] *Revivalist* carries the sense of renewed attention and new presentation (an orientation to the past), while *revitalist*—Hasidism has
been characterized as a revitalist movement—suggests new life or vigor
(a program for the future).[28] The distinction between *revivalist* and *revitalist* tends to blur, and the terms are sometimes used interchangeably
with each other, and with *renewal*. Both are often associated with youth
and countercultures, as is klezmer. While it would be going too far to
call them youth movements, Hasidism, and for that matter the Haskala,
attracted youthful followers during the early period of their formation.

Both professional and amateur bands often characterize the spirit of
their performances in terms of a religious experience—not the sedate
murmurings of polite synagogues but something more akin to ecstatic
possession or altered states of consciousness. The Klezmatics' most recent CD is titled *Possession*.[29] Appropriately enough, tracks nine through
seventeen are from the score created by the Klezmatics for Tony Kushner's adaptation of Sh. Anski's *A Dybbuk*, a play about possession by the
soul of a dead person—Kushner himself, in the liner notes, characterizes the music as "full of August Mystery."[30] Musicians and those who
write about them speak of madness, wildness, frenzy, hysteria, and passion. Call it the youthful enthusiasm of devoted aficionados. Here again
there are religious connotations: the etymology of *enthusiasm* is *inspiration*, and the primary definition of *inspiration* is "a divine influence or
manifestation that qualifies a person to receive and communicate sacred
revelation."[31]

Some bands have adopted names (and record titles) that invoke a generally spiritual or religious sensibility, or refer more specifically to Judaism or Hasidism and its musical repertoire. These include Frank London's Hasidic New Wave project, Fabrangen Fiddlers, Souls of Fire,
Thread of Blue, and Burnt Offering. Some of these bands are associated
with synagogues, others are not. In the case of Souls of Fire, a British
band, none of the members is Jewish. Giora Feidman, who debuted his
Jewish "soul music" in 1972 and his records of this music in 1973, has
used album titles such as *The Dance of Joy* and *The Magic of Klezmer*.
In claiming to distill the essence of "Jewish soul music" and to univer-
salize it, Feidman expresses a romantic mysticism reminiscent of the fin-
de-siècle orientalism of Martin Buber and his circle.[32] Since his religious
awakening, Andy Statman insists that what is now called *klezmer music*
was always religiously mandated and cites its role in the fulfillment of

the mitzvah of *simkhe* on the occasion of a wedding. This is the reason he gives for calling the music he plays today *Hasidic,* rather than *klezmer,* though one critic has characterized it as "a sort of Jewish/new-age fusion." [33]

Arguments over what to call the phenomenon and how to characterize the music were once dominated by the experience of rupture and recovery. The debates have intensified and their character has changed as the musical formation called (or not called) *klezmer* expands, diversifies, and matures.

HERITAGE, TRADITION, ORTHODOXY

To better understand the terms of these debates, the musical practices with which they are associated, and the historical processes of their unfolding, I explore three distinctions: feeling and ideology, tradition and ideology, and tradition and heritage. [34] "Tradition," the opening number of *Fiddler on the Roof,* performs the distinction between tradition and heritage simply by making such a fuss over what is otherwise taken for granted. Tradition can no longer be assumed because it is under attack. [35] When all is said and done, *Fiddler on the Roof* is a performance of heritage, not tradition, because the Broadway musical offers the disappearing and the gone a second life as an exhibition of itself. Heritage is coded at every level—diegesis (the narrative), mimesis (the representation), and the performance artifact itself.

Fiddler on the Roof is also a long way from contemporary orthodoxy, which Haym Soloveitchik distinguishes from tradition. Though he focuses on the transformation of contemporary orthodoxy, his distinction between tradition and orthodoxy is relevant to a consideration of the klezmer phenomenon. "A traditional society has been transformed into an orthodox one," when what was a matter of course (what was once absorbed and habitual) has become subject to rules, formal teaching, and scrupulous attention to textual authority. [36] The result is not "heritage," but a tendency toward stringency *(humra).* As a result, "Performance is no longer, as in a traditional society, replication of what one has seen, but implementation of what one knows." This trend started in the mid-fifties "and by the mid-Seventies was well on its way to being, if it had not already become, the dominant mode of religiosity." The result is what Soloveitchik calls "a performative spirituality, not unlike that of the arts, with all its unabating tension."

Soloveitchik uses an explicitly musical metaphor, "For spiritual life is an attempt, as a great pianist once put it, to play music that is better than it can be played."[37] Applied to klezmer music, the *humra* principle is most clearly expressed by Austrian-based Budowitz, an "ensemble of Klezmer veterans performing early Jewish repertoire and style on historical instruments."[38] Taking their cue from the early music movement, they perform music that Barrymore Laurence Scherer, music critic for the *Wall Street Journal,* described as "very pure." He compared their *tsimbl* accompaniments to "the kind of music that enthralled Bartok and Kodaly."[39]

The shift that Soloveitchik describes—"The aspiration will be . . . more to purity of ideology than of impulse"—is precisely the distinction that Raymond Williams makes between ideology and feeling.[40] Gone is the *yidishkayt* that was "something deep in the bone," a Judaism whose essence "lay not in law or ritual, but in a social vision *(yoysher)* and a moral standard of conduct *(mentshlikhkeyt)."* He attributes the end of "self-evident Jewishness" to a "rupture in the traditional religious sensibilities" once rooted in what he calls the "mimetic society."

Stringent orthodoxy is not the only response to the end of "self-evident" Jewishness, though it could be said that what counts as self-evident Jewishness has come to an end more than once. What I have been calling *heritage*—and klezmer music is in many ways a case in point—is a second outcome. Historians of European popular culture such as Peter Burke and E. P. Thompson have argued that pressures on "customary consciousness and customary usages" prompt the precipitation of "folklore" at emerging divides between high and low culture, as the upper ranks collect "folklore" from the lower ranks.[41] When the Haskala applied pressure on customary consciousness and practices, Jewish folklore emerged from the outtakes of reform.[42] What had been rejected as tradition would eventually be embraced as heritage.

An ideological relationship to tradition among *haredim,* ultra-Orthodox Jews, as well as among the new klezmers arises from a ruptured past that "gave them free rein to create a familiar past of which the present was simply an extension."[43] On the jacket of their first album, *East Side Wedding* (1977), The Klezmorim explained that "To rediscover the unashamed passion and hysteria of authentic Jewish music, you have to journey to the limits of living memory," which they identified with the period of mass immigration and "neglected manuscripts and forgotten 78 rpm recordings." On the jacket of their 1981 album, *Metropolis,* they declared, "We are The Klezmorim. We play klezmer music. It's been underground for fifty years. Now it's back."[44] Frank London has noted that The Klezmorim "never once mentioned Jews or being Jews. It was just klezmer, klezmer, klezmer," and he added in a later interview, "For years, many of the klezmer bands hid behind the word 'klezmer' as a way of avoiding the 'Jewish' word." [45] This is an astute observation.

The word *Jewish* does appear on The Klezmorim's first album, but strictly in an historical context. The "Jewishness" of their project is carried instead by the word *Yiddish* and the prominence of Yiddish terms, song titles, and lyrics. They are klezmers by affinity, rather than by descent or Jewish identification. Where bloodlines are absent—in contrast with Hankus Netsky, Judy Bressler, Henry Sapoznik, and Giora Feidman, who identify with Jewish instrumentalists and Yiddish performers in their families—affinities are invoked. Like their historical models, The Klezmorim explain, they started out playing in small bands, they improvise, they arrange their numbers communally and by ear, and they take pride in never playing a solo the same way twice.

In the absence of living models, particular importance is accorded texts (and, in the case of klezmer music, records). Defining the relationship of contemporary performance to past models as best they can be reconstructed is an ongoing concern. As London commented, "Whenever we think we are being very now, very new, we find out what we have done is actually very traditional." [46] The sense of newness in the old and oldness in the new is also conveyed in a band name like Brave Old World and characterizations like "making old-world music new." [47] Kapelye's first album was entitled *Future & Past* and carried the following dedication: "This album is dedicated to our families who have taught us that our future is our Jewish past." [48]

Anachronism is a productive principle, a musical aesthetic, which operates by unsettling temporal direction. There is no smooth continuity from yesterday's *klezmorim* to today's *klezmers*. There is no dramatic rupture, no simple sequence of life, death, and rebirth, as the term *revival* would imply. Instead, old and new are in a perpetually equivocal relationship. The future precedes the past, the new precedes the old, the revival precedes its historical models. While *klezmer revival* suggests the primacy of recovery, initially a copying of what can still be heard on old records and from elderly musicians, "It is the copying that originates," as Clifford Geertz has stated, even in the case of meticulous musical reconstructions. [49]

Klezmer musicians have felt a need to root present practice in a meaningful past, which is not the same as searching for roots, though for many the two come together. Even the term *roots music* conveys a sense of rootedness, rather than an exclusive claim to a singular origin. However much klezmer music offered clarinetist David Krakauer a "musical home," it was its fusion with jazz that gave his compositions what one reviewer characterized as a "thoroughly contemporary sensibility," no doubt because that fusion did not produce melting-pot music or a soft universalism or easy affirmation of a singular ethnic identity.[50] A sense of rootedness does not require musical monogamy.

While orthodoxy and heritage do not by any means exhaust the possible outcomes of rupture, they do force us to rethink any easy opposition between conservative and radical, tradition and innovation, custom and ideology. As Thompson notes for his period, the eighteenth and nineteenth centuries, "So far from having the steady permanence suggested by the word 'tradition,' custom was a field of change and contest, an arena in which opposing interests made conflicting claims . . . it is an arena of conflictual elements, which requires some compelling pressure —as, for example, nationalism or prevalent religious orthodoxy or class consciousness—to take form as 'system.'"[51] Not only religious orthodoxy but also the klezmer revival have taken form as system. Indeed, the klezmer revival is an example of what Neil Rosenberg, in his taxonomy of music revivals, calls a *named-system revival*—others include Balkan, old-time fiddling, blues, and bluegrass.[52] *System* in this context signals the shift from tradition to ideology.

What can be learned in this regard from the fate of eastern European Jewish instrumental music among Hasidim and haredim in America and Israel? While an earlier American generation considered even kosher versions of swing and jazz "alien to a 'Jewish rejoicing' (*yidishe simche*)," their children and grandchildren were open to rock beat and to kosher rock, that is, to rock with acceptable lyrics, a shift that Soloveitchik attributes to the embourgeoisement of American-born haredim.[53] Hoping to find klezmer music still going strong and without interruption among those who seem to hew to tradition most vigorously, Joel Rubin turned to haredim in Israel.[54] There are several reasons that he did not find what he expected, including the low status of professional musicians in haredi society and the rabbinical ban in the 1860s on instrumental music in Eretz Israel. In other words, Rubin found himself exploring music within a religious community, not a music scene. This is not to say that a religious music scene does not exist, whether here or in Israel, but only that klezmer music as such is not its focus.[55] According to Rubin, Hasidic and haredi communities in Israel are not part of the new klezmer scene, though there is some musical traffic, and Rubin himself is something of a bridge between the two worlds. Those worlds are separated by more than music.

CATALYTIC RUPTURES

A delay in the heritage process prior to the klezmer revival not only left Jewish party music to the vicissitudes of sensibility, but also spared it from the very ideological attachments, from the political and religious engagements, that gave other forms of Jewish music and musical practices a competitive advantage at the time. The music of American Jewish wedding musicians faded from view for some of the very reasons that would make it attractive to the generation that later picked it up. No movement, whether political or religious, had claimed this kind of music. Israeli music was sustained by the Zionist movement, the labor movement had its songs, mandolin orchestras, and choral groups, and both had their youth groups and summer camps. The synagogues had their cantors, choirs, and schools. In contrast, professional instrumentalists worked for a market, not a movement. Though movements also constitute a market of sorts, movements give precedence to ideological considerations.

To better understand why the lapse was catalytic, it is useful to compare the turning *to* klezmer music during the seventies, described by Frank London and Alicia Svigals (chapters 10 and 11 in this volume), with the turning *from* the "old but little-known *happy* Jewish music of the old country" that Mickey Katz was still playing in the fifties.[56] The two moments are deeply implicated in one another, both musically (Katz's material has made a kind of comeback) and in terms of structures of feeling (his stigmatized irreverence is a badge of honor for a subsequent generation). Don Byron, virtuoso clarinetist with the New England Klezmer Conservatory Band, explains that he was attracted to "the mischief in [klezmer] music" and found in Mickey Katz a master of mischief: "I tend to gravitate to whoever is playing the trickiest, outest stuff, and that's where I live," whether the music be "klezmer, jazz, big band, or improvisation."[57]

That the music was not previously picked up cleared the path for receiving it in purely aesthetic terms. This is how many musicians first became interested in it—London is emphatic on this point. So is John Zorn. A saxophonist and composer, Zorn curated the Radical New Jewish

Figure 7.2   Andy Statman and Zev Feldman's *Jewish Klezmer Music* (1979), the first "authenticity" album, marking the entry of the term *klezmer music*. Used with permission of Shanachie Entertainment.

Culture Festival at the Knitting Factory in New York City in 1993 and has issued klezmer/jazz/funk fusions on his Tzadik label. For Zorn, "All music is on equal grounds and there's no high art and low art." His compositional approach has been described as jumping "from style to style the way a television picture does when a deranged channel surfer has the remote control." [58] The "roots" of this radicalism are more likely to lie in avant-garde aesthetics and Jewish political activism than in religious orthodoxy or folkloric heritage, though there are exceptions like Andy Statman.

It could be said that Statman is reconfiguring the relationships between tradition, heritage, and orthodoxy in his live connection to Hasidic *nigunim*, spiritual take on jazz, and religious orientation to performance. Statman's recent CD, *Between Heaven & Earth: Music of the Jewish Mystics*, reclaims "klezmer as sacred music" and produces "a sort of Jewish/new-age fusion," according to Rogovoy.[59] As I noted earlier, Statman insists that this music was always religiously mandated and insists that it is Hasidic, not klezmer, music. Though he calls his band The Andy Statman Klezmer Orchestra, Statman has said, "I don't like to use the word 'klezmer.' It becomes very limiting," a statement that hints at shifts in aesthetic and not only religious sensibility.[60]

The very name of his ensemble aligns it with such early bands as the Abe Schwartz Orchestra, Harry Kandel's Orchestra, and Art Shryer's Modern Jewish Orchestra, rather than with the revival bands. Revivalists are more likely to invoke other musics (Yid Vicious, The Freilachmakers Old-Time String Band, Mazeltones, Jumpin' Jazzy Jewish Music). Revivalists tend to display a playful, even nostalgic, relationship to the tradition (Di Ganeyvim, Shir Fun, Kudzu Klezmer, Take the Oy Train). They are likely to identify with the immigrant history of the music and musicians (Greena Kozinas, Hester Street Troupe, and Ellis Island). And, most of all, they proudly identify themselves and their music as *klezmer,* a term that earlier generations of musicians considered an insult.

Whatever its status might have been when it was a functioning part of eastern European Jewish life, as outsider music (The Klezmorim called it "underground music"), the instrumental tradition was vulnerable to a rupture in transmission. That rupture has given shape and direction to the new klezmer music and its various sensibilities and ideologies. That the music was once stigmatized is an asset for a generation committed to new forms of radicalism like the Queer Yiddishist movement identified by Svigals (chapter 11 in this volume). For prominent Jewish klezmer performers like the Klezmatics and their Jewish audiences, klezmer music gives voice to what they call the Radical Jewish Culture movement.

Klezmer music has become the sound of particular forms of identification, as can be seen in the "Manifesto" which Svigals presents in chapter 11 of this volume. Whether defined positively (queer Yiddishism, socialist Jewish past, serious approach to the music) or negatively (no nostalgia, no "tourism of the past," no cuteness, no apologetics, no fetishizing of authenticity), "the identity music of Jewish American youth" envisioned by Svigals articulates distinctive sensibilities and their sounds. While the scene (actually several interlocking scenes) has many of the features associated with youth subcultures, as Svigals shows, it is also intergenerational, a feature that London specially values.

London, who now "draws pride in the secular, social activist Yiddish song tradition," did not start out that way. Quite the opposite. Klezmer music initially captured his interest because it is "good, just on its own terms." It is one of many kinds of music he plays. When he says of his first experience with the music that it "really started in the middle of nowhere," he is describing what it is like to engage with music that is literally separated from its source.[61] Recordings make it possible to circulate the sounds of music without circulating the musicians. This disjunction not only heightens the experience of "nowhere" that London describes, but also his sense that "one can study and assimilate the elements of *any* musical style, form, or tradition by ear," a legacy of the historical avant-garde.[62] Not only had the music been detached from its historical moorings, but his generation could come toward it with a detached attitude, an attitude they had willed and cultivated. "Nowhere" is a space of abstraction where sounds unmoored from other times and places can be engaged as sound for its own sake. In that place called *nowhere,* musicians can play anything. They do so in the "theme concerts" London describes. Jewish was a theme and klezmer music was a scene. Several contributors to this volume speak to the theme and the scene from the inside, as musicians who have been part of it, each in their own way, for almost two decades. It is telling that they speak in the spatial terms of *nowhere* (and *scene*), not in the temporal terms of *revival* and *heritage.* David Krakauer also uses a spatial metaphor when he says of klezmer music that "I felt in a certain way that I had found a kind of musical home," though it is not the only place he lives.[63]

The aesthetic practice of detachment, in the dual sense suggested here, is intensified by the situation of music without memory—or, in some cases, in spite of memory. If anything, being Jewish was actually an obstacle, because London's experience of growing up with Jewish music had left him feeling that it was corny. As a result, it was not roots and heritage, but technical challenge, fun, and the market that drove his initial interest in klezmer music, much as it did his captivation with jazz.

If London could play any kind of music, then anyone could play Jewish music—and they did, though doing so was not so straightforward. As Don Byron explained, "I've played klezmer music since 1980. But it hasn't been easy to feel *entitled* to play it. A white man plays world music, and no one questions the ethnic connection. But not too many brothers are playing music from Bulgaria. I spent hundreds of hours transcribing Katz's records: I feel entitled to the knowledge, entitled to participate. But what amazes people is that I'm a black guy doing the music of people who are supposed to be white."[64]

While he attributes the secret of the Klezmatics' success to their being "a great rock band—that is, they swing hard and get people emotionally," Michael Dorf, who owns the Knitting Factory, adds that "there is something in their music that reaches the Jewish part of me."[65] This statement marks the distance traveled from the sixties, when Milton Gordon in his study of assimilation in American life could still warn his readers that "the individual who engages in frequent and sustained primary contacts across ethnic group lines, particularly racial and religious, runs the risk of becoming what, in sociological parlance, has been called the 'marginal man.'"[66] Gordon's marginal man, derived from Chicago sociologists Robert Park and Everett Stonequist, who were working in the twenties and thirties, was a "social deviant" on the verge of a nervous breakdown. Nothing could be further from the sensibilities informing the klezmer music scene.

The Jewish part of Dorf is clearly not all of him. The other part, to which he attributes the Klezmatics' success, has helped the music travel far beyond the wedding circuit to which Jewish instrumental music had become confined. During the first half of this century, the music could be heard not only at simkhes, but also at banquets and social and political functions of various kinds, Jewish cafés, and restaurants.[67] By the fifties, it was most likely to be heard at weddings and in the English-Yiddish comedy shows by performers like Mickey Katz.

MULTIPLE TEMPORALITIES

Emphasizing a continuity they have worked hard to achieve in the wake of genocide and cultural obsolescence, pioneers of the klezmer revival repeatedly delineate the chronology of the music they have recuperated, a process that plays memory against history and autobiography against musical reconstruction. While the scene has a relatively short history, less than three decades, telling that history is integral to it. The founding figures not only tunneled to the past through archives, but also sought out living bridges to the music as it was once played. They apprenticed themselves to the last exponents of the tradition. Their acts of recuperation, preservation, documentation, and renewal affirmed Isaac Bashevis Singer's apothegm, "There's a big difference between 'dead' and 'dying,'" the "favorite quotation" of the Boston radio program, The Yiddish Voice (WUNR, Brookline, Massachusetts).[68]

The founders of the scene have a keen sense of the peculiar temporality of the revival. Unlike subsequent generations, which have grown up with neo-klezmer music, the founding cohort lived through the rupture and the recovery, an experience that heightened their historical awareness. Short and fast, the history of the scene is remembered in detail by those directly involved in it. Long and slow, the history of the music that inspires it has left spotty evidence. Those who have made the scene have also had to excavate the music. Their sense of one is infused with their sense of the other. While a history of klezmer music like the one provided by Hankus Netsky in this volume is narrated forward, from the "beginning" to the present, it is understood backward, from now to then. Younger musicians are forming their own sense of the music's temporality, as can be seen from the claim by Vurma, which models itself on "the pioneer group Klezmorim," that they are part of the second renaissance of klezmer. In an interview about ten years ago, about the time The Klezmorim disbanded, Kevin Linscott of The Klezmorim discouraged new groups from using his band's music as a model and encouraged them to go back to historical recordings.[69]

"Klezmer music," as it emerges from what is said and written and from the musical practices themselves, is what Williams calls an "initial shaping concept."[70] It bears, as he puts it, the marks of its formation and its unresolved problems, both of which tend to be taken for granted. Memory of the revival and history of the music are not the same thing, though they tend to converge in accounts that reflect the experience of first-generation klezmer revivalists and those who write about them. The founding narrative is stated in the starkest terms by Rogovoy, for whom klezmer is a phoenix rising from its own ashes. The music is marked by "its refusal to die" in the face of two assaults—the Holocaust and assimilation. The revival is the story of what happened to "old-world klezmer," whose "sonorities . . . evoked the simple joys and sorrows of shtetl life," in the hands of postmodern musicians. At the same time, he documents the nuanced sense of klezmer history expressed by Svigals, whom he quotes as saying, "Klezmer isn't the music of an extinct culture. . . . As contemporary living culture—as opposed to something extinct which has been curiously and artificially revived—klezmer is different than it was twenty years ago, and still more different than it was forty, sixty, a hundred years ago."[71] Rather than a bifurcated temporality—before and after the revival—a sense of differentiated historical layers is beginning to emerge.

As professional musicians become professional scholars, their historical vistas expand.[72] Rubin looks beyond the United States to Israel. James Loeffler (chapter 3 in this volume) looks beyond the "golden age" of the interwar recordings to the early period of mass immigration, during which the first Jewish musicians' union in the United States was established (1889). He opens a window on the working conditions and performance culture of professional Jewish musicians during this era and considers their mobility. As the musicians discussed by Loeffler entered the larger marketplace of music, Jewish music became even more of a niche market and some musicians, in their rising success, left this music (and the Jewish musicians' union) behind.

It is during the period of mass immigration that the Yiddish theater came into its own, musicians began making recordings, and Yiddish folk songs attracted increasing interest from scholars, artists, and publishers. Because these developments took place in the United States as well as in Europe, they did not precede immigration, but were coincident with it. It has been argued that the Yiddish theater and the instrumental music tradition as we know it from early commercial recordings flowered in the United States as performers and repertoire flowed across the Atlantic in both directions.[73] Moreover, during the period Loeffler considers, musicians played not only for simkhes but also on a wide variety of political, ceremonial, and social occasions. His account offers an important corrective to the current image of old-time klezmer music as strictly party music.[74]

Loeffler's evidence suggests that specialization was a response to a shrinking market. As they were no longer in demand for so wide a range of events, those musicians who continued playing for Jewish audiences came to depend more heavily on simkhes for their living.[75] They could do so because Jewish life-cycle celebrations—primarily the wedding, but also the bar mitzvah—had become much more elaborate. Those who still remember hearing the music before the revival associate it almost exclusively with simkhes. Many of today's klezmers and those who write about them project this image of the music back to the Middle Ages. Rogovoy, for example, states that "Strictly defined, klezmer is the Jewish instrumental music that was played by professional musicians in eastern Europe for occasions such as weddings and bar mitzvahs—a tradition that dates back at least as far as the Middle Ages."[76] As for weddings, the musical requirements were far more extensive than dance music, and still are in Hasidic communities today. During the nineteenth century (and earlier), wedding festivities could extend over a three-week period and require musicians and a varied repertoire for a series of events. As for bar mitzvahs, in eastern Europe they were generally low-key events, not the extravagant affairs they have become here.[77]

Complementing Loeffler's consideration of the working conditions of Jewish instrumentalists in the United States, Robert Rothstein (chapter 2 in this volume) attends to the occupational subculture of professional Jewish instrumentalists in eastern Europe as revealed through their argot. He presents *klezmer-loshn* from Sholem Aleichem's novel *Stempenyu;* in Joachim Neugroschel's 1979 English translation, the klezmorim sound like a couple of jazz hipsters rapping about chicks. The translator has substituted one musical argot (jazz) for another (klezmer), with the assumption that his readers in 1979 would recognize the lingo. Would the translation need to be updated for subsequent generations by substituting rap for jazz? If yes, something would be lost, for American exponents of the klezmer tradition played jazz. Many also referred to their *bulgars, doinas,* and *freylekhs* as Jewish jazz and many played both Jewish dance music and jazz on the same program.

Neugroschel's translation thus captures a musical convergence subsequent to the period represented in the novel, but meaningful to the later history of the music and to later readers. Many musicians have come to neo-klezmer music with formal training in classical music and jazz, and use what they know to create such new musical fusions as freestyle klezmer. Objections to the term *Jewish jazz* notwithstanding (Sapoznik quips that if klezmer is Jewish jazz, then jazz must be goyish klezmer), the relationship between the two musics suggests a history of reversals as much as revivals, with musicians moving from klezmer to jazz and back, while keeping both in play and creating new fusions.[78]

Future translations of *Stempenyu* may have to reckon with a new klezmer-loshn, the argot of the revival. Variations on the word *klezmer* (klez, neo-klezmer, klezmology, and klezmeroid) pepper discussions of the music. Band names play with even more possibilities: Klezmania!, Klezmatics, Klezical, Klezmechaye!, Klezmos, Klezmotones, Kleztet, Klezmeydlekh. KlezKamp is the affectionate name of the Yiddish Folk Arts Institute established by Henry Sapoznik in 1985 and Klezkanada the name of a similar venture in Quebec, established in 1996. The cyberhome of klezmer information is Ari Davidow's Klezmer Shack. This terminology has no parallel in Yiddish, as evidenced by entry 285 *(muziker)* in the monumental *Thesaurus of the Yiddish Language* and the 1913 "'Klesmer'sprache'" lexicons of S. Weissenberg and A. Landau.[79]

There is no klezmer-loshn in *Di vunderlikhe geshikhte fun r' shmelkele der klezmer* (The wonderful story of Reb Shmelkele the klezmer), a little chapbook published in Warsaw in 1910, about *eyn yidisher klezmer* (a Jewish musician) named Reb Shmelkele in the Prague ghetto in 1820. Shmelkele, a famous artist on the fiddle and paragon of piety, played so well that *"men hot gekent antshlofn vern fin ziskayt"* (one could fall asleep from sweetness). He was invited to play for the Chris-

tian nobility, who treated him with great honor and even sent their car-
riages for him. At night, in the privacy of his home, he would play "Al
Naharot Bavel" ("By the Waters of Babylon") with such *moralishkayt*
that he could rouse feeling in a stone. He was also handsome and hum-
ble. Not surprisingly, the tone of the chapbook is pious, not sardonic.[80]

Note that the anonymous author specified a "Jewish" klezmer, or
musician, but at no point did he refer to "klezmer" music. In Yiddish,
where *klezmer* means *musician,* the formulation *klezmer music* would
mean *musician music.* Nor does he play with ethnographic detail—
there is no musician's argot—though he does endow Reb Shmelkele's
performance with extraordinary, even divinely inspired, power. We do
not find Reb Shmelkele playing at Jewish weddings, but at elegant balls
and aristocratic mansions, the king's court and robber's den. These locales belong more to the world of the wonder tale than to the daily reality of Jewish instrumentalists, though klezmorim did perform for the
nobility. While this story cannot be taken as a baseline for the history of
klezmer music, it does reveal an historically specific musical sensibility
that values emotive effect.[81] This sensibility is allied with the sentimen-
tality of melodrama, a popular genre of Yiddish theater in the period
and even today in the Purim plays produced by Hasidic communities in
New York.[82]

The term, the category, the specific music, and the sensibility that we
associate with the words *klezmer music* are not only contemporary, but
new. Jewish instrumentalists before the revival characterized their music
in a variety of ways, but *klezmer music* was not one of them, a point that
Statman underscores when he says his band plays Hasidic, not klezmer,
music. However, Statman had to pass through the klezmer revival to get
to Hasidic music, and once he got there he has been moving in new directions that are difficult to name.

INCIPIENT HERITAGE

Albums produced in the fifties, sixties, and early seventies not only feature the performances of active wedding musicians, but also reveal an
incipient heritage orientation to the instrumental tradition. *Wedding
Dances,* featuring clarinetist Marty Levitt and his orchestra, promises
listeners "authentic Wedding Dances" and assures them that the music on this album will be as good "as when he performs in person at a
traditional wedding"—hopefully listeners would hire him and his orchestra for their simkhes.[83] Rudy Tepel's 1962 album, *Chassidic Wed-*

ding: Rudy Tepel and His Orchestra Play Dance Melodies of Vizh-nitz, Lubavich, Modzitz, Satmar, Skulen, Mea Shearim, also features the performances of an active musician.[84] Tepel claimed a repertoire of over six hundred Hasidic melodies and estimated that he had played close to five thousand weddings in a twenty-year period. He is still active today.

The liner notes, however, also suggest an emerging preservationist sensibility. They were prepared not by Tepel, but by the producers of the album, the husband and wife team B.-H. Stambler, who "have been active for the past fifteen years [i.e., since 1947] in gathering, preserving and creating Jewish music. They have pioneered in recording Hasidic and Sephardic music, and in the restoration of historic cantorial discs."[85] Accordingly, the notes tell the listener little about the musical numbers or the Hasidic dynasties and rebbes with whom they are identified, but a lot about each stage of the wedding festivities, information that insiders to the tradition would not need. Records targeted to Hasidic communities are more likely to focus on the history of a dynasty, its rebbe, and his melodies, and to carry the admonition "Please do not play this record on the Sabbath or holidays."[86]

The note for "Shpilt, Klezmorim!," the first number on Tepel's album, uses the opportunity to offer a little disquisition on klezmorim. After describing the sorry state of part-time amateurs in the old country, the note continues, "Life in the United States has made a tremendous change: today's klezmer is a successful, well-trained musician who devotes his full time to weddings; these in turn have become elaborately catered affairs." Rudy Tepel and his orchestra are characterized, not as klezmorim, but as "one of today's best-known wedding bands."[87] Consistent with this characterization, Tepel's biographical note refers to him as a *musician,* not a *klezmer.* Tepel expresses ambivalence in his careful distinction between the Old World amateurs (klezmers) he disavows and the American professionals (musicians) with whom he identifies, the noble heritage intentions of the Stamblers notwithstanding.

The liner notes for *Rejoice: Torah in Song / Wedding in the Old Country,* a collaboration of Israeli, American, and Canadian artists, most of them classically trained, describe Dave Tarras as "the greatest clarinet virtuoso of Jewish folk music."[88] This designation already suggests a shift of consciousness—neither Levitt nor Tepel described what they played as folk music, though Levitt did promise the "authentic" wedding dances that he plays at "traditional" weddings.[89] Tarras himself signaled the shift, as Mark Slobin has noted, when he titled one of his doinas "Wedding on Second Avenue," a reference to the Yiddish theater, which often included wedding scenes.[90] The wedding and its music were literally staged for the album.

A heritage orientation is even more explicit on Adele Margolin's album *Pages of History,* which featured "Living Torah" on one side and "A Wedding in the Old Tradition" on the other. Margolin, a mezzo-soprano and product of the Yiddish Folk Schools and Jewish Teachers Seminary, hosted a Jewish music program on radio stations WLIB and WEVD. The arrangements on *Pages of History,* played by the Hebrew Folk Ensemble, were intended to make the music "sound like the 'Kappelia' (miniature orchestra) which was the major part of the entertainment at these small town weddings. His [Amitai Ne'eman, arranger/ conductor] successful handling of the subject met with the approval of Folklorists who have been fortunate to hear a true Kappelia in the old country."[91] We see here the hallmarks of "heritage music." The music is not only performed but also exhibited, glossed, translated, and authenticated by "folklorists."

These recordings circulated in Jewish circles. So did reissues of great cantorial performances and artistic reworkings of Yiddish folk songs by cantors, luminaries of the Yiddish stage, and concert artists such as Jan Peerce, Herschel Bernardi, Sidor Belarsky and Masha Benya, Seymour Rechzeit and Miriam Kressyn. Their approach grows out of earlier efforts in Europe, Palestine, and the United States to create art music based on Jewish sources.[92] Lazar Weiner was a living link to the eastern European concertizing tradition. Born in Kiev in 1897, Weiner went to New York when he was seventeen. His settings of Yiddish folk songs, whether he arranged them for chorus or accompanied them on piano, "elevated" these songs to the level of classical music.[93] His approach was consistent with the efforts of Jewish composers in Saint Petersburg at the turn of the century to use Yiddish folk song as the basis for creating a Jewish national music.[94]

SIMPLE NOISE

Sensitivity to musical hierarchy also informs the instrumental tradition, not only historically, as Loeffler shows in his discussion of the stigma associated with the term *klezmer* (chapter 3 in this volume), but also within certain sectors of the klezmer revival today. According to the liner notes for his 1977 album, Giora Feidman "took an ancient art of the klezmer, an unschooled, Eastern European Jewish musician, from the folklore plateau of amateurism and elevated it to artistic heights, amazingly sophisticated, profound in style and virtuosic eclat." [95] This is a long way from the avant-gardism of a John Zorn, who considers all music equal—"there's no high art and low art." It's also a long way, for that matter, from the ethos of the folk song revival, which turned the hierarchy upside-down, but did not get rid of it.

Inclusive as the folk song revival was, it could not find a place for the Jewish instrumental tradition. Why not? Clues may be found in debates over the definition of *folk song*, the aesthetic of simple noise, and the celebration of amateurism. Above all, for the revivalists, folk song did not require elevation. On the contrary, unadorned performance was a statement in its own right, a critique of the exclusive culture of classical music. There was still a musical hierarchy, but in reverse. "Low" music was good just as it was, and maybe even better than "high" music.

Reacting to the idea that folk song needed to be dressed up for the concert stage, performers such as Theodore Bikel brought an unvarnished voice, self-taught guitar, international repertoire, and entertaining spiel to their performance of folk song. Musical virtuosity was not the point. Of his own abilities as a folk singer, Oscar Brand wrote in a playfully self-effacing tone, "I even learned to play the guitar in order to cover my vocal deficiencies." [96] A Canadian Jew who moved to the United States, Brand began performing professionally after leaving the United States Army in 1945. He can still be heard today on WNYC 820/AM (Saturday, 7:30 P.M. EST), where he hosts "Folksong Festival with Oscar Brand."

In his 1962 account of the "tidal wave of folk singing," Brand defines the folk song in terms of sound, what he calls "simple noise," not provenance.[97] Though oral transmission will gradually wear away "the unreal, the phony, and the unnecessary," the patina of an antique musical form can be fabricated instantly by those who know how to achieve an "artless, unself-conscious quality" and "special ring of truth" in their compositions and performances. The locus classicus of "simple noise" is the Anglo-American ballad. Brand is explicit on this point: "I can usually recognize this simplicity when I meet it in American and Canadian song, but I find myself less sure when I encounter the folk music of foreign lands. I can humbly confess that most Chinese songs sound alike to me. And the difference between a Kirghiz art song and a Kirghiz folk song is beyond my comprehension." [98] A few generations later, musicians such as Walter Feldman would be able not only to tell the difference, but also to perform the music.

With its emphasis on storytelling, rather than virtuosic musicianship, the ballad was considered a song anyone could sing. The ethos of participation was so strong that Professor Robert J. Potter, whom Brand quotes, insisted that folk music "by its very nature doesn't make perfectionist demands with respect to performance, but is in some ways even 'better' if it is not perfect—imperfection makes it more folksy." It requires "no more than average ability" or even "*less* than average ability." Behind this overstatement of the inclusiveness of the folk song revival is a critique of musical exclusivity: "Our nation is peopled with unfortunates who were tagged as 'listeners' by harried kindergarten teachers, and, consequently, fear the sound of their own voices raised in song."[99] Judging from the surge of guitar sales, the enormous audiences at the Newport Festivals, and the popularity of singing along, many people did ride the wave of folk song interest.

Brand was not alone in defining folk song by effect, an approach that separated the purists from the popularizers. It was not long, however, before effect was confounded with affectation and both were subjected to parody and criticism.[100] The purists objected to an approach that was essentially theatrical, however much it affected the effect of simple noise. Not surprisingly, several singers, among them Theodore Bikel, were also professional actors. To some extent Bikel approached his international repertoire the way a character actor approaches a role. While audiences were responsive, Bikel has complained in his autobiography, *Theo,* that key figures in the movement, such as Alan Lomax, took him to task: "Alan never seemed comfortable with me as a folk performer, grudgingly accepting my Hebrew, Yiddish, or Russian songs, but little else among the twenty-one languages in which I perform, especially any Anglo-Saxon material."[101] Reflecting on the time when Lomax prevented him from performing at a ceremony in Washington, D.C., honoring recipients of the National Heritage Awards in the Folk and Traditional Arts, Bikel commented, "One more example of the folk purist fearing contamination from 'show biz.'"[102]

The international repertoire and musical sensibility of a Theodore Bikel was more like continental cuisine than local cooking, and it was down-home food prepared by native cooks that the purists were after. Bikel's performances were highly mediated by a set of aesthetic practices specific to the revival itself. But so too were the performances of an Almeda Riddle or Huddie Ledbetter, however different those practices might be.

FAULT LINES OF SENSIBILITY

The decades immediately preceding the klezmer revival are generally viewed as a wasteland for the music. Traditional Jewish instrumental music fell out of favor, and the folk song and music revivals of the period showed no interest in it. Viewed as a lull in musical interest, little remains to be said. Viewed as a plenum of sensibility, the period holds clues to the klezmer revival that followed. To track the careers of Theodore Bikel, a rising professional folk singer, and Mickey Katz, a veteran instrumentalist/comedian, is to trace the fault lines of changing structures of feeling.

In his recent autobiography, Bikel chronicles his rise as a folk singer and dramatic artist. Born in Vienna, Bikel left for Palestine with his family in 1938, when he was fourteen years old. His parents, ardent Zionists, were from Czernowitz, a city in the eastern part of the Austrian-Hungarian empire before World War I and in Romania after the war. Bikel was born on Theodore Herzl's birthday and was named after him. Active in a Zionist youth movement, he learned Hebrew songs from Zionist propaganda films in Vienna and added to his repertoire in Palestine, where he completed school, lived on a kibbutz, and acted in the Hebrew Theater. In 1946, he moved to London, where he studied at the Royal Academy of Dramatic Art and pursued a career in the theater.[103] Both in London and in Paris, which he visited frequently, he sought out folk music and musicians in cafés and bars, particularly Russian expatriates who played Gypsy music. He also encouraged friends and acquaintances, including key figures in the British and American folk song revivals, to perform at parties in his home. Before long, he was singing folk songs in public. Within days of arriving in New York in 1954 to perform in the Broadway play *Tonight in Samarkand*, he attended a Pete Seeger concert at Columbia University and introduced himself to Seeger —the Weavers were still blacklisted at this time, and their recordings and performances were few and far between.

Bikel quickly became a part of the revival scene. While Jewish repertoire may not have been central to the folk song revival, Jews certainly were. They owned and managed clubs and record companies. They were composers, performers, agents, and managers. They were writers and critics. Moses Asch, son of Yiddish writer Sholem Asch, established Folkways, a preeminent recording company that specialized in traditional music. Jac Holzman and Leonard Ripley ran Elektra, another primary source of both traditional and contemporary folk recordings. Kenneth S. Goldstein issued innumerable recordings of songs from the field. Israel Young ran the Folklore Center on MacDougal Street. Aliza Greenblatt, the mother of Woody Guthrie's former wife Marjorie, was a published Yiddish poet; she wrote *Der fisher,* which has become a favorite in the Yiddish song repertoire.[104] Jean Richie's husband, George Pickow, a Jew from New York, made her an improved mountain dulcimer. The list goes on.

Bikel recorded nineteen albums for Elektra, the first of which, *Folksongs of Israel,* appeared in 1955. As already noted, he sang in twenty-one languages (he did not speak all of them) and was a gifted impersonator. As he says of himself, "I was a character actor and considered my craft to demand chameleon techniques." He brought a similar approach to his international repertoire of songs and manner of presentation, explaining that he could "assume authentic accents" but was sometimes faulted for his "willingness to make a song accessible and palatable to an audience unfamiliar with the material, instead of keeping the aloof stance of a purist."

The staged images on his album covers are consistent with his theatrical approach to folk song performance. In his autobiography, Bikel explained that *"Folksongs of Israel* showed an Israeli pioneer girl walking through fields of the Jordan Valley. She was actually a New York model, and the fields were on Long Island." Describing the cover of his first album of Yiddish songs, he recalls that it "shows me leaning on a guitar in front of a Lower East Side brick wall with a theater poster on it, listing the songs in Yiddish, and speaking to a young yeshiva boy. The boy looked right, but was hardly likely ever to see the inside of a yeshiva; when I called him over to offer him a few dollars to pose with me saying, 'Come here, *yingele* [kid],' he asked, '*¿Qué quiere?*' (What do you want?) in pure Puerto Rican." [105] Just before the photograph was taken, Bikel added a little graffiti to complete the scene: "I took a crayon and wrote a word on the wall next to the Jewish poster. The word consisted of three Hebrew letters: pe, aleph, kof. Pronounced, that comes out 'fuck'. It was an in-joke that very few people caught." However irreverent the in-joke, neither the image nor the music were in-your-face, in contrast with the sensibility of some neo-klezmers.

Bikel performed concerts at Town Hall, was featured at Newport Festivals, and collaborated with leading revivalists such as Pete Seeger and Oscar Brand. Classically trained soprano Martha Schlamme presented similar material in the same locations. During the fifties, they not only included Jewish songs on records with titles like *Folk Songs from Just about Everywhere* (Bikel) and *Songs of Many Lands* (Schlamme), but also issued records devoted exclusively to what they called "Jewish folk songs." (When klezmer bands list the wide range of what they play—the Mike Eisenstadt Band declares "Our speciality is anything!"—they mean musical and performance style and not just repertoire.)[106]

Like Bikel, Schlamme spent her early years in Vienna, but unlike him, she took a classical approach. She favored orchestral accompaniment or flute and piano for her Yiddish, Hebrew, and international songs. Shortly before her death, she performed Yiddish songs with David Krakauer. Though Bikel generally accompanied himself on guitar, he occasionally performed with orchestras and bands—Bill Lee, the father of film maker Spike Lee, accompanied him on bass and traveled with him on a concert tour through the South during the sixties. If Bikel popularized a folk sound and Schlamme concertized, Ruth Rubin was the purist. Given that Yiddish folk song is a largely a cappella tradition, what were singers headed for the stage to do? All three of them located the Jewishness of their material in song, and specifically in melodies and words. Only Rubin was to focus exclusively on Yiddish folk songs, which she collected from oral tradition. Only she consistently performed these songs without accompaniment. She recorded Yiddish folk songs, both her field recordings and her own performances, for Folkways. She also presented her extensive research in songbooks, published as early as 1950, and in *Voices of a People: The Story of Yiddish Folk Song*, which first appeared in 1963.

Not surprisingly, Rubin was the most attentive of these three singers to the traditional vocal styles of those from whom she collected the songs. Schlamme was the professionally trained singer, while Bikel's style owed more to the Parisian café and Greenwich Village coffee house, where he learned much of his repertoire. He was more inclined than Rubin to learn songs from other professional singers and to use instrumental accompaniment. In this way, revivalists integrated the songs into an international repertoire suitable for concert stage and hootenanny alike. A constitutive feature of this approach was precisely the recognition that the song (words and tunes) did not emanate from the same source as the performance (vocal style, setting, arrangement, accompaniment). The result was not the eclectic fusions we see in the klezmer revival or the incongruous juxtapositions of parodies of the period, but *the sounds of the revival itself.*

The singers of Jewish repertoire that we remember from this period were solo vocalists, with or without accompaniment, not ensembles. Despite the popularity of these performers, Yiddish folk song remained one of the most vulnerable genres in the Jewish musical repertoire. It had already begun the process of becoming "heritage" during the late nineteenth century, if not earlier, with efforts to collect, record, and arrange it for artistic performance. Needless to say, few klezmer performers today grew up speaking Yiddish, the sine qua non of the a cappella Yiddish folk song tradition. While training in classical music and jazz, and experience playing Balkan and Appalachian traditional music, may have prepared them for the instrumental requirements of klezmer music, those who choose to sing must also master enough Yiddish for the task. Interestingly, more than one klezmer revival musician has characterized the musical instrument, particularly the clarinet, as a human voice, and the music itself as a language. David Krakauer has said, "I realized that klezmer music was the Yiddish language in music," and he hears in it "the sound and inflection of my grandmother's very heavily Yiddish-tinged English." [107] For Alicia Svigals, klezmer is "a musical abstraction of the Yiddish language, and it simply sounds 'Jewish' to our ears." [108]

PERFORMING OBSOLESCENCE

As Benjamin A. Botkin has noted, "Every revival contains within itself the seed not only of its own destruction (in our mass entertainment the destruction proceeds from repetition and dullness as much as from catering to the lowest common denominator) but also of the new revivals." [109] An indication that a revival (or other kind of musical movement) has run its course is parody. The Jewish music identified with Bikel became a prime target. The comedy album *Allan Sherman's Mother Presents My Son, the Folk Singer* (1962) was so funny and insightful, according to journalist Richard Gehman, that it was sure to "send Theo Bikel into another line of work." [110] A year earlier, Bob Dylan had launched an attack on the kind of music identified with Bikel when he performed "Talkin' Hava Negeilah Blues," which one critic characterized as mocking "the quintessential American Jewish tune"—it is the one Jewish tune that David Krakauer can remember hearing when he was growing up. Dylan's version was "an epitaph for the Hebrew folk songs sung by folk singers like Theodore Bikel and the Weavers as a vaguely leftist, working-man's ethnic repertoire. The mockery was prescient: the left would not be strumming love songs about Israeli soldiers much longer. Dylan, with his inspired instinct for the authentic, was first to smell the phonies."[111] So could Al Capp, "who introduced a new character into his widely syndicated comic strip 'Li'l Abner' named 'Joanie Phonie,'" based on Joan Baez.[112]

Some of the first neo-klezmers shared this sensibility. NAMA Orchestra, based in Los Angeles, explained on their 1978 album, *Mazltov!*, that what made their music special and rare was precisely its departure from "existing records of Yiddish songs [that] tend to feature either operatically trained vocalists accompanied by symphony orchestras, or folk singers with a guitar."[113] Unlike them, NAMA's Pearl Rottenberg "sings in a strong natural voice, accompanied by a small folk orchestra, such as might have been found in the villages of Eastern Europe." The term *klezmer* does not appear. The Jewish numbers are part of the band's repertoire of largely Balkan folk music.

While Allan Sherman and Bob Dylan were quick to parody the Jewish music they identified with Bikel, it could be said that Bikel and Schlamme marked out a place for Jewish music within an international folk music scene, a place that would later be filled by klezmer music. So, too, did the parodies. Parody is an integral part of the heritage complex, a "museum" in its own right. The Jewish parodists, not the revivalists, were the ones in the fifties and sixties to compose new material and set Jewish/Yiddish lyrics to popular tunes. At the same time, the parodists recognized that they were working with "heritage music." The cover for *Mickey Katz Plays Music for Weddings, Bar Mitzvahs and Brisses* shows Katz "sitting in a baby carriage, presumably after my own *bris*, smoking a cigar."[114] However, this was not a comedy album, but strictly a recording of instrumental numbers. Recalling the late forties and fifties, when he cut the English-Yiddish comedy records for which he is so vividly remembered, Katz said of this album, his second for Capitol, "Every note of the album breathes the flavor of the old but little-known *happy* Jewish music of the old country, yet all the tunes are original."[115] Parody also anticipates the irreverence and eclecticism that would become hallmarks of the klezmer revival.

The mapping of sensibility in this period—serious music was respectful, irreverent music was comic—was upturned as some of the new klezmers took irreverence seriously. They produced not the Shtetl Lite of *Fiddler on the Roof,* but what has been called Heavy Shtetl or "the new, in-your-face Jewish music."[116] They and their fans relished the mischief of Don Byron's performances of Mickey Katz's music and the *Klezmer*

Madness of David Krakauer. The promotional copy on The Klezmorim's *Metropolis* album describes their models as musicians who "played like demons," stirred "dancers to a frenzy," and exhibited a style "full of unorthodox tonalities and crazily interlocking rhythms—the rollicking, vodka-soaked sound of a steam calliope gone mad." Three groups have named themselves Klezmania! (San Francisco; Boston; and Melbourne, Australia) and a New England high school band calls itself Klezmaniacs.

Parody is an example of what Steven Mullaney has called a rehearsal of culture—namely, a performance that is self-consuming in the sense that it is "ultimately organized around the elimination of its own pretext." [117] As ethnographic burlesque, which has a long history and was a tool of the Jewish Enlightenment, such parody displays its target in extraordinary detail and makes that display a vehicle for sensibility, which is what animates the parody in the first place. *Stempenyu,* discussed by Rothstein in chapter 2 of this volume, is a case in point.

The Jewish wedding has long been the focus of such treatment. A kind of primal scene of Jewish survival, the wedding is where the promise and crisis of cultural reproduction and biological survival get addressed both in reverential and parodic performances of Jewish wedding music. Recordings of wedding parodies were all the rage in the twenties, as Slobin has noted, and not just among Jews. [118] A comparison of Jewish wedding parodies over time would chart a history of changing structures of feeling, from David Fränkel's "Gallery of Obnoxious Abuses, Shocking Customs, and Absurd Ceremonies of the Jews" in *Sulamit* during the early nineteenth century, to *Der mesader kedushin* and *Di boyberiker khasene* in the twenties, to Mickey Katz's affectionate lobs of the fifties. [119] Seen as musical performances of cohort awareness, these displays of cultural connoisseurship in the breach chart the generational structure of sensibility and its sounds. No one exemplifies this moment more vividly than Mickey Katz.

In his roles as musician, comedian, and radio host, Katz presided over the obsolescence of what he called "the old but little-known *happy* Jewish music of the old country." [120] Katz, who was born in 1909, had been doing English-Yiddish parodies of fairy tales on the radio as a teenager in Doc Whipple's big band in Cleveland in the twenties. But it was only in 1947, after he broke up with Spike Jones, that Katz made English-Yiddish parody a speciality. The Barton Brothers had brought out several parody records, which made Katz think there might be a market for his own routines. Jewish executives at RCA were taken with the idea, and Katz proceeded to record parodies of current hits. The first singles by Mickey Katz and His Kosher Jammers were, by his own account, a sell-out success: "I had given the Jewish record-buying public something they evidently wanted and up to now hadn't had." [121] There followed the Borscht Capades, with his son Joel Grey, and a stint as a "kosher disc jockey" in Southern California from 1951 to 1956.

In addition to his own records, Katz's radio show featured everything from Al Jolson's "The Anniversary Waltz" and Yiddish recordings by operatic cantors to symphonic arrangements of Jewish folk music, songs about the Holocaust, and Israeli recordings. Summing up the experience, Katz writes: "The greatest personal satisfaction I got from my radio show was its wide appeal. Thousands of people of all faiths loved the *haimish* ('homey') Jewish music and the lively *frailachs*." [122] Though Katz did most of his talking in English, the Yiddish flavor of the show and the repertoire he featured would have appealed to an older generation. This assumption is borne out by the joke he tells about his audience:

> Jewish mamas and papas have always loved waltzes. There's a wonderful story about the old couple who were dancing in Miami Beach. In the old days all the hotels there had "dancing classes." And since it was Florida, the dancing classes usually featured Latin music. Well, one day our elderly couple were dancing to Pupi Campo's band at one of the hotels, and Sam, trying to keep up with the lively Latin rhythm, was stepping all over his wife's feet. Finally, she said, "Waltz a little faster, Sam; they're playing a fox-trot." [123]

While the show's success was a vindication of sorts, by the early fifties, Katz was finding it "slow going." He was encountering resistance to his routines. After his first show at Slapsie Maxie's in Los Angeles, the owner-manager came to Katz's dressing room and declared, "There will be no Yiddish done in this club!" and Spike Jones suggested Katz supply a libretto for the Yiddish-challenged. [124] The Jewish manager of a radio station in Los Angeles refused to play Katz's records. He said they were insulting and besides, "I don't play *any* ethnic records," which was not the case—he did play Mexican music. A Philadelphia station manager (not Jewish) refused to play Katz's records because "some of our listeners are offended. . . . I will not play any record with Yiddish in it. Yiddish is the language of the ghetto."

Katz, in the autobiography from which I take these accounts, attributes the hostility he encountered to shame on the part of Jews and anti-Semitism on the part of non-Jews—he also acknowledged that not everyone in his audience could understand Yiddish. What he does not address is precisely what some people found so funny and others so "insulting" and "offensive." This is a subject worthy of a study in its own

right. Suffice it to note that Katz's parodies of incompetence were highly
virtuosic. They required a mastery not only of multiple linguistic and
musical idioms, but also of incongruous juxtapositions.[125] This art, gov-
erned by a different sensibility, lives on in such recordings as *Rechnitzer Rejects,* also known as Schlock Rock, which were produced in the
eighties.[126]

Katz's Yiddish humor appealed to a contracting circle of "insiders"
as well as to the children of Yiddish speakers for whom just the sound
of Yiddish was funny or offensive, quite apart from the meaning of the
words. Uriel Weinreich has noted how obsolescent languages acquire
esoteric value and comic associations: "Among children of American
immigrants, the mere utterance of a word in their parents' language easily evokes laughter."[127] Whatever status Yiddish may have had as a primary medium of communication, it is as an obsolescent language, a stylistic specialization, that it figures in Katz's English-Yiddish routines. It
is characteristic of obsolescent languages that "colorful idiomatic expressions, difficult to translate, with strong affective overtones, whether
endearing, pejorative, or mildly obscene," turn up "in discourse that is
informal and uninhibited by pretensions of high social status."[128] Food
terms are likely to be part of the mix. (Sure enough, they turn up today
in the humorous names of neo-klezmer bands such as Nosh, Lox &
Vodka, Hot Latkes, and Shawn's Kugel.) Setting Yiddish lyrics to a hit-
parade tune intensified the comic effect.

The mixed responses to Katz's performances in the fifties point to
shifts in sensibility. During the Cold War, Jews had good reason to be
nervous. Obsolescence is one thing, genocide is another. As early as
1943, Maurice Samuel described *The World of Sholom Aleichem* as an
act of necromancy, a calling up from the dead.[129] He converted what
Sholem Aleichem's nineteenth-century readers had read as satire into
elegiac ethnography. *The World of Sholom Aleichem* was one of several such treatments of a destroyed world that appeared in the forties
and fifties. Others include Bella Chagall's *Burning Lights* and Abraham
Joshua Heschel's *The Earth Is the Lord's: The Inner World of the Jew
in Eastern Europe,* both of which appeared in Yiddish and in English
translation, and *Life Is with People: The Culture of the Shtetl,* the first
major ethnography of eastern European Jewish culture to appear in English.[130] Ambivalence about that world, an ambivalence that informed
both the immigrant experience and the Zionist movement, was put to a
severe test after World War II. It was one thing to be ambivalent about
a way of life that posed a threat to success in America or the establish-

ment of a Jewish homeland. Condemning a destroyed world to oblivion was another matter.

Evocations of a vanished world reached their apogee in *Fiddler on the Roof* (1964), which, together with Marc Chagall's imagery, made the klezmer the icon of an irretrievable world—and, from then on, albums of Yiddish song often included songs from this popular musical, as did Jewish weddings. It is surely no accident that Theodore Bikel would come to perform the lead role of Tevye some 1600 times in the decades that followed. However sentimental such elegies may seem to us today, they attempted to deal with what came to be known as the Holocaust before it was possible to deal directly with the genocide. In a period where memory vacillated between sad nostalgia and outraged horror, hope attached itself to establishing a Jewish homeland and creating a new life there or elsewhere.

No wonder Mickey Katz had a difficult time finding a niche for his English-Yiddish parodies. They spoke to the experience of an earlier generation of immigrants, those who had come far enough to be able to laugh at the "incompetence" Katz performed with such virtuosity. That experience had become irrelevant, if not embarrassing, to a suburban-ized generation of respectable Jews. The Yiddishists of the Yiddish day schools and summer camps, Workmen's Circle, and YIVO Institute for Jewish Research considered Borscht Belt culture vulgar. It was a threat to the Yiddish civilization for whose very survival they fought. As for the newest Yiddish speakers to arrive on the scene, a young generation of refugees and survivors, what were they to make of Katz's parodies as they struggled to learn English? In the wake of the Holocaust, those routines had become an irreverent tombstone, a sacrilege, an affront to changed sensibilities. In the fifties, Bikel could write obscene graffiti on the record cover of his first album of Yiddish folk songs. Forty years later, he would begin his autobiography with the Holocaust, not with his birth, and write of his own narrow escape, "Maybe I was meant to use my voice as a warning that history must not repeat itself." [131]

THE JEWISH SPACE

Since the Holocaust, there have appeared innumerable evocations of "vanished communities," eleventh-hour documentaries of the "last Jews" of eastern Europe, and, increasingly, Holocaust memorials. Those memorials, seen historically, also reflect shifts in sensibility, particularly as the children of survivors find their own voices. Art Spiegelman's *Maus* is but one example of what Gilad Melzer calls "irreverent memory." He considers the problem of representing the Holocaust "properly" in relation to new generational sensibilities, citing the "Holocaust rock music" of such Israeli musicians as Yehuda Poliker.[132] Today, central and eastern Europe are no longer the nowhere of an evacuated Yiddishland. Not only is there a modest renewal of Jewish life and communities and a major influx of Jewish tourists, but also "the 'Jewish space' in Europe . . . is increasingly attracting non-Jews," in the words of historian Diana Pinto.[133] They are the primary audience in Europe for klezmer music, particularly as performed by American Jewish musicians, but also by bands with names like Klezgoyim. In the estimation of Alan Bern, the virtuosic accordionist in Brave Old World, some non-Jewish musicians perform klezmer music "better than Jewish musicians who count as leaders of the revival." [134] If, as Liberman declared, old-time klezmorim "bridged the cultural abyss between the ghetto and the world," the neo-klezmers are filling a new kind of Jewish space, no less imagined than the topoi of ghetto and shtetl.[135]

A hero of the contemporary European klezmer scene is Giora Feidman. While The Klezmorim, based in San Francisco, are generally credited with being the first to record neo-klezmer music in 1977, Feidman was recording his Jewish "soul music" as early as 1971[136] and issued his first klezmer album in 1973. "King of Klezmer in the world today," Feidman bases the purity of his performances of klezmer music not on scrupulous attention to reconstruction but on distilling the "essence" of what he calls "Jewish soul music." [137] Born of a romantic mysticism, his ethereal musical interpretations depend more on inspiration than on fidelity to an authoritative musical "text." The preciousness of his performances is better suited to the concert stage and movie sound track, than to the dance floor or downtown club. While his fans embrace his music as a "universal language" and medium of international brotherhood, his critics object to his rarefied treatment of an earthy musical idiom. They object to his sensibility; liner notes for his early albums refer to "Jewish Folk Music" and "little worlds" (among them *Fiddler on the Roof* and contemporary Israel), and his repertoire draws from film scores as well as Hasidic Music Festivals and the music of Middle Eastern Jewish communities living in Israel.[138]

"Maestro Feidman," as he is referred to on his albums and on The Giora Feidman Home Page, is not of the same cohort as the American neo-klezmers. Born in Argentina, Feidman immigrated to Israel in 1957 to accept an invitation to join the clarinet section of the Israel Philharmonic Orchestra. While he describes himself as a fourth-generation klezmer, it is precisely this *yikhes* (and his extraordinary talent as a classical musician) that authorizes his distillations and the bold claims he makes for them. His largest followings are in Germany and Israel, where relationships to the eastern European Jewish past are particularly fraught, whether as the legacy of Nazism or of Zionism.

Groups like the Klezmer-Gesellschaft e.V., founded in Berlin in 1990, and their Klezmer Orchestra, established in 1995, are attracted to Feidman's celebration of klezmer music's universality because it gives them "permission" not only to play the music, but also to claim it: klezmorim, they explain, "usually were Jewish, but not necessarily. They usually played at Jewish celebrations—but not only. And that was why they integrated into their repertoire the traditional music of their surroundings. The style of playing and the repertoire are characterized by both the tradition, vivid modifications, and new perceptions. That is exactly what we now call klezmer music." [139] The Klezmer-Gesellschaft was founded by musicians who took Feidman's workshops, and Feidman is also a member of the society. He is an active teacher and has issued numerous instructional recordings and books.

In the United States, Balkanarama has created a slot for klezmer music in a list that includes Albania, Bosnia, Bulgaria, Croatia, Greece, Hungary, Macedonia, Romania, Serbia, Slovenia, and the Roma (Gypsies). The topos of music as place, a site of imagined community, can be found in the instruction, "Welcome to the Republic of Balkanarama. . . . Please surrender your passport now." [140] The place is then—a dreamy chronotope of Jewish Gypsies, fiddling their way from place to place, picking up the sounds around them, and fusing them into a zany foot-tapping musical icon pierced by the soulful cry of a fiddle or clarinet.[141] The place is not now.

Moreover, the music, once it has been universalized, is no longer even Jewish—"Klezmer is not Jewish music," Feidman has said. He explains, "Everyone is born a singer. God gave to us an instrument of song, our body. *This* is klezmer." [142] Nothing could be further from the sensibility of American neo-klezmers. Or from the sensibility of those who remember hearing the old-timers, some of whom were young at the time and alternated playing Jewish and jazz gigs. The "indigenous music" of klezmorim, which Hentoff defined as "improvising Yiddish musicians," reminded him of jazz, but with a critical difference: "The cadences, the timbres, the swirling rhythms went back to far different places and times than the jazz I also loved. It was more from these sounds than from any

reading that my sense of the old country first began to be vivid." [143] If
the music took Nat Hentoff back to Minsk and Pinsk and offered David
Krakauer a "musical home," it lets Don Byron "take you to a place you
may have avoided and make you feel comfortable there." [144] That place
is out. It is on the edge. It is radical in the contradictory senses of rooted
and extreme. Such are the fault lines of sensibility defined by klezmer
music of the nineties.

NOTES

I would like to thank John Czaplicka, Max Gimblett, Harvey Goldberg, Marion
Jacobson, Mark Kligman, Elliott Oring, and Mark Slobin for their careful reading and thoughtful comments on this paper and Robert Freedman for providing
discographic information.

Please note that web pages are by their very nature ephemeral. The text and
navigation change with updating and redesign. URLs change. Some pages disappear completely. This has happened to many of the sites since I first consulted
them in 1997. I have addressed in two ways the problem of attributing quotations from web sites that have changed or disappeared. First, I updated the URLs
for sites that still contain the material quoted here. Unless otherwise indicated,
I last accessed each site in January 2001. Second, I noted when the cited material can no longer be found, because the site has changed or disappeared. In such
cases, I indicated the date that I originally accessed the site. Citations to such
sites appear in the endnotes, but not in the bibliography.

1. Nat Hentoff, "Indigenous Music," *Nation,* 14 January 1978, 28–29. Excerpts from Hentoff's 1978 review of The Klezmorim's first recording appeared
on the jacket of their second album, *Streets of Gold* (Arhoolie Records, 3 011,
1978). Hentoff was no stranger to music revivals. He had commented on the
earlier American folk song revival. See also Nat Hentoff, "The Future of the Folk
Renascence," in *The American Folk Scene: Dimensions of the Folksong Revival,*
ed. David A. De Turk and A. Poulin, Jr. (New York: Dell, 1967), 326–31.

2. Ari Davidow, comp., "Memories of the Klez Revival and 'The Klezmorim,'" excerpts from e-mails from Lev Liberman and David Julian Gray, 1999,
http://www.klezmershack.com/articles/klezmorim.hist.html (January 2001).

3. Quotes in this paragraph are from Raymond Williams, *Marxism and Literature* (New York: Oxford University Press, 1977), 132–33. The relevant chapter is "Structures of Feeling," 128–35.

4. Haym Soloveitchik, "Rupture and Reconstruction: The Transformation
of Contemporary Orthodoxy," *Tradition* 28, no. 4 (1994): 90.

5. For a rich discussion of klezmer music in central and eastern Europe today, see Ruth Ellen Gruber, *Filling the Jewish Space in Europe,* International
Perspectives, no. 35 (New York: American Committee, 1996).

6. Raymond Williams, *Keywords: A Vocabulary of Culture and Society,* rev.
ed. (New York: Oxford University Press, 1983), 15.

7. Seth Rogovoy, "Andy Statman's Hasidic Jazz," *Boston Phoenix,* 21 March

1997, http://www.berkshireweb.com/rogovoy/interviews/statman.html (26 January 2001). Also Gruber, *Filling the Jewish Space*, 32.

8. Vurma home page, http://hem.passagen.se/vurma/. This Swedish-language site, under construction in January 2001, no longer contained the passage that I found there on 30 May 1997.

9. The Klezmorim, *Metropolis* (Flying Fish, FF 90258, 1981). Quote is from jacket copy.

10. Joel Lewis, "Heavy Shtetl: The New In-Your-Face Jewish Music," *Moment* 20, no. 4 (August 1995): 46.

11. Seth Rogovoy, "The Klezmatics: Outing Klezmer," *Boston Phoenix*, 16 May 1997, http://www.berkshireweb.com/rogovoy/interviews/klezmat.html (January 2001).

12. The program, Sunday Morning Klezmer & Other Jewish Music, airs on Sundays, 6:00 A.M. to 10 A.M., Eastern Time, on WBZC-FM, 88.9 FM (Burlington County College, New Jersey). It has been hosted and produced by Jacob Freedman since 1995. The site has changed since I consulted it in 1997 and is at http://www.angelfire.com/nj/WBZCFMsndymrnngklzmr/ (16 January 2001).

13. Unless otherwise indicated, all characterizations quoted in this paragraph came from the band list reached through Ari Davidow's KlezShack in 1997. As of January 2001, this site, now known as Ari Davidow's Klezmer Shack, is located at http://www.klezmershack.com/.

14. Information on Cayuga Klezmer Revival comes from entries on Ari Davidow's Klezmer Shack web site (see n. 13) and from Mika Kovalainen, "Mika's Klezmer Pages," http://www.astrakan.hig.se/~kryp/klezmer.htm (26 January 2001).

15. Mickey Katz and Hannibal Coons, *Papa, Play for Me: The Hilarious, Heartwarming Autobiography of Comedian and Bandleader Mickey Katz* (New York: Simon and Schuster, 1977), 164, 165.

16. Walter Zev Feldman makes this point in his important essay on the bulgar, "Bulgărească/Bulgarish/Bulgar: The Transformation of a Klezmer Dance Genre," *Ethnomusicology* 38, no. 1 (1994): 5–6. For a revised version of this discussion, see chapter 6 in this volume.

17. Robert Cantwell, "When We Were Good: Class and Culture in the Folk Revival," in *Transforming Tradition: Folk Music Revivals Examined*, ed. Neil V. Rosenberg (Urbana: University of Illinois Press, 1993), 36. For the earlier history of the revivals of the postwar period, see David E. Whisnant, *All That Is Native and Fine: The Politics of Culture in an American Region* (Chapel Hill: University of North Carolina Press, 1983).

18. Quoted by Seth Rogovoy in "The Klezmer Revival: Old World Meets New," *Berkshire Eagle*, 31 July 1997, http://www.berkshireweb.com/rogovoy/interviews/klez.html (24 January 2001).

19. Henry Sapoznik and Pete Sokolov, *The Compleat Klezmer* (Cedarhurst, N.Y.: Tara Publications, 1987), 5.

20. Sapoznik and Sokolov, *The Compleat Klezmer*, 5.

21. Sapoznik and Sokolov, *The Compleat Klezmer*, 14.

22. Barbara Kirshenblatt-Gimblett, "Theorizing Heritage," *Ethnomusicol-*

ogy 39, no. 3 (1995): 367–80, and the chapter "Destination Museum" in her *Destination Culture: Tourism, Museums, and Heritage* (Berkeley and Los Angeles: University of California Press, 1998), 131–76.

23. Hentoff, "Indigenous Music," 29.

24. I curated the Jewish program, which included *haredi* instrumentalists from Israel, but neither American Jewish wedding musicians nor the new klezmers. See Barbara Kirshenblatt-Gimblett, the chapter "Objects of Ethnography," in her *Destination Culture: Tourism, Museums, and Heritage,* 17–78. The pages cited here are 70–72.

25. Seth Rogovoy, "Making Old-World Music New," *Berkshire Eagle,* 22 August 1996, http://www.berkshireweb.com/rogovoy/popcorner/pop8-22 .html (23 January 2001).

26. Seth Rogovoy, "David Krakauer's Klezmer Incites, Provokes," *Berkshire Eagle,* 30 August 1996, http://www.berkshireweb.com/rogovoy/concerts/ klezmer.html.

27. This point is made by Neil V. Rosenberg, in *Transforming Tradition,* 17.

28. S.v. *revival* and *revitalize, Webster's Seventh New Collegiate Dictionary* (Springfield, Mass.: G. and C. Merriam Company, 1976).

29. Klezmatics, *Possession* (Green Linnet Records/Xenophile, XENO 4050, 1997). Note the instruction on this CD: "File under: World/Klezmer."

30. The quote comes from the liner notes. Following its premiere in 1995 at the Hartford Stage, Connecticut, this production of *A Dybbuk* was performed at the Public Theater in New York in 1997. Frank London has also said of the Klezmatics, "We come from this ecstatic standpoint on Jewishness, gender and sexual politics." Quoted in Seth Rogovoy, "Andy Statman's Hasidic Jazz."

31. S.v. *inspiration, Webster's Seventh New Collegiate Dictionary.*

32. See Paul Mendes-Flohr, "Fin de Siècle Orientalism, the Ostjuden, and the Aesthetics of Jewish Self-Affirmation," in *Divided Passions: Jewish Intellectuals and the Experience of Modernity* (Detroit: Wayne State University Press, 1991), 77–132.

33. Rogovoy, "Andy Statman's Hasidic Jazz."

34. For "feeling and ideology," see Raymond Williams, *Marxism and Literature,* 132–33; for "tradition and ideology," see Soloveitchik, "Rupture and Reconstruction," 90.

35. For a more extended discussion of *Fiddler on the Roof,* see Barbara Kirshenblatt-Gimblett, "Imagining Europe: The Popular Arts of American Jewish Ethnography," in *Divergent Centers: Shaping Jewish Cultures in Israel and America,* ed. Deborah Dash Moore and Ilan Troen (New Haven: Yale University Press, 2001), 155–91.

36. Quotations in this paragraph from Soloveitchik, "Rupture and Reconstruction," 71, 72, 74, and 73, respectively.

37. Soloveitchik, "Rupture and Reconstruction," 73.

38. From entry for Budowitz, under Performing Groups and Individual Artists, at Sacred and Secular, Jewish Music WebCenter, 14 January 2001, http:// www.jmwc.org/jmwc_performinggroups.html (24 January 2001).

39. Barrymore Laurence Scherer, "Country and Eastern," *Wall Street Journal,* 28 December 1994, Eastern edition. A11.

40. Quotes in this paragraph from Soloveitchik, "Rupture and Reconstruction," 81, 90, 103, and 86, respectively.

41. See E. P. Thompson, *Customs in Common* (New York: The New Press, 1991), 1–15, and Peter Burke, *Popular Culture in Early Modern Europe* (New York: New York University Press, 1978).

42. Barbara Kirshenblatt-Gimblett, "Problems in the Early Historiography of Jewish Folkloristics," in *Proceedings of the Tenth World Congress of Jewish Studies,* ed. D. Assaf, Art, Folklore and Music, Div. D, vol. 2 (Jerusalem: World Union of Jewish Studies, 1990), 21–32.

43. Soloveitchik, "Rupture and Reconstruction," 82.

44. The Klezmorim, *East Side Wedding* (Arhoolie, 3006, 1977) and *Metropolis.*

45. For the first Frank London quotation, see Chris King, "Klezmatics to Appear at Washington U.," 11 September 1996, http://www.klezmershack.com/articles/king.klezmatics.9609.html (23 January 2000). For the second, see Rogovoy, "The Klezmatics."

46. Ibid.

47. Seth Rogovoy, "Making Old-World Music New."

48. Liner notes for Kapelye, *Future & Past* (Flying Fish, FF 249, 1981).

49. Clifford Geertz, "Epilogue," in *The Anthropology of Experience,* ed. Victor W. Turner and Edward M. Bruner (Urbana: University of Illinois Press, 1986), 380.

50. Seth Rogovoy, "Making Old-World Music New."

51. Thompson, *Customs in Common,* 6.

52. Rosenberg, *Transforming Tradition,* 177–82. Klezmer revival pioneers came to the music through just such "named-system revivals"—Appalachian music (Sapoznik), bluegrass (Statman), jazz (Netsky, Byron, London), Balkan (Brody, Brotman), Greek (Svigals, Feldman), and other musics, rather than through Jewish music, though there are exceptions.

53. Soloveitchik, "Rupture and Reconstruction," 75.

54. Joel Rubin, "Rumenishe Shtiklekh: Klezmer Music among the Hasidim in Contemporary Israel," *Judaism* 47, no. 1 (Winter 1998): 12–23.

55. See Mark Kligman, "On the Creators and Consumers of Orthodox Popular Music in Brooklyn," *YIVO Annual* 23 (1996): 259–94.

56. Katz and Coons, *Papa, Play for Me,* 132.

57. These quotations are from "Biography of Don Byron," *European Jazz Network,* http://www.ejn.it/mus/byron.htm. The entry has been updated since the 1997 version that I originally consulted, which is no longer online.

58. John Wankoff, "Biography of John Zorn," *Contemporary Musicians* 15, http://www.musicblvd.com/cgi-bin/tw/9339107872835211_108_215723 (November 1995). This page no longer exists at this address.

59. Rogovoy, "Andy Statman's Hasidic Jazz." Also Andy Statman Quartet, *Between Heaven & Earth: Music of the Jewish Mystics* (Shanachie Records, 64079, 1997).

60. Rogovoy, "Andy Statman's Hasidic Jazz."

61. The separation of sounds from their sources has been termed *schizophonia* by R. Murray Schafer, *The Tuning of the World* (New York: Knopf,

1977), and applied to world beat by Steven Feld, *From Schizophonia to Schismogenesis: Notes on the Discourses of World Music and World Beat,* Working Papers and Proceedings of the Center for Psychosocial Studies 53, ed. Greg Urban and Benjamin Lee (Chicago: Center for Psychosocial Studies, 1992).

62. See Barbara Kirshenblatt-Gimblett, the chapter "Confusing Pleasures," in her *Destination Culture,* 203–48.

63. Rogovoy, "David Krakauer's Klezmer Incites, Provokes."

64. Jeremy Wolff, "A 'Cat' from the Bronx Makes His Mark on Klezmer," *Wall Street Journal,* 19 September 1991, Eastern edition. A12.

65. The Klezmatics Home Page, http://www.jewishmusic.com/kle.htm, which I accessed in 1998, no longer exists.

66. Milton Gordon, *Assimilation in American Life: The Role of Race, Religion, and National Origins* (New York: Oxford University Press, 1964), 56–57.

67. Andy Logan, "Profiles: Five Generations," *New Yorker,* 29 October 1949, 32–51.

68. "The Yiddish Voice," WUNR, 1600 AM (Brookline, Massachusetts), http://www.yiddishvoice.com/.

69. The Lark's March (pseud.), "Klezmorim Interview," Lark in the Morning, http://www.larkinam.com/MenComNet/Business/Retail/LarkNet/ArtKlezmorimInterview (24 January 2001). Lark in the Morning is a musician's service founded in 1974.

70. Williams, *Marxism and Literature,* 12.

71. Seth Rogovoy, "The Klezmer Revival."

72. Henry Sapoznik was one of the first to reissue 78s of Jewish instrumental music, document those recordings, and combine historical documentation with practical advice for the musician. He has since published his own history of klezmer music, *Klezmer!: Jewish Music from Old World to Our World* (New York: Schirmer Books, 1999). Walter Feldman has prepared meticulously researched liner notes, record reviews, and historical essays. Joel Rubin has released important albums of historical recordings and substantive liner notes, including a revisiting of Moshe Beregovski's prewar collection of instrumental transcriptions, as well as a book: Rita Ottens and Joel Rubin, *Klezmer-Musik* (Kassel: Bärenreiter, 1999). Hankus Netsky is writing his doctoral dissertation in ethnomusicology at Wesleyan University on the history of klezmer music in Philadelphia. Seth Rogovoy, who has reported extensively on klezmer music, has just issued his own book on the subject: *The Essential Klezmer: A Music Lover's Guide to Jewish Soul Music, from the Old World to the Jazz Age to the Downtown Avant-Garde* (Chapel Hill, N.C.: Algonquin Books, 2000).

73. Mark Slobin, "Fiddler off the Roof: Klezmer as an Ethnic Musical Style," in *The Jews of North America,* ed. Morris Rischin (Detroit: Wayne State University Press, 1987), 95–104.

74. Loeffler deals with this subject in depth in his splendid senior thesis, "A Gilgul fun a Nigun: Jewish Musicians in New York, 1881–1945," Harvard Judaica Collection Student Research Papers, no. 3 (B.A. thesis, Harvard University, 1997).

75. For the range of occasions that called for Jewish instrumental music, see

Loeffler in this volume (chapter 3) and Moshe Beregovski, *Old Jewish Folk Music: The Collections and Writings of Moshe Beregovski,* ed. Mark Slobin (Philadelphia: University of Pennsylvania Press, 1982).

76. Seth Rogovoy, "The Klezmer Revival."

77. See Jenna Weissman Joselit, *The Wonders of America: Reinventing Jewish Culture, 1880–1950* (New York: Hill and Wang, 1994), 89ff.

78. The quip from Sapoznik appears on the jacket of Kapelye's *Jakie Jazz 'Em Up: Old-Time Klezmer Music, 1912–1926* (Global Village Music 101, 1984).

79. Samuel Weissenberg, "Die 'Klesmer'sprache,'" *Mitteilungen der Anthropologischen Gesellschaft in Wien* 43 (1913): 133. Also Alfred Landau, "Zur russisch-jüdischen 'Klesmer'sprache,'" *Mitteilungen der Anthropologischen Gesellschaft in Wien* 43 (1913): 143–49, and Nahum Stutchkoff, *Der oytser fun der yidisher shprakh* (New York: Yidisher Visnshaftlekher Institut-YIVO, 1950).

80. I discovered this extremely rare, ephemeral publication through the catalogue of the YIVO Institute for Jewish Research and have not been able to find traces of it in the Library of Congress. No author is indicated. The binding obscures a word that refers to the publisher, although the colophon indicates that it was printed by Sikora i Mylner.

81. See also Beregovski, *Old Jewish Folk Music.*

82. Indeed, this story is similar in structure to Hasidic purim plays. See Shifra Epstein, "Drama on a Table: The Bobover Hasidim *Piremshpiyl,*" in *Judaism Viewed from within and without: Anthropological Studies,* ed. Harvey Goldberg (Albany: State University of New York Press, 1987), 195–217, and Barbara Kirshenblatt-Gimblett, "Performance of Precepts, Precepts of Performance," in *By Means of Performance: Intercultural Studies of Theatre and Ritual,* ed. Richard Schechner and Willa Appel (Cambridge: Cambridge University Press, 1990), 109–17.

83. Marty Levitt, *Wedding Dances* (Tikva Records, T94, [1960s]).

84. Rudy Tepel, *Chassidic Wedding: Rudy Tepel and His Orchestra Play Dance Melodies of Vizhnitz, Lubavich, Modzitz, Satmar, Skulen, Mea Shearim* (Collectors Guild, CGL-623, 1962).

85. Liner notes for Tepel, *Chassidic Wedding.*

86. See David Werdyger, *Cantor David Werdyger Sings New Bobover Nigunim Composed by the Bobover Rebbe (Rabbi Solomon Halberstam) Shlita,* accompanied by The Epstein Brothers Orchestra and The Bobover Chassidic Choir, musical arrangements by conductor Velvel Pasternak, supervised by Rabbi Moses Kessler (Aderet Records, LPW 303, n.d.).

87. Tepel, *Chassidic Wedding.*

88. *Rejoice: Torah in Song/Wedding in the Old Country* featured clarinetist Dave Tarras. It was conducted by S. Fershko and produced by Michael Golan (Heritage Records, CH501). The quotation comes from the liner notes by Mike Silverman.

89. Liner notes for Levitt, *Wedding Dances.*

90. Slobin, "Fiddler off the Roof," 98.

91. Adele Margolin et al., *Pages of History* (Heritage Records, L.P.DC 477).

92. See Philip V. Bohlman, *"The Land Where Two Streams Flow"*: *Music in the German-Jewish Community of Israel* (Urbana: University of Illinois Press, 1989).

93. See A. Z. Idelsohn, "Artistic Endeavors," in *Jewish Music in Its Historical Development* (New York: Schocken, 1967), 461–68; Avraham Soltes, "The Hebrew Folk Song Society of Petersburg: The Historical Development," in *The Historic Contribution of Russian Jewry to Jewish Music,* ed. Irene Heskes and Arthur Wolfson (New York: National Jewish Music Council, 1967), 13–27.

94. For example, see Herschel Bernardi, Shoshana Damari, Netania Davrath, Leon Lishner, Jan Peerce, Martha Schlamme, Abraham Ellstein, Gershon Kingsley, Robert De Cormier, and Vladimir Golschmann, *The Yiddish Dream: A Heritage of Jewish Song,* 2 discs (Vanguard, VSD 715/716, 1971).

95. Giora Feidman, *Long Live Giora, His Clarinet and His Soul Music* (Star Record ST AE 76 A/B, 1977).

96. Oscar Brand, *The Ballad Mongers: Rise of the Modern Folk Song* (New York: Funk & Wagnalls, 1962), first page of his preface.

97. Agnes De Mille refers to the tidal wave on the third page of her foreword to Brand, *The Ballad Mongers.* Brand discusses the concept of "simple noise" in *The Ballad Mongers,* 3–16.

98. Brand, *The Ballad Mongers,* 10, 14, and 15.

99. Quotations in this paragraph come from Brand, *The Ballad Mongers,* 56–57.

100. See David A. De Turk and A. Poulin, Jr., *The American Folk Scene: Dimensions of the Folksong Revival* (New York: Dell, 1967).

101. Theodore Bikel, *Theo: The Autobiography of Theodore Bikel* (New York: HarperCollins, 1994), 88.

102. Bikel, *Theo,* 89.

103. Bikel studied at Mikve Israel, a two-year agricultural college established by the Alliance Israélite Universelle in Jerusalem. He went on to study theater at the Studio, which was run by the director of Habimah, Tsvi Friedland, before entering the Royal Academy of Dramatic Art in London.

104. According to Bikel, Marjorie supported Yiddish and even launched a project to preserve Yiddish books. Information in this paragraph and the two following paragraphs comes from Bikel, *Theo,* 157–58, 108, 186, 107, 156, and 155, respectively.

105. Bikel is referring to the jacket for Theodore Bikel, *Theodore Bikel Sings Jewish Folk Songs* (Elektra ELK 141, 1959).

106. S.v. Eisenstadt, "Bands and Performing Groups: Klezmer, Jewish, and Related or Derivative Musics," Ari Davidow's Klezmer Shack, http://www.klezmershack.com/contacts/klezbands_e.html (24 January 2001).

107. Quoted in Rogovoy, "Making Old-World Music New." The talking instrument is also found in Sholem Aleichem's *Stempenyu* and other literary accounts of klezmorim.

108. Svigals quoted in Rogovoy, "The Klezmer Revival."

109. B. A. Botkin, "The Folksong Revival: Cult or Culture," in *The American Folk Scene,* ed. David A. De Turk and A. Poulin, Jr., 99.

110. This quotation appears on the jacket of Allan Sherman, *Allan Sherman's Mother Presents My Son, the Folk Singer* (Warner Bros., W 1475, 1962), where Sherman states that "These songs are what would happen if Jewish people wrote all the songs—which, in fact, they do," a tongue-in-cheek acknowledgment that Jewish songwriters were a visible presence on the American scene.

111. Larry Yudelson, "Dylan: Tangled up in Jews," *Washington Jewish Week,* 7 July 1997, http://www.well.com/user/yudel/Tangled.html (24 January 2001).

112. Rosenberg, *Transforming Tradition,* 10.

113. NAMA Orchestra and Pearl Rottenberg, *Mazltov!: Yiddish Folk Songs* (NAMA 3, 1978). The additional quote in this paragraph comes from the web page for the *Best of NAMA* (NAMA 5 CD, 1999), featuring (according to the jacket) "Balkan, Klezmer, and American Songs and Dance Music, 1974–1983." From http://ourworld.compuserve.com/homepages/owensmohr/nama .htm: "The NAMA Orchestra, an offshoot from the Aman Folk Ensemble, was from 1974 to 1986 probably the country's best known Balkan folk dance band, and part of the klezmer revival of the 1970's. Here are their 'greatest hits'— Serbian, Macedonian, Bulgarian, Greek, Israeli, Yiddish, klezmer, American, and Latin—by a remarkable group of musicians."

114. Both quotes in this paragraph come from Katz and Coons, *Papa, Play for Me,* 132. Mickey Katz, *Mickey Katz Plays Music for Weddings, Bar Mitzvahs and Brisses* (Capitol T-1021, 1958).

115. Katz and Coons, *Papa, Play for Me,* 132. Katz published his autobiography in 1977, when he was sixty-eight years old. He made English-Yiddish comedy a specialty when he was in his fifties.

116. See Sapoznik and Sokolov, *The Compleat Klezmer,* 14, and Joel Lewis, "Heavy Shtetl," 46.

117. Steven Mullaney, *The Place of the Stage: License, Play, and Power in Renaissance England* (Ann Arbor: University of Michigan Press, 1995), 69. Discussed in the chapter titled "The Rehearsal of Cultures."

118. Slobin, "Fiddler off the Roof," 99.

119. I discuss Fränkel's column in my essay "Problems in the Early Historiography of Jewish Folkloristics." Marc Caplan compares the wedding parodies of Goldstein and Katz in his insightful "Borsht-Belt Badkhonim: Carnival Performance Recordings of Gus Goldstein and Mickey Katz" (unpublished essay, 1997).

120. Katz and Coons, *Papa, Play for Me,* 132.

121. This quotation and the information following come from Katz and Coons, *Papa, Play for Me,* 123, 155.

122. Katz and Coons, *Papa, Play for Me,* 157.

123. Katz and Coons, *Papa, Play for Me,* 156.

124. Quotations in this paragraph from Katz and Coons, *Papa, Play for Me,* 127, 128, 130.

125. On code-switching and Jewish immigrant humor, see Barbara Kirshenblatt-Gimblett, "Culture Shock and Narrative Creativity," in *Folklore in the Modern World,* ed. Richard M. Dorson (The Hague: Mouton, 1978), 109–22.

126. See Elliott Oring, *Jokes and Their Relation* (Lexington: University Press

of Kentucky, 1992). The relevant chapter is "Rechnitzer Rejects: An Unorthodox Humor Of Modern Orthodoxy," 67–80.

127. Uriel Weinreich, *Languages in Contact: Findings and Problems* (The
Hague: Mouton, 1968), 95.

128. Weinreich, *Languages in Contact,* 95.

129. Maurice Samuel, *The World of Sholom Aleichem* (New York: Knopf,
1943).

130. For a history of these works in relation to one another see my intro-
duction to the 1995 edition of Mark Zborowski and Elizabeth Herzog, *Life Is
with People: The Culture of the Shtetl* (New York: Schocken, 1995). When *Life
Is with People* first appeared in 1952 (International Universities Press), it was
subtitled *The Jewish Little-Town of Eastern Europe.* See also Abraham Heschel,
The Earth Is the Lord's: The Inner World of the Jew in Eastern Europe (New
York: Henry Schuman, 1950) and Bella Chagall, *Burning Lights,* trans. Norman
Guterman (New York: Schocken, 1946).

131. Bikel, *Theo,* 12.

132. See Gilad Melzer, "Past Impossible: Irreverence in the Representation
of the Holocaust, from 1970 to the Present," Ph.D. dissertation, New York University, in progress. On the history of changing sensibilities in relation to Holocaust memory, see Jeffrey Shandler, *While America Watched: The Holocaust on
Television* (New York: Oxford University Press, 1999).

133. Pinto's quotation can be found in Gruber, *Filling the Jewish Space,* 1.

134. Gruber, *Filling the Jewish Space,* 35.

135. Liberman's quotation can be found in Hentoff, "Indigenous Music," 29.

136. Feidman's compilation CD *Rabbi Chaim's Dance: Traditionals* [*sic*]
from Israel (RCA International, AAD 71-75, 1996) features recordings made
between 1971 and 1975 with his ensemble, Jewish Soul. The ensemble consisted
of Giora Feidman on clarinet, Ami Frenkel on bass guitar, and Yossi Levi on guitar. Their Tel Aviv debut was in 1972 and selections from their concert program
appeared on Giora Feidman, *Jewish Soul Music* (Hed-Arzi Ltd., BAN 14297,
1972), shortly thereafter.

137. The Giora Feidman Home Page, http://jewishmusic.com/cgi-bin/
SoftCart.exe/gfe.htm?L+jmcom+rvlf4776+973218246, has been updated and
no longer contains the quoted passage.

138. Quotations come from the liner notes for Feidman, *Jewish Soul Music.*

139. The Klezmer-Gesellschaft e.V., http://www.geocities.com/Broadway/
1791/. (As of February 2002, this site is now called the "German Klezmer Page,"
and is located at www.ta-deti.de/klezmer/.) While the material quoted here no
longer appears on the web page that I consulted in August 1997, the same ideas
are still expressed, albeit in different words. For a guide to the klezmer scene in
Germany, see Virtual Klezmer, http://www.klezmer.de/index.html.

140. Balkanarama, http://www.troutdream.com/balkanarama/ (4 January
2001). This site has been been redesigned since I originally visited it in August
1997, and no longer carries these words on its opening screen. On the notion of
imagined community, see Benedict R. O'G Anderson, *Imagined Communities:
Reflections on the Origin and Spread of Nationalism,* rev. ed. (London: Verso,
1991).

141. On the notion of chronotope, see M.M. Bakhtin, "Forms of Time and of the Chronotope in the Novel," in *The Dialogic Imagination: Four Essays,* trans. Caryl Emerson and Michael Holquist, ed. Michael Holquist, 41–83 (Austin: The University of Texas Press, 1981).

142. Found in Gruber, *Filling the Jewish Space,* 32.

143. Hentoff, "Indigenous Music," 28.

144. Wolff, "A 'Cat' from the Bronx," A12.

CHAPTER 8

KlezKamp and the Rise of Yiddish Cultural Literacy

HENRY SAPOZNIK

At the outset of the klezmer renewal in 1976, an arm of the American Jewish Congress, called the Martin Steinberg Center, received a federal grant under President Carter's CETA program to fund the study of Jewish culture. As musicians, filmmakers, writers, poets, painters, puppeteers, and playwrights made their way to the old carriage house on East 85th Street that housed it, the center became a short-lived oasis for young Jews seeking self-expression and Jewish continuity through the arts.

For me, CETA was a dream come true of research, documentation, and study in the largely uncharted field of klezmer music. But if that research had remained academic, klezmer music today would be a relic, a curio piece viewed with nostalgia, instead of the vibrant musical form it has once again become. And if efforts to learn to play the music had remained similarly formalistic—limited, say, to what could be gleaned from listening to old 78s—the depth of our understanding and performance of it would be no greater than the thickness of the discs.

Fortunately for my mission at CETA, the preeminent source for Jewish cultural research, the YIVO Institute for Jewish Research, was located just around the corner. YIVO housed a jumble of unlistened-to 78s, and my days were given over to playing, cataloging, and documenting them. This method of research was not new to me. As an ethnomusicologist/banjoist specializing in old-time music, I'd spent much time perusing the scratchy 78s of American popular music from the turn of the century—the raw and vital first sounds of Appalachian fiddlers,

Figure 8.1 KlezKamp, 1988. Lorin Sklamberg (piano), Alicia Svigals (violin), Margot Leverett (clarinet), Pete Sokolow (keyboard), Dave Licht (drums); others unknown. Photo by Albert J. Winn, used with permission.

banjo-playing blackface comics, and hot early jazz bands. But the YIVO collection of 78s was surrendering to me the music of my forebears, the passionate and unfettered first American klezmorim.

Simultaneously new and old, the records were a passport to a vanished land. However, the sort of face-to-face collecting and observation of continuity through which I'd researched old-time music in numerous field trips to North Carolina was not possible for the study of this music. There was no Old Country to go back to, no Poland, Ukraine, or Rumania where I might find Jewish old-timers tenaciously holding onto their repertoire against all modern influences. These delicate shellacs were three-minute musical Rosetta stones that unearthed a musical language that offered entrée to the klezmer tradition; they in effect *were* the Old Country, a ticket back to that time and place. And they led to even richer passage when, in delivering the knowledge gleaned from such research, I happened upon the primary source for learning what klezmer was, and is, all about.

One of my tasks in the CETA program was to give lectures on klezmer music at various senior centers and nursing homes in the New York City area. While translating some theater ads from vintage Yiddish newspapers, I had come across a reference to cellist Joseph Cherniavsky and his Hasidic-American Jazz Band. What a wonderful and incongruous name—I loved it! Who were they, though? Thereafter I made sure to mention the orchestra in all my lectures, including one on a spring day in the Bronx in 1978.

The audience comprised dozens of seniors, some listening, some dozing, some talking. One woman sat up front, knitting furiously. When I mentioned the Cherniavsky outfit, without looking up, she said aloud, "Oh, them. My husband used to play drums with them."

"Your husband. Is he . . . all right?" I asked, fearing that she, like so many of the older women, was a widow.

Again without looking up, she replied, "He was when I left him in the back playing pinochle." Putting down her knitting, Grace Helfenbein headed to a back room of the Bronx Senior Center to fetch her husband, Joe.

Thus began my first lecture to an audience that included someone who had lived the experience. Would the man consider this the height of chutzpah? I needn't have worried. Joe Helfenbein's radiant, attentive smile was the best assurance that the world he'd known was being accurately portrayed.

After the lecture, Helfenbein and I went together to the rear of the center. My tape recorder, only moments before expelling the sounds of antique recordings, was now turned on Helfenbein himself, to document his vital memories of the days when those recordings were new. We settled down in a quiet corner with the cassette machine humming, the ambient sound of pinochle-playing replaced by recollections of a faraway time in 1925.

So Joe Helfenbein came to provide the first of the oral histories through which the story of klezmer unfolded itself to me. When I went to the Bronx to visit with him, he and Grace would lay out a lavish spread that culminated with my taping Joe as Grace sat by his side, smiling—and knitting.

Helfenbein was a true professional who, until his last days, assiduously practiced his *paradiddles,* the daily rhythm regimen of the serious drummer. Years later, I brought percussionist David Licht of a new band called the Klezmatics to meet him, and Joe was elated. He took out his practice pad and proudly demonstrated his paradiddles for Licht, who expressed genuine admiration for his limber acuity. Facilitating this exchange between a veteran klezmer musician and an up-and-coming younger player delivered a deep joy and satisfaction I would come to experience again—in spades.

I personally had felt the impact of such a quintessential music lesson back in 1979, when I began studying fiddle with Leon Schwartz, who taught children in his home in Sunnyside, Queens, and whom I'd chanced to hear of through a fellow CETA worker, singer/researcher Carol Freeman. What he taught was classical music, but what Freeman knew—and the reason I was there—was that Schwartz's real love was for the traditional music of his homeland: Bucovina, the region of the Austro-Hungarian empire bisecting Rumania and the Ukraine. When Schwartz raised fiddle to chin, even the vanilla notes of a simple scale exploded with the flavorful essence of Yiddish music, marking him as one of the great interpreters of klezmer music.

Slightly amazed that anyone would be interested in studying klezmer music, Leon Schwartz agreed to teach a bit of it at the conclusion of our lessons, provided I had run the gauntlet of classical exercises. I desultorily agreed and slogged through colorless drills while trying to keep my true enthusiasm in check: the thrill of being taught klezmer music by a master.

As the power and value of this transmission became ever clearer, I resolved to make it happen wide-scale by organizing an event that would tie Yiddish tradition and culture to its music. For the past three summers, I had taught banjo at a camp in Ashokan, New York, run by fiddler Jay Ungar, who went on to score Ken Burns's PBS documentary, *The Civil War*. Ungar's "Root" camp taught traditional Appalachian music, dance, and song in a beautiful woodland setting. The music and people were great and provided an ideal environment to learn and play this music. As was so often the case in the New York folk music scene, the vast majority of participants—teachers and students alike—were Jewish, and though I did manage to sneak in some klezmer music (I arranged "Freylekh fun der Khupe" for five-string banjo), a surreptitious mix was not what I was after.

In 1983, the East European Folklife Center sponsored a Balkan music and dance camp at Ashokan, and I went as a student. The camp was similar to Ungar's Fiddle and Dance Camp in that the teachers for the most part studied the culture but were not necessarily of it. And although again a majority of students and teachers were Jews, eastern European Jewish music was not on the menu. This puzzled me. I hardly expected it in the old-time country music scene, because folks there knew little about European music traditions, but members of the eastern European scene who were aware of Old World Yiddish music traditions chose not to present them.

Missing in traditional music camps in general was a sense of transmission within a community context. They were almost all exclusively peer-driven, a vast departure from the way music and culture typically gets passed on. I also sought a humanizing factor that would put a face on the folk music, as opposed to treating the tunes as a mere commodity, another tune to play at some jam session. And much as I liked working with my peers, I wanted younger players to get the same experience I had had: learning from senior musicians, so they would get an accurate take on what this music was about. This was music played by living, breathing people.

In 1982, by which time I was on staff at YIVO as director of the archives of recorded sound, I formally proposed a Yiddish music camp to the powers that were. Through a curriculum of classes in Yiddish language, crafts, and various aspects of this rich, diverse culture, the event aimed to place Yiddish music and dance within a larger context. The program was initially called the Yiddish Folk Arts Program, but with my weakness for nicknames (I referred to the YIVO as "the 'Vo"), my shorthand for it was KlezKamp, the name by which most people have come to know it.

The original idea of the Folk Arts Program was to offer musicians, singers, and Yiddishists a place to learn, exchange, and create Yiddish music in an enthusiastic and challenging intergenerational environment. It also came to serve as payoff for students who had just completed YIVO and Columbia University's rigorous six-week intensive summer Yiddish-language program. For one week, these students would be able to use the language they learned with some of the leading lights of Yiddish music and folk art culture—and have a great time.

I also saw the camp as a way of making the sound archives—and YIVO itself—more activist. Instead of waiting for people to discover the institute and utilize its vast resources, KlezKamp would go out and find them, creating an easily accessible dynamic bridge to the institute. Underlying these more altruistic reasons for creating KlezKamp was my own selfish desire to assemble some of the world's greatest klezmorim and play wonderful music with them.

Adrienne Cooper, then the assistant director of YIVO, had immediately understood the import of the program and ran interference for it. By February 1984, Cooper and I were meeting with Becky Miller, hired to coordinate KlezKamp. I had already lined up veterans Ruth Rubin, Max Epstein, Leon Schwartz, Bronya Sakina, and younger players like Michael Alpert, Lauren Brody, Hankus Netsky, and dance ethnographer LeeEllen Friedland to serve as its staff.

After some looking around, I had heard that a well-known summer

Yiddish socialist camp in Dutchess County, New York, had fallen on hard times and recently been sold to a New Age group. I went up to see the new owners and was surprised by how many of the original Yiddish accoutrements they'd preserved. "It's great karma," they said, that we were bringing a Yiddish camp back to this place.

Being as big a fan of great karma as the next guy, I arranged for the first Yiddish Folk Arts Program to take place 4–10 August 1984, at the newly opened Omega Institute in Rhinebeck, New York. With help from the YIVO mailing list and one from the East European Folklife Center, we sent out several thousand brochures and hoped for the best.

But as the Yiddish Folk Arts Program started drawing more and more people, the New Age folks at the camp, in a decidedly Old Age kind of way, began overcharging us. By the end of June, it was clear that if this kept up, the bigger our success, the less money we'd make. I reluctantly canceled the program.

Disappointed but not stymied—the event had to happen—I shifted my focus. What was another large time slot that could accommodate a multiday event like this? It occurred to me that the most readily available time slot in the Jewish world had yet to be tapped. Why not run the event over Christmas? No period in the calendar year alienates and marginalizes Jews as much as the week surrounding December 25.

In late August, Becky Miller and I made a grand inspection tour of hotels in the Catskills. We visited all the large resorts: the Concord, the Raleigh, the Nevele. None was what we wanted—a warm, homey place reminiscent of the old-time hospitality the region had made famous. The final hotel on our list was the runt of the litter: the quirky little Paramount, in Parksville. At its peak in the 1920s, the town of Parksville boasted more than fifty hotels, but now all that was left was the Paramount. The last of the family-owned hotels, the place had somehow managed to avoid changing since the mid 1950s. It was like a time capsule, with its round center-lobby couch and walls covered in green carpeting reminiscent of Spanish moss, thick red-and-amber water glasses on every dining room table, and heavy kosher comfort food pouring from the kitchen.

Built and expanded on over the years, the hotel is a crazy quilt of construction. The jumble of impetuous additions has resulted in some remarkably odd room numbering. For example, room 64 is down the hall from room 211, while 25 and 26 are on opposite ends of the hotel. The surest method to finding your way back to your room is to memorize the carpet pattern in your section of the hotel: like fingerprints, each is unique and never repeated. Even owner Fred Gasthalter's name was amusingly ideal: in Yiddish, *gasthalter* means "hotelier." Straight out of central casting right down to his ubiquitous cigar, Freddy, short and brusque, runs the Paramount like the Borscht Belt fiefdom it is, the last major employer in the area.

When Becky and I approached the Paramount with the idea of bringing in a Christmas trade, they were elated. The place was seriously underutilized at that time of year, hosting only a tiny group of folk-dancers and a B'nai B'rith Youth Organization convention of raging-hormone teenagers. The employees, usually tapped for funds to buy Christmas gifts, were thankful for this eleventh-hour burst of income.

Picking up where we'd left off with the ill-fated summer KlezKamp, we sent out a new mailing, hoping to reattract some of the 70 people who had replied to our earlier announcement. To our amazement, we exceeded that number, corralling some 90 people from around the country, most of them musicians. With the 30 staff members we hired, the first KlezKamp community comprised a nice, cozy 120 people.

On 21 December 1985, the day before the event was to open, staff convened at the hotel in a definite "Hey, kids, let's put on a show!" atmosphere, everyone pitching in to make it happen. We ran roughshod through the Paramount, renaming rooms in Yiddish and posting directional signs drawn in the old-time "finger-pointing" style throughout the serpentine hallways.

The first KlezKamp was rough and clunky, but tremendously *heymish* and fun. The participants loved it; the staff loved it. In the months following the event, I put out a small, short-lived KlezKamp newsletter and planned the second KlezKamp, with the help of Lynn Dion, a one-time ethnomusicology student at Brown University drawn to YIVO by her strong interest in Yiddish. Meanwhile, Becky Miller got kicked upstairs, working for Adrienne Cooper, and was replaced by my old Martin Steinberg cohort Chava Miller, brought in to help run KlezKamp. The following KlezKamp was bigger still, attracting almost 150 registrants, many of them returning participants and many of whom brought family members.

The best break for the future of KlezKamp happened in 1987, when Cooper hired Lorin Sklamberg. Already an accomplished singer and devotee of Yiddish music in Los Angeles, Sklamberg was also a founding member of New York's newest klezmer group, the Klezmatics. Happily, as soon as he got settled in, Sklamberg started working with me on

KlezKamp 3. It didn't take us long to find that our work styles and temperaments greatly complemented each other's.

By this time, we began to notice a subtle but important shift in our constituency. For the first few years, the ages of the registrants—mostly musicians—mirrored the average ages of the younger staff members. Though musicians still made up the bulk of staff and participants, their overall percentage was shrinking. We were now starting to attract more sixty- to eighty-year-olds and upward, many born in Europe.

There were all sorts of these older, mostly retired, KlezKampers. Some had grown up within reach of this old culture and now basked in the delight of reclaiming it; others, either denied it by assimilated parents or having spurned it themselves, were experiencing Yiddish culture for the first time. And a precious few were those rare *folksmentshn,* people born and raised in eastern Europe who actively retained crystal-clear access to that lost world and could transmit it to a new generation.

So KlezKamp was a win-win. For this older generation, it offered not only a cultural coda but the assurance that their stories, songs, accrued wisdom, and experience would be carried forward. For the younger participants—many of whom had never met anyone with an eastern European Jewish accent—it was their chance to experience people from the world that had produced the music they loved, to touch and be touched by a person who had lived in that vanished place, to become a part of that continuity. KlezKamp was attracting not only the greatest Yiddish musicians in the world, it was also attracting the greatest Yiddish audiences in the world.

Because the older participants were largely nonmusical, we began offering more and more general courses: more history, folklore, and "intro" courses. (My "Klezmology 101" class became a big draw for uninitiated and seasoned musicians alike.)

In another unanticipated shift in Kamp demographics, the positive word-of-mouth message that had helped solidify our base of support spread strongly throughout the long-disenfranchised Jewish gay and lesbian community, which by 1989 had come to represent a definable portion of Kamp registrants and staff. Contemporary Jewish homosexuals had found themselves polarized between two worlds: in left-of-center groups, they felt marginalized by cohorts who used anti-Zionism as a politically correct way to mask anti-Semitism; Jewish organizations and groups, meanwhile, often eschewed gays and lesbians because of their sexual preferences. KlezKamp, with its focus on Yiddish culture, gained the reputation of being gay- and lesbian-friendly, helped in no small part by Sklamberg's openly gay identity. But the active presence of *freylekhe* —as the community came to dub itself—at KlezKamp led several feature writers to emphasize that seeming incongruity at the cost of the true diversity of the event.

Nonnationals made up a third surprise element in our constituency. The first KlezKamp had only three people from outside the United States, and they were Canadians. The list of attendees from abroad quintupled the very next year, and by 1987, thanks to the growing number of European klezmer concerts, lovers of Yiddish culture from Germany, Switzerland, and England had become KlezKamp regulars. The continued growth of a European constituency—mostly German and the majority non-Jews—has been most telling. That the KlezKamp community is some 15 percent non-Jewish is a testament to the program's appeal. Eventually it was not unusual to have participants from Israel, South America, and even Asia.

YIVO's sponsorship of KlezKamp came in the form of paying for my and Lorin Sklamberg's time, printing and mailing the brochures, and not a lot more. The rest of the cash had to be culled from registration, which forced a dilemma. We knew that in order to attract people in the arts —who were usually young and broke—we'd have to keep the cost of Kamp low, but that if we did, the event would never pay for itself and wouldn't survive. If we charged a bigger fee, we'd have a good fiscal buffer by drawing mostly retired and well-to-do older folks, but at the cost of young families or people in the arts. So we needed to find an equitable way of attracting all of these vital constituencies.

I sought the support of the folk arts divisions of the New York State Council on the Arts and the National Endowment for the Arts (NEA). Both agencies had supported YIVO projects in the past, in keeping with the limits of their modest operating budgets. To become eligible for funding, we agreed to have auditors from the NEA and NYSCA come down and see what we were about. The auditor for the NEA, a devotee of eastern European culture then in the eighth month of her first pregnancy, arrived at Kamp just as an impromptu swaddling workshop was being conducted by my mother and the late Russian émigré Bronya Sakina. That fortuitous bit of active folklore set the tone for our long-running relationship with the NEA, an undersung hero in the fostering and encouragement of America's folk communities.

By the fourth KlezKamp, in 1988, registration for the folklore class alone equaled the first Kamp's entire registration. And by 1989, the waiting list to get into the event surpassed that number. But we had reached an impasse: with 350 attendees, KlezKamp had outgrown the hotel. We didn't want to move—the hotel staff had never been anything less than helpful and supportive, and the Paramount's administration bent every which way to accommodate our ever-growing needs. They adjusted, even letting us commandeer their kitchen to run classes on Jewish cuisine. The fact was that we filled the hotel, and they didn't want to lose us. So they started building again. And again. And again. We, meanwhile, found ourselves expanding in new ways.

Since the beginning of KlezKamp, we had always made a schedule allowance for a children's program, at first a catch-as-catch-can affair, depending on the number and ages of kids who showed up and the resources we had at our disposal. But as more and more of our peers became parents, it became clear we needed to craft a multiage-appropriate program for children. There were some models available; New York City's Pripetshik after-school program was one, but because it dealt with a regular group of children over the course of a school year and we met for just four days, it did not entirely serve. The more we tried to meet the needs of this community, the more kids showed up. By the third year, a full-time kids' staff was in place.

On the precipice of the 1990s, we looked back at our five years of KlezKamp to see a tremendous diversity of people totaling some fifteen hundred participants. *Community* no longer meant the physical limitations of region or neighborhood, but bespoke a shared literacy and cultural consciousness. For the few days of each event, our near-perfect mélange of kids and grandparents, musicians and artists, looked, acted, and reacted like a "real" community, coexisting in a way that evidenced a new method of jump-starting a culture's near-moribund processes. KlezKamp was finding new adherents not just from the powerful word-of-mouth it had generated, but from its inclusion in several documentaries made about the klezmer scene.

A phone call came to my office at the YIVO in 1984 from a young Boston-area filmmaker named Michal (rhymes with *nickel*) Goldman, who was making a documentary about klezmer music. She had heard the Klezmer Conservatory Band play at her sister's wedding and, transfixed by the music, decided to do a documentary featuring them. She asked me to be the consultant on the film, *A Jumpin' Night in the Garden of Eden.*

In an effort to amplify Goldman's desire to show klezmer music in its social context, I encouraged her to film her first KlezKamp as an insider.

These scenes of dance classes, music instruction, and "Klezmer Fake-lore," a panel discussion on the image of the klezmer featuring folklorist Barbara Kirshenblatt-Gimblett, are among the most compelling in the film.

Another film that came to KlezKamp was the BBC documentary *Fiddlers on the Hoof* (1989). Part of a British series called "Rhythms of the World," director Simon Broughton came to the subject as an assignment, bringing no knowledge of Yiddish music or its culture to the project, just his experience from a previous segment on Romanian music. He visited me at YIVO and retained me as a consultant.

Since its creation, KlezKamp has served as a yardstick on many levels—of itself, of the klezmer scene, and of Yiddish cultural literacy. The event keeps growing, and though we've been courted by numerous larger hotels to bring our business there, we still like the size and cozy, slightly frayed ambience of the Paramount.

The process of organizing KlezKamp, though straightforward, is time-consuming, requiring some nine months of preparation by our setup staff. With a cadre of top-drawer teachers, we continue to craft diverse programs, interesting themes, and challenging combinations of offerings.

The goal of KlezKamp was to create a community in which every aspect of Yiddish culture, from music to movies and from folklore to forklore, was given equal recognition and focus. By avoiding overemphasis of one aspect of the culture over another, we were able to broaden our community from one of primarily musicians to a deeply textured and variegated population encompassing seniors and toddlers, Jews and Gentiles, straight and gay, religious and secular.

KlezKamp's resonance in the extended Jewish community has been made tangible in the explosion of registrants wishing to celebrate life-cycle events at Kamp. Over the last few years, participants have opted to share these very personal and community-based events in the context of KlezKamp. Over the years we have hosted baby namings, an *opshern* (the ritual haircutting of a three-year-old boy), even a wedding.

But the most profoundly moving event was when KlezKamp veteran Lincoln Shnur-Fishman asked to have his bar mitzvah at the event in 1995. His family had been coming to the KlezKamp since he was a child, and his world view had been shaped by it. "I wanted my bar mitzvah to feel like I'm surrounded by Yiddishkayt," Lincoln said in his bar mitzvah speech. "KlezKamp, for me, means doing my part to carry on, keeping alive the souls of my grandparents' grandparents. . . . I wouldn't have done my bar mitzvah here if it didn't really mean something to me. I've chosen to have the most important milestone in my life here because I'm saying, 'I'm committed.'"

Another big bonus is the myriad instances of people who came to the Yiddish Folk Arts Program as registrants and worked their way up to staff and from there to worldwide prominence. This includes musicians like fiddler Alicia Svigals; clarinetists Margot Leverett, Merlin Shepherd, and Sherry Mayrent; and drummer David Licht; as well as dance instructor Steve Weintraub and standup Yiddishist Michael Wex.

Further evidence of KlezKamp's success are the events that borrow its format and content and even the staff. Events like the late Buffalo on the Roof, the Workmen's Circle's Mame Loshn, or the Los Angeles–based Yiddishkayt festival, billed as "the West Coast's largest festival of its kind," have their roots at KlezKamp: all were inspired and founded by one-time KlezKamp staff or attendees.

Several years ago, we were visited by a doctor from Montreal, who, though he had never been to KlezKamp, knew of it and wanted to run a similar event in Canada. Because of its cachet, he sought the use of our name for an event he wanted to call KlezKamp Kanada. I demurred. First, I told him, we wouldn't allow the name of our program to be used without having input into its operation, which he refused. And second, unless he sought an unwanted clientele, it was unwise to run an event whose initials were KKK. Mercifully, he changed the name to the less inflammatory KlezKanada.

Another Canadian event inspired by KlezKamp is the weeklong Ashkenaz festival, held every other year in Toronto. After attending Klez-Kamp for several seasons, Ashkenaz founder David Buchbinder reasoned that a modified version of KlezKamp would work well in his central Canadian city. Since its founding, Ashkenaz, like its model, has been a focus of much international interest of fans and performers of Yiddish music and culture.

The influence of KlezKamp has extended beyond North America. When Dutch poet and playwright Mira Rafalowicz went to KlezKamp in 1995, she took back with her what she learned there to found Amsterdam's International Yiddish Festival, which she ran for two years until her recent death. In 1996, when our theme was "Jews of Russia," we hosted several Yiddish activists from Saint Petersburg. Unacquainted as they were with the kind of open environment within which America's Yiddish culture has been created in the past few decades, these young people left with a fervent desire to replicate at home what they experienced in the Catskills. In 1997, the Saint Petersburg–based KlezFest was

born, with the assistance of KlezKamp staff Adrienne Cooper and Zal-
men Mlotek, who helped the Russian Jews mount their modest program.

KlezKamp is more than the sum of its parts—the bands that had their
beginnings there, from Brave Old World to the newly minted teenage
KlezMinors; the numerous people inspired to learn Yiddish; and the
multitudes who have carried back the essence of Yiddishkayt to their
communities around the world. The prime factor is the kids who grew
up attending Kamp and have come to see it as just another event, like
Passover, Rosh Hashanah, and Chanukah, in the firmament of the Jewish calendar—a new generation that assumes the mantle of cultural heritage with great aplomb and for which Yiddish and its culture is no
revival but simple continuity. By recontextualizing Yiddish culture, Klez-
Kamp has itself become a context.

NOTE

This article has been adapted from Henry Sapoznik, *Klezmer!: Jewish Music
from Old World to Our World* (New York: Schirmer Books, 1999).

CHAPTER 9

Newish, Not Jewish

A Tale of Two Bands

MARION JACOBSON

Following a successful tour in Germany, Brave Old World accordionist and musical director Alan Bern returned home to find the following e-mail message regarding the band's upcoming concert at a Toronto synagogue.

> We have heard that your repertoire has become too serious and artistic, and there are deep concerns in our congregation that your music will not be what we expect from klezmer. Please assure us that there will be plenty of opportunity for the audience to dance and sing along during the concert, or we will be forced to cancel the contract.[1]

Conflict simmers beneath the social contract that is a concert agreement. Klezmer is at the center of conflicting visions of its value. Some see it as the living expression of Jewish musical heritage, making any concert a celebration. Others conceive of concerts as a place for personal artistic expression, where listeners appreciate more than they participate. This might be less fun.

This paper plays off such tensions by presenting the careers of two major bands, The Klezmorim and Brave Old World, which emerged partly or wholly from the little-known California context of the 1970s. Drawing on interviews and song texts, I imagine how klezmer music evokes emotion and makes experiences of "Jewishness" reverberate with both fondness and a sense of loss.

Klezmer, originally referring just to the musician, now extends to

Figure 9.1 Brave Old World. From left: Kurt Bjorling, Alan Bern, Michael Alpert, and Stuart Brotman. Used with permission of Pinorrekk Records.

genres, venues, and expectations of twenty-first-century Jewish and non-Jewish audiences. At traditional weddings and other events, a set of dance pieces was performed in a fixed sequence. As an individual musician, a klezmer can be a flexible and spontaneous performer who incorporates a wide variety of song styles, from Balkan to world beat to jazz or rock, with electric guitar accompaniment. In recent years, groups like Brave Old World and the Klezmatics have been active in exploring new traditions by composing vocal parts and singing in Yiddish and English. Performers like David Krakauer and his trio Klezmer Madness, and John Zorn's Masada have expanded the role of solo improvisation. The two bands discussed below take different social-aesthetic positions. The Klezmorim have described themselves as a brass band. They honed their style by playing Balkan music and a variety of different jazz styles, perfecting a style of presentation that has been considered odd and quirky. Their work is offset against that of Brave Old World, an ensemble that has dedicated itself to traditional Yiddish folk singing in addition to old-time klezmer music while exploring the architecture of classical musical forms.

In this article, I give my attention to two groups whose music is neither completely open-ended nor tacitly traditional. As I examine the intersection of and distinction between klezmer as Jewish heritage music and personal expression, I draw in some of the language that musicians use. I examine emotional and artistic experience as it is verbally described and musically conveyed at the level of sound and event. "Identification" helps me to think about how a person constructs and reproduces something that one might call *the self*. It implies that identity is never fixed, but wraps itself around social and historical circumstances. It is a way of reconfiguring the self, a way of orienting one's mind to its surroundings. Ethnomusicologist Mark Slobin suggests that musicians in an ensemble can drift between affinities with their listeners and their ties to fellow band members.[2] These studies intersect my own questions regarding how klezmer music is made, how it works, and how it resounds.

I first met Alan Bern and Brave Old World at KlezKamp, the annual Yiddish folk arts program in the Catskills. At the time, my knowledge of klezmer music and the klezmer scene was shaped by the paradigm of "revival" revealed in apocryphal stories from the New York–based musicians I had come to know when meeting klezmer band leaders and musicians such as Henry Sapoznik and Andy Statman, hearing them play with their respective groups, and reading Sapoznik's personal accounts.[3] Slobin's theory of klezmer music as a marker of Jewish identity also provided a major impetus for my approach, as well as a major motivation for my graduate studies in ethnomusicology.[4] Indeed, this early literature on the "revival" showed how the new resurgence of Yiddish dance music provided a kind of sound track for the reawakening of American ethnic identity and the sense of its being linked to *yidishkayt* (cultural "Jewishness"), including Old Country Jewish culture and the Jewish immigrant experience, a heady mix of nostalgia, romanticism, and a sense of longing.[5] Over the next few years, I heard Brave Old World play at the Krakow Jewish Heritage festival in 1995, where klezmorim Michael Alpert and Stuart Brotman also jammed with traditional Carpathian mountain fiddlers. I took lessons from the Klezmatics' violinist Alicia Svigals, who honed her approach to the klezmer fiddle by performing a variety of folk and ethnic styles, including Greek popular music. At the same time, I puzzled over The Klezmorim's Balkan-brass-band-as-klezmer sounds and perused thoughtful e-mails from Lev Liberman about the band's meanderings at Balkan camps and the vibrant, chaotic Venice Beach, California, performance scene. Slobin's notion of eclecticism, explored in his early articles on the klezmer revival, certainly fits here. Slobin, along with Barbara Kirshenblatt-Gimblett (see chapter 7 of this volume), convincingly illustrates how klezmer has accommodated a range of forms, including eastern European, Western art music, and jazz.

However, there is no consensus among scholars and musicians on the minimum requirements for being a specialist on the klezmer circuit. These might include a broad repertoire and quick reflexes for audience response. The implied credo of eclecticism suggests that just about any kind of musics have the potential to be included in the klezmer musician's arsenal. In practice, however, musicians create their own mixture of styles, sounds, and possibilities for musical expression, and these processes have been little studied and understood. The musician's training, background, religious orientation, and musical knowledge come into play. I understand the complexity and variety of the klezmer genre not so much as a product of eclecticism, but as ways that performers make choices and negotiate meaning in sound and spectacle. Kirshenblatt-Gimblett's use of Raymond Williams's "changing structures of feeling" in accounting for the sensibilities of klezmer musicians prompts our interest in knowing more about what musicians play and what they do.[6] Like their counterparts—the Klezmatics, John Zorn's Masada, and David Krakauer's Klezmer Madness—the two groups whose work I discuss here have helped to manipulate sounds and signifiers of art music and Jewish authenticity in a way that ultimately helped to reconfigure klezmer music beyond its traditional reception as ethnic heritage music. This musical current begins in the freewheeling environment of the California performance scene of the 1970s with The Klezmorim.

THE KLEZMORIM: RUBBER CHICKENS, RHETORIC, AND RADICALISM

The Klezmorim, founded in 1975 in Berkeley, California, was one of the first Yiddish bands to become active in arranging, recording, and touring, and certainly the first to use the word *klezmer* in its name.[7] Around the same time on the East Coast, "revivalist" bands such as Kapelye and the Klezmer Conservatory Band began rallying for the inclusion of klezmer in mainstream Jewish consciousness, following decades of neglect.[8] The Klezmorim began to recognize in klezmer the ingredients of an irreverent, idiosyncratic, and distinctly California counterculture. Unlike Kapelye and the Klezmer Conservatory Band, both groups that have tended to focus exclusively on Yiddish dance music and Yiddish theater tunes, The Klezmorim latched onto a diverse repertoire, of which Yiddish dance music of eastern European Jews was a single part.[9] This repertoire, as Liberman describes it, had its origins in "our early experiments with tight ensemble playing, improvisation, klezmer/jazz fusions, neo-klezmer composition, street music, world beat, and New Vaudeville." [10]

According to Liberman and his colleagues, Stuart Brotman and Michael Alpert of Brave Old World, the heady environment for musicians living on the West Coast during the 1970s inspired these experiments. There, Jewish music mainly thrived within other subcultures: the alternative acoustic music community, the Dixieland revival, and the world music scene. The streets of San Francisco, especially the area around Fisherman's Wharf and the Cannery, regularly came alive with experimental performances. Two members of The Klezmorim frequently played al fresco: Rick Elmore, a.k.a. Professor Gizmo, the One-Man Band, and Brian Wishnefsky, a.k.a. Hairy James, the Trumpet-Playing Gorilla. [11] The Klezmorim met Gizmo while sharing the stage at the Freight and Salvage (a renowned East Bay folk club, where The Klezmorim were one of the house bands) together with R. Crumb and the Cheap Suit Serenaders. At the same time, the orientation toward musical preservationism also reverberated in the mix. San Francisco had been an outpost of the Dixieland revival, in which local groups like Turk Murphy played a significant role in promoting an older polyphonic jazz style. Liberman puts it this way: "Think of a Barbary Coast/Haight Ashbury recycled thrift-store 1920s novelty-music aesthetic." If this sounds rather noncommercial, it was so deliberately. "We had always had a kind of agit-prop/Theater of Poverty aesthetic, even in 1975 when we were first coalescing into a band and nobody cared if we lived or died." In addition, the Renaissance Faires, sponsored by the Society for Creative Anachronism, were drawing crowds of ten thousand to twenty-five thousand people. "It seems that Stuart Brotman, . . . Levy, . . . Miller and Stew Mennin [were] donning vests and playing Yiddish instrumental tunes on clarinet, sax, peckhorn, and violin."

Like the early music revival that fueled such events, the burgeoning folk music scene thrived on patronage from within academia. During the 1960s, the emerging discipline of ethnomusicology at the University of California at Los Angeles was carving out a niche for Balkan and eastern European music. One manifestation of the student performance scene was the Aman Orchestra, which toured the West Coast doing a "sort of . . . multinational extravaganza which included Bulgarian and Russian choral music, instrumental dances, wedding vignettes, etc.," as Liberman recalls. When The Klezmorim at last "discovered" Yiddish dance music, first at Berkeley's Magnes Museum, where Liberman was working in 1974, and on a set of 78s belonging to Berkeley professor Martin

Schwartz, they heard it as a more familiar strain of eastern European
and Balkan folk and popular musics. "The emotionalism intrigued us,
as did the quasi-vocal stylings of the instrumentalists. . . . [C]ertain Anatolian subsets struck our ears as kinda klezmish. The whole gestalt con-
firmed that klezmer music was a fusion music to begin with, and that
one could learn a lot about how to play it by examining the music of coincident indigenous cultures." [12]

The rough outlines of these varied influences, and an attempt to
grapple with klezmer as an instrumental vocabulary, are apparent on
The Klezmorim's early recordings. *The Klezmorim* and *East Side Wedding* (1976–78) offer a mix of Serbian, Romanian, Greek, and Jewish
tunes. By 1981, the Grammy-award–nominated album *Metropolis* (for
"best ethnic, traditional or folk recording") marked the group's transformation from a string band (in the mold of the Cheap Suit Serenaders)
to an urban brass band. In those days, the band's top priority was re-
fining the role of collective improvisation, to make it happen in the
rhythm parts and internal lines as well as in the solo lead. Rehearsals in
the early eighties were rigorous exercises aimed at improving ensemble
playing and spontaneity. [13]

> Call-and-response exchanges, round-robin doinas, transposing to new keys
> on the fly. We knew from literature and history that the old-time klezmorim
> improvised, and that their general demeanor was kinda flamboyant. We lis-
> tened to 78s hundreds of times in an effort to understand how the klezmer
> players THOUGHT. We listened to what they listened to. We tried to play their
> music from the inside, as if reinventing it. We played the way they would have
> played if they'd been us. We also flirted with minimalism . . . African rhythms,
> Schoenberg, Prokofiev, Stravinsky, and free form, collective composition. . . .
> Horns, Constantinopolitan, improvisational, urban, jazz. [14]

Toward the mid 1980s, The Klezmorim began plotting a new kind of
rigorously theatrical stage presentation. Folk music performance, Liberman believes, had been overdetermined and fossilized by the "pretensions of an ethnomusicological style of presentation, i.e., 'this next tune
from the Skopje region of Macedonia is played in 13/8 time, and the lyrics describe the curdling of goat cheese in February.'" [15] The Santa Cruz
and Berkeley street scenes offered plenty of inspiration in the burgeoning fields of experimental outdoor performance, and Northern California's generally sunny weather cooperated. In 1984, The Klezmorim
joined forces with a group well known on the Venice boardwalk, the Flying Karamazov Brothers. Their joint theatrical run combined juggling
with brass-band music. Recalls Liberman, "These guys' bizarre humor

left its mark on us permanently. We loved performing in fezzes and tossing rubber chickens into the crowd. . . . Yes, we did conduct a mock Socialist rally, holy-roller revivalist meeting, and kabuki drama onstage." [16]

The collaboration with the Karamazovs provoked The Klezmorim to new levels of antic in their own performances.

> We moved constantly on stage because we were a 6-piece band playing 9- or 10-piece arrangements. Essentially, everybody played bass lines, rhythm, counter-rhythm, melody, harmony, and counter-melody. . . . [E]ach of these functions would require a different physical alignment onstage—mostly so we could hear one another and maintain eye contact . . . but also to help the audience see what they were hearing. . . . [W]e pulsed like Betty Boop cartoon characters . . . to synchronize sight and sound. And then you know, it dawned on us that the moves made us interesting—i.e., correlated with vast improvements in our sex lives—we got into this competitive macho thing and became absolutely shameless. So we'd run onstage and play in midair, and hold high notes 'til we turned blue, and use our horns as swords and oars and telescopes and whatnot. [17]

These techniques come to the fore in their album *Jazz-Babies of the Ukraine* (1986), a hodgepodge of musical themes, quotations, and shtick from the live show that generates a kind of surreal antibiography for the band.

> We started out as members of two rival bands, in the city of Minsk, 1905. The police charged us with attempted music, and attempted to revoke our artistic license. We took refuge in the Minsk Opera House. There, we murdered the classics, and once again became fugitives from justice. So we stowed away aboard the mysterious Orient Express and had a hair-raising brush with Bulgarian royalty. We got off the train in New York City and got a straight shot of Harlem jazz. I remember it all as if it really happened. [18]

The Klezmorim stage this cartoonish slapstick through narration, sound effects, and music. The resulting chain of parodies links vignettes with brief quotations from opera, waltz, tango, and Bulgarian and Yiddish dance music. Offset by the sounds of speeding trains and other dramatic sound effects reproduced on percussion and brass, these are woven together tightly, occurring in seamless, rapidfire succession like a cartoon sound track. As the "conductor" announces the final stop in Harlem, The Klezmorim invite their audience to imagine themselves as a Cotton Club audience. There follows the only complete song performance in this segment, Cab Calloway's novelty hit "Minnie the Moocher." Thus the journey that began with a disgraced klezmer band's expulsion from the Old World culminates in an exuberant jazz performance drawing on

features common to both big-band jazz and klezmer music: the collective improvisation of a densely polyphonic texture.

This kind of spectacle enabled The Klezmorim to break out of the
"moribund folk circuit" and into musical theater, concert halls, music
festivals, arts residencies, national TV, rock, and jazz arenas. Says Liberman, "It made us visually appealing, it was a media hook. It made us
not just a band but an event."[19] In a sense, sequences like the one on
Jazz-Babies allow The Klezmorim to consider their own reception by the
public and to spoof routine publicity and press coverage.

As Liberman describes it, the event did not really work for their Jewish audiences. The Klezmorim did reach some Jewish listeners, although
mostly of the atypical variety, by playing a venue known as Ashkenaz in
Berkeley in the 1970s. Founded in 1973 and modeled after a Polish Jewish wooden synagogue, it served as a center for eastern European folk
dancing and musicmaking for Yiddish and related cultures. In fact, the
strongest showing of enthusiasm for The Klezmorim came from Europe.
Beginning in the 1980s, the group relocated to Paris, where they found
themselves "minor pop stars in Europe."[20] By Liberman's account, The
Klezmorim had finally found listeners who could accept the juxtaposi-
tion of performance art with Jewish folk music. Unlike the American
Jewish audience, which brought to the music certain expectations of
"authenticity" based on what they had heard from older recordings and
at celebrations, the European audiences brought few preconceived no-
tions to their hearing of the music. According to Liberman, they could
simply enjoy the blend of klezmer and shtick. In Liberman's terms, the
relationship of the Jewish community to Jewish music posed a problem.

> I think it's significant, and a sign of those times, that most [Jewish musical
> colleagues] were playing every kind of music in the world except Jewish. In
> the 1970s, the Jewish music scene in America was freighted with all kinds of
> agendas—political, ideological, religious—which drove away some talented
> musicians. Basically, every Jewish music gig was about something besides mu-
> sic: a wedding, a religious ceremony, a political rally, a holiday, the grand
> opening of a deli, yadda, yadda. . . . [B]y and large, the music was simplistic
> and boring and hackneyed and was played perfunctorily or amateurishly, and
> the musicians were treated like coolies.[21]

Indeed, The Klezmorim thought they subjected themselves to further
scorn for not sounding Jewish or traditional enough, said Liberman. Yet
Liberman argues that their antics with rubber chickens did nothing to
compromise the authenticity of the music: "At some level, I remained a
folk purist and amateur musicologist. . . . [W]e honestly tried like hell to

penetrate the mindset of the old players, and do what they would have done . . . if they'd been us."[22] However, Liberman does recall that the band "went over terrifically well with African American audiences in jazz venues in the Bay Area. . . . I think they dug the bluesey modes and ensemble playing . . . and with East Indians. I am convinced that there's a klezmer/Indian connection via the Gypsies."[23]

The Klezmorim drew upon a vast range of sounds and genres and a broadly theatrical approach to musicmaking. Above all, their music staged their commitment to virtuosity and mastery of many different kinds of music. On some occasions, they led the audience to question their expectations of a reverent presentation of Jewish folk traditions. On others, they offended their listeners and fellow musicians, some of whom have commented to me that The Klezmorim played neither Jewish music nor klezmer. The Klezmorim never reconciled their often-tangled arguments about their authenticity and purism, and they reveled in the art of making manifestos. Eventually, as Liberman himself admits, these manifestos escalated into shrill and incomprehensible rants that were lost on their followers.[24]

The Klezmorim's unique performance style provides a cornerstone for what followed in the work of other bands, including Brave Old World. Like The Klezmorim, Brave Old World considered themselves to be in the vanguard. But Brave Old World presented their music in a way that came across as more refined, polished, and palatable, owing to its references to high art and classical music, and their struggle to shape their message for the audience.

BRAVE OLD WORLD: "NEWISH" MUSIC

Partly sharing The Klezmorim's roots in California counterculture, the quartet Brave Old World (Michael Alpert, vocals/violin; Stuart Brotman, bass; Kurt Bjorling, clarinet and cimbalom; Alan Bern, musical director, piano/accordion) also draws upon a startlingly wide range of sounds and performance styles. The early careers of Brave Old World's band members Alpert and Brotman strikingly parallel those of players in The Klezmorim. Brotman, a bassist, was a member of the Los Angeles–based band Kaleidoscope, founded by David Lindley. Since its founding in 1966, Kaleidoscope had experimented with an array of styles: jug-band, folk-rock, and an early prototype of world music fusion.

While The Klezmorim honed a theatrical performance aesthetic that drew on *Jewish* as a single category of historical phenomena, Brave Old

World's music privileges a complex philosophy of musical Jewishness: "In my view, the value of 'musicality' and 'creativity' [has] equal priority to that of 'Jewishness.' True, we wanted to leave behind all two-dimensional caricatures of Jews and Jewish music (kitschy, weepy, wacky, etc.) and restore a three-dimensional sensibility based on the variety and depth of Jewish culture. But not as 'authentic re-creators,' rather as creative contemporary musicians."[25] Bern's comment suggests that the band's notion of Jewish heritage forms the basis for larger and broader self-perceptions as artists. Brave Old World emerged from linking two collaborations: Joel Rubin and Alan Bern in Europe, and Michael Alpert and Stuart Brotman in the United States.[26] Rubin, a clarinetist who had studied at the California Institute of the Arts and the Music Conservatory at SUNY Purchase, was seeking a departure from the "monotony of the classical music world."[27] His family musical lineage (his biographical statement accounts for cantors and musicians in his ancestry) prompted him to explore Jewish music. Several years before Rubin had approached him about the possibility of forming a duet, Bern had left the Klezmer Conservatory Band and decided not to perform klezmer anymore.

> I was already unhappy with the artistic aims and level of existing [klezmer] bands. . . . There just wasn't enough musical care. So that the shared common language settled into something very unnuanced. . . . [I was also] frustrated at not having enough creative room for myself as pianist and accordionist in a music where those instruments had a rigid and restricted role to play, and I'd become more interested in developing my theoretical interests. . . . Joel turned out to be a fine clarinetist who was happy to play the melody rock solid while I noodled around like crazy. So the association with Joel set loose a chain of events that changed my life.[28]

Soon after this pivotal encounter, the pair decided to form a band, linking up with Stuart Brotman and Michael Alpert, who (like Bern and Rubin) had also played Bulgarian music during the 1970s and were linked to the UCLA ethnomusicology scene. Like Rubin, both Alpert and Brotman came from strongly identified Jewish and musical families (Brotman's maternal grandfather stemmed from a long line of Romanian cantors), and their route to a discovery of Jewish music clearly began with the Balkan music and dance scene. Brotman says:

> At Balkan camps, a number of us found ourselves jamming Jewish tunes. When Kaleidoscope dissolved, my wife and I went to Europe, sleeping in the back of a car every night. I recorded village bands in Romania at twilight, and

the music felt so Yiddish-inflected. I had a sound in my head when I came back, and when I played it for people, it fit into the Jewish tunes that people knew from Kammen. People started playing them at Balkan camps, and passed them around among friends.[29]

Alpert says that the eclectic strains of musicmaking were shaped by a distinctly home-grown attitude: "It was a very L.A. thing, what was coming together. A lot of us played Russian and East European music, because it was organic to the community. There was a consciousness of a smorgasbord or panoply of ethnic musics. I also grew up with Mexican music."[30]

Indeed, while Alpert and Brotman were aware of the Jewish heritage of klezmer, they never identified with that music themselves, at least not until they realized that what their coreligionists were playing at celebrations couldn't be further from the "real thing." Alpert remembers passing through a large catering hall in Los Angeles on the way to a birthday party. "We passed by a room that had a sign announcing the Goldman-Silverman wedding. The doors swung open, and suddenly what came out was a band playing Stevie Wonder's 'You Are the Sunshine.' I was a hippie, and we didn't go to weddings. I thought, holy shit! It's the seventies, and this is what they're playing at Jewish functions!"

If the Jewish community's mainstream musical tastes were unpalatable, their right-wing politics were intolerable. As an actively gigging musician, Brotman had been hired to play a number of Israeli fundraising events in the Jewish community, until a realization stopped him in his tracks.

> An Israeli consul general described Israeli political outreach to the guests: "Thanks for your contributions, which help us buy bombs and planes to kill Arabs." I thought, "These are not my people." That made me realize that I didn't feel comfortable anymore with an Israeli-Jewish identification. The West Coast Jewish community was starting to turn religious, and move to the right politically. While the East Coast supports different Jewish communities, in California you were in the straitjacket of an Israeli-oriented community, and everyone else was disenfranchised.[31]

Brotman and Alpert realized then that klezmer music could be a Yiddish-rooted alternative to the middle-class Jewish mainstream of the time, with all of its Israeli resonance. "I wanted to re-Ashkenize the culture scene here," says Brotman, "and klezmer was the way to do it." Throughout the 1980s, both Brotman and Alpert were active in the klezmer scene. Brotman played with Ellis Island in the Bay Area, while

Alpert was in New York's Kapelye, one of the first klezmer bands to tour internationally.

Shortly after it was formed in 1989, Brave Old World became one of the most visible and groundbreaking klezmer groups on the international scene. While they play much that could be considered traditional Yiddish dance repertoire, neither the term *klezmer* nor the commonly used prefix *klez-* are in the band's title. Indeed, their instrumentation and the absence of a drummer is more evocative of a classical chamber music ensemble than a klezmer group. The billing of Bern as musical director is also a kind of classical signifier, as well as a way of formally structuring Bern's and the group members' creative contributions to the compositional process. As Bern explains, "It rarely happens that someone brings in a finished arrangement to teach the others. Usually someone brings in a text or melody and through an improvisation process [that] I direct we create an arrangement together." [32] Indeed, the refined, worked-out quality of their arrangements and their chamber music–like texture is part of what makes Brave Old World unique. Explains Alpert, "In taking a musical tradition from wedding hall to concert stage, we augmented the instrumental repertoire with related Yiddish song traditions and brought our diverse musical sensibilities to bear on it." [33] One of Brave Old World's contributions to the contemporary Jewish music scene is to present itself as a different kind of band. Brave Old World does not like to use the word *klezmer* to describe the category of music it plays. "I think it should be called 'newish' music," remarks Alpert.

Brave Old World has released three of its own albums: *Klezmer Music, Beyond the Pale,* and *Blood Oranges.* [34] Michael Alpert has served as musical director for two klezmer compilation albums featuring Itzhak Perlman, as well as the PBS documentary program *In the Fiddler's House.* Perhaps the most significant of all their work is the 1994 album *Beyond the Pale,* featuring the band's arrangements of traditional Yiddish dance tunes as well as original vocal and instrumental compositions. *Beyond the Pale* is built around a core of what might be characterized as traditional Jewish material: Hasidic melody ("A Tish-Nign," "Bobover Wedding March"), Yiddish ballads ("Borsht," "Di Sapozhkelekh"), and dance tunes ("Brave Old Hora"). The album opens with Alpert and Bern's composition, "Berlin Overture," which is reprised at the end. The last three numbers make up an original suite that draws together the band's experiences of both familiar and exotic musical places. "Rufn Di Kinder Aheym" ("Calling the Children Home") is described in the liner notes as a jazz-flavored, Buddy Bolden–influenced reinterpretation of a Jewish wedding march. "Doina Extravaganza" is a suite of klezmer tunes, beginning with a *doina*, a traditional eastern European solo improvisation. The doina is divided into four solos, and the sections of the solos are linked by unison melodies drawn from the material that follows. While the traditional doina centers on limited, formulaic improvisations for a solo instrumentalist, Bern and Bjoerling instead shape their doina into spectacular extended group improvisations.

The opening piece on the album, "Berlin Overture," is built around a simple melody in waltz time that evokes a tune from the Yiddish folk song or theater repertoire. This evolves into a fully elaborated chamber music piece, featuring Bern on piano and Alpert on guitar. Bern fills his accompaniment with rhapsodic arpeggios and flourishes, emphasizing the dark lower registers. Alpert sings the words with conviction, infusing his lavish musical surroundings with directness and immediacy. The Yiddish words describe the experiences of an American Jew casing the Berlin marketplace and observing Gypsies and refugees from Turkey and Poland. The narrator realizes that his own people once found themselves in the same predicament. "Berlin Overture" closes these somewhat fragmentary observations with the injunction, "Sing, my fiddle, sing a sweet Diaspora song," to which Alpert's violin responds with a mournful obbligato. In the album's interior sections, composed of traditional eastern European folk material, "Sweet Diaspora Song" bubbles to the surface in material drawn from Jewish weddings, Sabbath *zmirot* (table songs), and other traditional settings. Paired with these exuberant commentaries on the strength and vitality of Jewish musical heritage and homeland are some thoughts of a different nature. "Imagine the Holocaust never happened," read the song notes to Stuart Brotman's elegant, gossamer-textured composition, "Waltz Român à Clef." "You're on a cruise ship on the Danube. Erik Satie on piano and Joseph Moskowitz on cymbalom are the house band. It's the last waltz of the evening. . . ."[35]

"Berlin 1990" reprises the opening number. The words extend the fleeting observations at the Berlin marketplace into a more elaborate meditation on what it is like to play "here in Germany" and earn the admiration of "today's children of yesterday's enemy." But Alpert also comments that his own heritage, and his own fate, consequently, is tied to that of the "enemy": "If not for the wars, pogroms, slaughter / I too would have been Europe's progeny."[36] At the end of the song, Alpert elegizes the guestworkers and immigrants of Germany, drawing a parallel between the prewar pogroms and contemporary demonstrations of anti-foreigner sentiment. Framed by the two Berlin pieces, the album chronicles a mythical sonic journey, traveling between history and dream, concluding with a dissonant strain of reality in present-day Germany. In fact, Alpert recycles a harangue from a real-life "xenophobic Frankfurt cabbie": "*Was wollen Sie hier in Deutschland?*" ("What do you want here in Germany?") Indeed, Alpert and Bern themselves have played the part of guestworkers: until recently, Bern was a resident of Germany, where he also worked as musical director in theater, and Alpert has spent much time there and is married to a German woman.

The German phrase forms a single part of Brave Old World's rich palette of languages. Michael Alpert and his fellow band members are all native English-speakers, but Yiddish plays a special role in *Beyond the Pale.* Alpert, Bern, and Brotman were raised in Yiddish-speaking homes, and Yiddish is indeed the "language of home," compared to those klezmer albums that confine themselves to instrumental pieces. For the folk songs, Yiddish texts are given with transliteration and English translation. The album's title is translated into Yiddish on the cover. Hebrew words slice through the Yiddish texts in the form of fleeting references to prayer and *halakha* (Jewish law). In "Berlin 1990," Alpert follows the first line, "I've played here in Germany, many's the time," with a line from the traditional *havdalah* service (separating the Sabbath from the weekday), *hamavdil beyn koydesh lekol,* or "he who divides the sacred from the worldly." Invoking his own Jewish past, Alpert invokes a Hebrew-Yiddish epithet used as a term of respect for a dead person, *zikhroyne levrokhe* (of blessed memory).

As Brave Old World mix and match languages and styles, they pursue a distinct agenda—the Polish song, meditations on the Holocaust and Jews, and Roma ("gypsies") and Turks in contemporary Germany—and they address themselves to explicit political concerns. The album's back cover offers the Yiddish dedication, *Gevidmet di ale iber der velt, vus zey kemfn far pluralistishe gezelshaftn,* or "to all those everywhere who strive for just and pluralistic societies." As musicians playing Jewish music, as both guestworkers and welcome visitors and entrepreneurs in present-day Germany, Brave Old World comments on the nature of power structures (Nazism, the New Europe, xenophobia, etc.). But as secularists and non-Zionists, they offer an alternative mode of Jewish consciousness. The album's rhetoric severs Yiddish language and Yiddish music from their nostalgic, "schmaltzy" connotations, instead linking them to the development of anti-Zionist sentiment and radical political consciousness. Hebrew and the imagery of traditional Judaism are offered only with a trace of wistful irony and only as fragmentary memo-

ries. In *Beyond the Pale,* traditional klezmer sounds interlock with Western classical and pop idioms to create a dense texture. Political messages
mingle with sounds and textures aimed at good craftsmanship and aesthetic pleasure for its own sake. As Alpert puts it, "We are trying to
make a world-class artistic statement rooted in Jewish music." [37]

Performing the music from *Beyond the Pale,* and from their more
recent album *Blood Oranges* (1997), for the concert stage, Brave Old
World encounters a different set of issues: how to present a music for celebration in fixed-seating halls where the audience may be more passive
than at a Jewish celebration. "My basic conviction is that performing
decontextualized Jewish music on a concert stage is artificial, and the
concert stage is [both] too determinate and too impoverished to simply
let the music 'take care of itself.' That means considering what we do
at a performance, with everything that implies about staging, lighting,
presentation and even how we contextualize the performance for the audience." [38] Brave Old World sometimes feels that the North American
Jewish community is not interested in hearing a performance, as the let-
ter from the synagogue director cited above indicates. In fact, the group
is busiest touring in Europe, especially Germany, "where people want
art and klezmer." [39] "At a concert we did [in New York's] Merkin Hall
in 1994, a friend was selling our CDs at intermission, and a woman told
her that she wanted more klezmer and less art. We talk about getting a
'walking ovation' from Jewish audiences" (Alpert 1997). The tide may
be changing, however. Since their mid-1990s collaboration with Itzhak
Perlman, Brave Old World has had requests for more performances at
home in the United States and in Canada. Concerts at large synagogues,
once a rarity, have been turning up on their schedules, and Alpert spoke
triumphantly of a Jewish community center concert in Houston where
the audience seemed to appreciate "deep yiddishkayt . . . speaking to
what they'd expect from a chamber or jazz concert, as well as to the Jewish part." [40] And the outcome of that contract with the Toronto synagogue? As it turned out, the congregation's worries were justified. No
dancing or singing took place, but the band received both standing ova-
tions and warm praise from synagogue officials.[41]

If The Klezmorim chose to label themselves with the Hebrew/Yiddish
word for klezmer musicians, embracing its outsider connotations, Brave
Old World chooses to make a music that often blends and harmonizes
different musical ideas and ideologies. Clearly, The Klezmorim and Brave
Old World have played an important role in mediating the transition of
klezmer music from its role as expression of Jewish American identity to

a palette that is both richer and more confusing. Mark Slobin describes the conflicts that result when musicians blur the boundaries between "banding," where musicians explore the roles of "musical adventurers" and "ambassadors to the superculture," and "bonding," where musicians link themselves to an affinity group, such as the Toronto synagogue.[42] The musicians discussed here recognize themselves both as bearers of Jewish culture and as artists fully conscious of their unique, idiosyncratic musical sensibilities.

As the locus of klezmer performance has shifted away from life-cycle events to staged concerts, klezmer groups have explored new ways of engaging a sedentary audience. The Klezmorim's tactic, as seen, was to create live events as frantic and busy as three-ring circuses, with live albums to match. Brave Old World also treats the klezmer concert as a kind of theatrical event. In doing so they have refined their own approach, in which classical structural devices such as overtures and finales frame fluid, seamless numbers. As The Klezmorim orchestrated and even costumed their presentations, they choreographed their own version of spontaneous revelry. Klezmer groups sometimes find themselves struggling to make their music meaningful within the space between Jewish celebration and formal concert.

In this liminal space, klezmer stages the tensions between Jewish music's particularity as ethnic music and its inclination toward fusions with rock, jazz, world beat, and classical idioms. The Klezmorim set the stage for this drama. Their strategy was to ventriloquize the Jewish musical experience, that is, to signify it indirectly through the sounds they drew from Balkan peoples, Gypsies, and American jazz musicians and composers such as Duke Ellington. Brave Old World has availed themselves of an equally broad musical palette. But in contrast to The Klezmorim, they are especially drawn to the music's particularity as "Jewish"-sounding. Where to find this Jewishness and how to perform it is by no means a clear-cut endeavor. The two bands have drawn on new sources of yiddishkayt not traditionally explored by klezmer musicians, such as Yiddish labor songs and revolutionary anthems and art music, and they have even incorporated strains of new Israeli-Sephardic pop and other "oriental" musics. These groups expanded the boundaries of klezmer, which people have conventionally associated exclusively with the eastern European Jewish and American immigrant experience. The "schmaltz-free" label on Brave Old World's *Beyond the Pale* marks their desire to subvert an overtly nostalgic approach to the presentation of klezmer. Negotiating the chasm between the margin and the mainstream, between the fusion and the melting pot idioms, is a major risk. It has prompted many (especially the Klezmatics) to posit an alternative legitimacy denied them in mainstream writings on klezmer music (see chapters 10 and 11 in this volume).

Finally, klezmer musicians have confronted the tension between their commitment to cultural work and their need for personal artistic expression in the music. The positive affirmation of Jewishness in the rhetoric of Brave Old World (and the Klezmatics) is linked to support for causes such as gay rights. Brave Old World's musical meditations on the contemporary klezmer as drifter, refugee, and champion of dreams of liberation addresses itself to broad, humanistic concerns by expressing solidarity with "all those who strive for just and pluralistic societies." In line with this idealistic viewpoint, The Klezmorim impressed on its audiences the potential of this music to sound fresh, original, and idiosyncratic. These undertakings carry a certain risk that the blend of multiple modes of expression will be lost on audiences. Brave Old World has followed this example, leaning toward lyrical, rhapsodic statements laden with arpeggios and other classical flourishes. This band especially showcases the talents of its musical director, Alan Bern, who creates carefully structured, seamless musical events inspired by large-scale classical symphonies and operas and crafted in collaboration with the other band members.[43]

How is it that a symbol of Old World crudeness can be transformed into symbols of diversity and universality, and of artistic freedom? Klezmorim enjoy not only freedom of expression, but greater freedom of geographical movement as they tour increasingly in Germany, Poland, and the former Soviet Union and, recently, to Latin America and South Africa. This spreading popularity is an official acknowledgment of an unofficial art form, one with the power to rally intense feeling and interest on the part of listeners, viewers, and album buyers. Brave Old World works over the klezmer's image, purifying it so that it can become a symbol fit for ethnic and transnational identity. The Klezmorim's refusal to launder its image and to cater to the audience's expectations of klezmer caused many pitfalls in their music and career.

As Kirshenblatt-Gimblett has pointed out in chapter 7, sensibilities have transformed. And so has the practice of klezmer bands. Neither outcast from nor index to Jewish identity, klezmer musicians find themselves a valued, if appropriated and somewhat anomalous, symbol of Jewishness. If the contradictions prove to be combustible, they reach a dead end, like The Klezmorim. If they are successful, like Brave Old

World, they may effect personal transformations from the role of klezmer musician to the status of artists while still embodying the notion of a strong Jewish collective identity.

NOTES

1. Alan Bern, "From Klezmer to New Jewish Music: The Musical Evolution of Brave Old World," *Mens en Melodie* 1 (1998): n.p.

2. Mark Slobin, *Subcultural Sounds: Micromusics of the West* (Hanover, N.H.: University Press of New England, 1993), 98.

3. Henry Sapoznik with Pete Sokolov, *The Compleat Klezmer* (Cedarhurst, N.Y.: Tara Publications, 1987).

4. See Mark Slobin, "Fiddler off the Roof: Klezmer as an Ethnic Musical Style," in *The Jews of North America,* ed. Morris Rischin (Detroit: Wayne State University Press, 1987), 95–104, and Mark Slobin, "Klezmer Music: An American Ethnic Genre," *Yearbook for Traditional Music* 16 (1984): 34–41.

5. See also Lynn Dion, "Klezmer Music in America: Revival and Beyond," *Jewish Folklore and Ethnology Review* 8, no. 1–2 (1986): 2–8.

6. Barbara Kirshenblatt-Gimblett, chapter 7 in this volume, and Raymond Williams, *Marxism and Literature* (New York: Oxford University Press, 1977).

7. I use the past tense throughout for The Klezmorim because the group disbanded in the mid 1990s. David Thornton took over as group leader from Lev Liberman, who left the group in 1988.

8. I use the term *revivalist* because these bands focus on Yiddish dance music repertoire and, occasionally, Yiddish theater tunes, and they often emulate the style of first-generation klezmer musicians in the America of the 1920s and 1930s.

9. Clarinetist Kurt Bjoerling is not Jewish. He has spoken, though, of how he identifies with Jewish culture by way of his Dutch relatives, who hid Jews during World War II.

10. Lev Liberman, "Memories of the Klez Revival and 'The Klezmorim,'" http://www.well.com/user/ari/klez/articles/klezmorim.hist.html (30 November 1995); see also Sources, Internet Resources, under Ari Davidow.

11. Material in this paragraph drawn from Liberman, "Memories of the Klez Revival"; information within quotes comes from Lev Liberman, personal e-mail correspondence with author, 22 April 1997.

12. Material in this paragraph within quotes comes from Lev Liberman, personal e-mail correspondence with author, 30 March 1997 and 2 April 1997.

13. The Klezmorim, *The Klezmorim: First Recordings, 1976–78* (Arhoolie CD 309, re-release 1989), *East Side Wedding* (Arhoolie 3006, 1977), and *Metropolis* (Flying Fish FF 90258, 1981).

14. Liberman, e-mail, 30 March 1997.

15. Ibid.

16. Liberman, "Memories of the Klez Revival."

17. Ibid.

18. The Klezmorim, liner notes for *Jazz-Babies of the Ukraine* (Flying Fish FF 465, 1987).

19. Lev Liberman, personal e-mail correspondence with author, 22 April 1997.

20. Ibid.

21. Ibid.

22. Liberman, "Memories of the Klez Revival."

23. Liberman, e-mail, 30 March 1997.

24. Liberman, e-mail, 22 April 1997.

25. Alan Bern, personal e-mail correspondence with author, 18 June 1999.

26. Joel Rubin left Brave Old World in 1992.

27. Joel Rubin, telephone interview with author, 17 June 1999. Further information about Rubin is available on the World Wide Web at www.ourworld .compuserve.com/homepages/simontov.

28. Alan Bern, personal e-mail correspondence with author, 15 July 1999.

29. Stuart Brotman, personal e-mail correspondence with author, 26 April 1997. The Kammen International Dance Folio series, originally published in the 1920s, are widely circulated collections of lead sheets for international music, highlighting Yiddish dance tunes; they have been reprinted.

30. Material within quotes in this paragraph and the next comes from Michael Alpert, personal e-mail correspondence with author, 15 April 1997.

31. This quotation and material within quotes in next paragraph come from Brotman, e-mail, 26 April 1997.

32. Alan Bern, e-mail, 18 June 1999.

33. Michael Alpert's quotations in this paragraph come from Alpert, e-mail, 15 April 1997.

34. Brave Old World has released three of its own albums: *Klezmer Music* (Flying Fish FLY 560, 1990), *Beyond the Pale* (Rounder CD 3135, 1994), and *Blood Oranges* (Pinorrekk Records PRCD 3405027, 1997).

35. Liner notes for Brave Old World, *Beyond the Pale* (Rounder CD 3135, 1994).

36. Ibid.

37. Michael Alpert, personal communication with author, 1996–99.

38. Bern, e-mail, 18 June 1999.

39. Alpert, e-mail, 15 April 1997.

40. Ibid.

41. Bern, "From Klezmer to New Jewish Music," n.p.

42. Slobin, *Subcultural Sounds,* 99.

43. Bern, e-mail, 18 June 1999.

CHAPTER 10

An Insider's View

*How We Traveled from Obscurity
to the Klezmer Establishment
in Twenty Years*

FRANK LONDON

I first became actively aware of Jewish music around 1970. Majoring in African American trumpet at the New England Conservatory of Music, I was part of a larger scene loosely centered around Ran Blake's Third Stream Music Department. We studied a mixture of classical and jazz, as well as lots of other stuff—pop, folk, and ethnic musics—while developing a practical philosophy that still guides my own musical life and that of many of my peers. The idea is that one can study and assimilate the elements of *any* musical style, form, or tradition by ear. You listen over and over to a Charlie Parker solo or a Peruvian flute player and learn to replicate what you hear. We went through lots of tape players—especially those with the ability to play music at half speed. We became cultural consumers. No music was off-limits.

Assorted theme concerts were organized, including a concert of Jewish music. Hankus Netsky invited me to join in an ensemble performing a few klezmer and Yiddish vocal tunes. I was already playing salsa, Balkan, Haitian, and other musics. Why not Jewish? It's interesting; people assume there's some connection, I must have been brought up Jewish—no, no. My parents spoke English. Any association I had with Jewish music was corny.

As was the usual practice of the day, all the band members received cassettes of the songs—repertoire or "rep" tapes—from old 78s whose level of surface noise made the task of learning parts akin to deciphering hieroglyphics without the Rosetta stone. It was insane, but you get

Figure 10.1   The Klezmatics. From left: David Licht, Alicia Svigals, Frank
London, Lorin Sklamberg, Matt Darriau, and Paul Morrisset. Courtesy of
Alicia Svigals and Frank London.

through it. The concert was a smash! We, a group of students with a
shared repertoire and knowledge of three—count 'em, three—Jewish
tunes, were besieged with offers to perform at concerts, parties, and
weddings. Newly named the Klezmer Conservatory Band, we rolled up
our sleeves and got down to the serious work of learning the style and nuances of klezmer and Yiddish vocal music. It really started in the middle
of nowhere: no search, no anything, three songs, a few gigs, you learn
some more songs, and then we slowly became aware that we were part
of a "scene," dubbed "the klezmer revival" by the media and others, with
groups and individuals who had been researching and performing all aspects of Yiddish music, including Kapelye, The Klezmorim, Andy Statman, Zev Feldman, Giora Feidman, and others. More often than not,
they had come to Jewish music after playing other American or eastern
European folk musics. It's interesting that, twenty years later, many of
the newer bands contain alumni from that first generation of bands.

I believe that for myself, and many of my peers whom I've spoken to,
the focus was on trying to play the music, trying to play it well, trying to get better on the nuances. Others were saying, "Oh, that's not
why you were trying to do it; you're carrying on your ancestors' legacy,
you're reigniting this torch that went out"—they were getting very heavy

about this. But no; we were trying to play some music, make some money, and have some fun. Many of the musicians who were doing klezmer music weren't Jewish, so they weren't discovering their roots. A lot of them were in it for technical reasons, particularly the clarinetists, as in the case of Don Byron. Here was a music that was technically challenging, fun to play, and had a market.

There seemed to be an unquenchable thirst for Yiddish music, as if it could fill the void created when American Jews divested themselves of their ethnicity in order to assimilate into the mass culture. Much of our work was playing weddings for young Jews who, in the wake of *Roots* and the rise of identity politics, were seeking to redefine their own cultural and religious heritage. They were alienated aesthetically and politically from a Jewish American tradition that seemed overly schmaltzy, dominated by Israeli culture and ideas, and unrelated to the rest of their lives. This "klezmer music," played by people to whom they could relate, perfectly fit the bill.

A little over twenty years has elapsed since this scene and its first recordings emerged, and now there are dozens if not hundreds of bands playing Yiddish music. Klezmer is Jewish music; it has gone from an underused term to being overgeneralized. Now young people come up to me after a concert and say they grew up with klezmer music. This means their parents are basically my age and listened to our recordings for the last seventeen or twenty years, so they grew up actually listening to klezmer music, a statement that used to apply only to people over sixty whose parents were from "the Old Country" and who grew up hearing Yosele Rosenblatt and Molly Picon 78s. Now "growing up with it" refers to college-age people who are as familiar with Yiddish music and culture as I am with the rock and roll and hippiedom of my youth. They feel comfortable radically reinterpreting their identity: writers create queer Jewish 'zines and thrash bands deconstruct holiday songs. I worked with a writer whose poetry used the word *klezmer* as a metaphor, a symbol as rich and intoxicating as *jazz* was for the beats. Yiddish culture has become one very strong, visible component of our postfeminist, postmodern artistic/musical/cultural/political environment.

One of the best aspects of the klezmer scene is its intergenerationality. At weddings today, the music forms a new bond between the oldest and youngest members of the family. Klezmer concerts forge an unlikely alliance between seniors and punks in rock clubs and formal concert halls. It's not unusual for a contemporary klezmer recording to feature older Jewish musicians who have been performing this music for over

fifty years alongside rock guitarists, Latin or African percussionists, and
Gypsy accordionists. Many of today's bands have had mentor relationships with older klezmer musicians: Kapelye with Sid Beckerman and the
late Leon Schwartz, the Klezmatics with Ray Musiker, Andy Statman
with Dave Tarras, Brave Old World with the late Ben Bazyler, Joel Rubin
with Max Epstein.

For some klezmer musicians, it's an outgrowth of their secular, cultural Jewish identity, while for others it's an expression of Jewish spirituality. Some people draw pride, as I do, from the secular, social activist
Yiddish song tradition, while others are drawn to mystical, trance-
inducing Hasidic nigunim. Some look for that nostalgic, warm feeling,
while others look for answers as large as the Holocaust, or why Yiddish
culture died, or why it was killed off. When you look at klezmer, particularly when you go from contemporary klezmer to the old 78s, you have
the beautiful phonographic, photographic view of the premodern era.

For many klezmorim, Jews and non-Jews, it's an exciting musical tradition, it's fun to play, and it's a source of income. That's a very strong
reason why people play klezmer, and why people call what they play
klezmer, whether it is or not. I believe this is the same as it was a hundred or two hundred years ago. You get to travel, you get to go all over
the place—Australia, Brazil, Israel, Scandinavia. There's a new resurgence I've seen coming from many parts of eastern Europe, including the
former Soviet Union. It's interesting, because it's due in equal parts to
identity issues and to economic issues. If you talk to people there, they
say, "We're playing klezmer now, because we know we can go to the
hard currency markets, and we weren't getting those gigs when we were
doing our Ukrainian folk music."

There's a big down side to all of this. A combination of self-serving
commercial interests and basic ignorance has led many music critics,
record labels, concert promoters, and even certain musicians to jump on
the bandwagon and use *klezmer* as a buzzword that refers to anything
that is remotely Jewish-identified or features a clarinet or sounds exotic
or oriental. Musician's warning: inclusion of an augmented-second in-
terval may lead to your music being labeled *klezmer.* Music that *functions* as klezmer is klezmer. If an eastern European Jewish community
needs the lambada at a wedding, then it's klezmer. This is obviously fa-
cetious, but it's a step closer than another definition I've heard, which is
that *anything* is klezmer. Klezmer is George Gershwin's "Rhapsody in
Blue" or a baby crying. However, there is no need to panic. Many of today's hard-core klezmerists are serious about studying all aspects of the

music—its history, performance practice, sociological context, and more
—and are creating a wide diversity of music that is both enjoyable and
can creditably be labeled *klezmer,* as it is clearly derived from the instrumental music that eastern European, Yiddish-speaking Jews performed
for their simkhes and other rituals.

There will always be those who claim that certain klezmorim play the
music more "traditionally," more "authentically" than others, but these
terms are open to a wide degree of interpretation. "Traditional" and "authentic" are important terms, and they're also politicized terms. They're
also power terms. I hear a lot of people trying to sell their product, the
one they like, because it's more "authentic." I can't get certain grants
because I'm not "traditional" or "authentic" enough. For me, to be traditional is to be "in the tradition." To sound like a 1925 Jewish band in
New York is to be traditional, but for me, it means to be informed by
the past and to be part of it, but to be moving into the future, to be both
part of the music, but also part of the grander scheme in which the music functions. Everything else is just someone trying to sell you something. "Tradition" does not always equal "good." Today's crop of bad
disco songs about Moshiach—ubiquitous at all religious Jewish weddings while unknown to the outside world—are totally traditional Jewish music, but who really wants to listen to them?

Often, what we think of today as "traditional" Jewish music was not
perceived as such in its own time. Jews at a *khasen*e in nineteenth-century Poland requested that the klezmorim play the contemporary, non-
Jewish polka-mazurkas and waltzes popular at the time. Today, because
they've been around long enough and were recorded by the older klezmorim, these songs are perceived as being part of the klezmer tradition
and repertoire. Maybe, in a hundred years, Kool and the Gang's "Celebration," one of the most requested songs at many simkhes I play, will
be perceived as klezmer. And what about authenticity? Don't get me
started. Suffice to say that if (as some allege) only Jews can authentically
play klezmer, then only people born 150 years ago in Europe can play
classical or Romantic music, and Yo-Yo Ma should throw away his cello.
But rumor has it that he too is starting to play klezmer.

People ask, "Why klezmer?" What many miss is that when I listen to
this music, I get aesthetically interested. It cuts through all the schlock,
all the schmaltz, all the things about Jewish music that never interested
me, all the Israeli music, all the Yiddish theater music, about all that sen-
timentality. Why klezmer music? Because it's good, just on its own terms.

CHAPTER 11

Why We Do This Anyway

Klezmer as Jewish Youth Subculture

ALICIA SVIGALS

In this chapter, I expand on some of the points Frank London has made, in his overview of the revival, regarding the variety of motivations for "reviving" klezmer among performers and audiences. I also offer my own understanding of why we're doing this to begin with. I look at the phenomenon of the klezmer revival from a sociological point of view, in the context of some larger trends in American Jewish life that have been emerging over the past two decades, and I'll speak not as a scholar presenting research (which I'm not) but as one of the participants in the phenomenon and someone who has promoted a particular use of klezmer and a direction for its future. I'll finish with my own personal klezmer manifesto.

I'm not going to try to cover all the reasons people have been drawn to klezmer, so I'm not going to talk, for example, about the fact that many musicians and listeners, both Jewish and non-Jewish, take a purely musical interest in the genre; what I'm addressing here specifically is the role of the revival in the American Jewish cultural scene.

Since the social upheavals and the ethnic-identity or "roots" movements of the 1960s and 1970s, American Jews, especially young American Jews, have been looking for new ways to negotiate our Jewishness in America. Three movements in particular have emerged that address the needs of Jews who reject the assimilationist model of the previous generation, but who haven't felt an affinity for, or haven't felt satisfied by, the Israel-centered alternative, and who want to create a new, strong sense of Jewish identity and community. I situate the klezmer revival within the framework of these three movements.

The first two are made up of Jews who identify with the progressive left. These are people who are looking for a way of being Jewish that is consonant with their feminist, gay-positive, and other new-left values and that does away with the social strictures of the past: that is, a way of being Jewish while still being themselves. They approach the problem from two very different directions.

The Havurah/Jewish Renewal approach locates the social conservatism of the traditional Jewish world in traditional Jewish culture. It selectively revives religious observance, but leaves out the traditional overtones that evoke an old-fashioned and restrictive way of life. This model conceives of religion as timeless spirituality and seeks to distill it from the culture to create a new kind of religion-centered Jewishness. Jewish renewal folks have modified the liturgy to reflect their progressive and feminist worldview and have sometimes drawn on non-Jewish sources, such as eastern religions and New Age concepts, in reworking religious material. The result is Judaism without much Yidishkayt.

The cultural secularist model, which I'll call Yiddishism, on the other hand, locates the conservatism of traditional Judaism in the religion. It looks to Ashkenazic Yiddish culture as the source of a rich Jewish identity and proposes to salvage that culture—its language, literature, and, most importantly for our purposes, its music—but for the most part discards religious observance.

These two movements clearly have their antecedents in Reform and Reconstructionist Judaism and in YIVO and Workmen's Circle Yiddishism, but the advent of the new left, ethnic consciousness, and identity politics has put a whole new spin on those old ideas.

Finally, there's the traditionalist model of the Ba'al T'shuvah movements, which embraces both the culture and the religion of the past unabashedly as a source of identity and community, without concern for the issues with which Jewish renewal and secular cultural Jews are grappling.

Of these three movements—the one that discards the culture and keeps the religion, the one that discards the religion and keeps the culture, and the one that uncritically embraces both—I would argue that the klezmer revival has been the province of the second, of the "cultural Jews." Of course, the audience for klezmer isn't limited to that group—in fact, it has a wide appeal for all kinds of Jews, not to mention plenty of non-Jews. But there's a special relationship between the klezmer revival and the secular Yiddishist movement that I want to explore here.

In fact, all three of these movements have inspired or embraced a whole range of new Jewish music, not just klezmer. The Jewish renewal movement, for example, is associated with singer Debbie Friedman, whose songs are a perfect musical reflection of the Jewish renewal philosophy: she sets religious texts, modified to reflect a feminist sensibility, to beautiful, spiritual melodies that for the most part draw on an American popular-music vocabulary. Some of her songs have an Israeli flavor, but none of them is in an eastern European Jewish idiom. Her songs are included in the liturgies of so many congregations, by the way, that many people now think of them as "traditional."

Then there are such artists as the orthodox Piementa brothers, whose music is an unselfconscious and spirited amalgam of anything and everything that appeals to them, from orthodox Jewish melodies to jazz, rock, and Middle Eastern pop, all in the service of a religious message that appeals to a modern orthodox, Ba'al T'shuvah, and Hasidic following.

But the klezmer revival has been the most vibrant and active Jewish music scene to emerge in decades, and it has provided the musical sound track for the construction of a new progressive, secular, Yiddishist youth culture. Its origins in the late 1970s can be found in the confluence of the larger American "roots" and folk music movements, "folk music" being the musical department of the alternative youth scene at that time. The musicians who initiated the klezmer revival to a large extent started out playing bluegrass, old-timey, and other American traditional music genres, and these musicians jumped at the chance to have their very own folk music (as in the famous story about Kapelye's Henry Sapoznik and his watershed conversation with elderly old-timey fiddler Tommy Jarrell, who prompted the start of Henry's klezmer journey when he asked, "Don't you people have none of your own music?"). The musical renaissance has gone hand in hand with a Yiddish language and literature "roots" revival, comprising such phenomena as the growth and success of KlezKamp and the other camps that it has inspired, the National Yiddish Book Center, the YIVO Institute for Jewish Research's summer Yiddish course, and the new Yiddish-language programs at colleges across the country. This rekindled interest in eastern European Jewish culture and the Yiddish language, which began for many as an extracurricular activity, has since turned into the cornerstone of a new Jewish identity. KlezKamp, for example, which has been the fertile crescent of the Yiddishist and klezmer renaissance for over a decade, was given a name twelve years ago that had a recreational connotation (*camp*). On the other hand, Ashkenaz, a Yiddish culture festival of more recent vintage, goes by a name that implies a nation, an ideology, and a way of life. As the participants in this renaissance have gained more cultural literacy and confidence, they've shifted their focus from study and imitation to the creation of new works of music and literature that draw on traditional material. (Ashkenaz bills itself, in fact, as a New Yiddish Culture festival and invites artists to present new works.)

There's something ironic—and very American—about the Jewish renewal and the secular Yiddishist movements, since they both depend upon a notion of the separability of religion and culture that didn't exist in traditional Jewish life. The irony jumps out when one compares, for example, Debbie Friedman's latest album and Yiddish singer Adrienne Cooper's: Friedman, whose texts are all religious, chooses not to utilize traditional Jewish musical materials, while Cooper's singing is deeply Jewish but her subject matter is almost exclusively secular. The uneasiness of this separation is reflected, in fact, in the way that people actually do float between the two movements. There is a tremendous amount of overlap (for example, I recently had the opportunity to work with Debbie Friedman when I arranged string quartet parts for her concert at Carnegie Hall and was surprised to notice a fair number of KlezKampers in the audience) and probably a lot of unarticulated desire for a community that would harmonize these two strains in Jewish life. In particular, there are many people who wish they could be culturally Jewish, spiritual, and progressive all at once. They secretly long for a congregation that would be a cross between a B'nai Jeshurun—a synagogue on Manhattan's Upper West Side that boasts progressive politics, religious tradition, a big youthful crowd, and sappy liturgical music of the Israeli Europop variety—and one of those shuls deep in the heart of Brooklyn that features great *khazones* (cantorial singing) but most decidedly doesn't marry gay couples.

Clarinetist Andy Statman's artistic development and career trajectory is an interesting illustration of this interplay of religious/cultural scenes and musical genres. He started out as a bluegrass mandolinist who then became one of the pioneers of the klezmer revival. When he turned to orthodox Judaism some years later, he expanded his musical horizons to include the music of his new community. His latest album, *Songs of Our Fathers* (which he recorded with former bluegrass colleague David Grisman), incorporates both repertoires and offers in its title a poetic reflection of the Ba'al T'shuvahs' comfort with the values, and in particular the gender roles, of the past: the music is identified with their fathers, but dedicated in the liner notes to their mothers, in a respectful but separate arrangement.

In a conversation I had recently with Mark Slobin, he brought up the question of why klezmer is considered an appropriate musical choice for progressive secular American Jews. The old-time klezmorim themselves, after all, weren't necessarily the most progressive of individuals. I think it's because, given the inextricable nature of religion in traditional Jewish culture (in the language, in the rhythm of daily life), klezmer instrumental music, being textless, is as close as we can get to secular Jewish music, along with Yiddish folk, theater, and art song—which, not surprisingly, have also been included in the repertoire of the klezmer revival. Although this may not be true of all the individuals in it, as a movement, the revival has been staunchly secular. When religious sources are drawn upon, like cantorial singing or Yiddish Hasidic folk songs, their appeal is basically as cultural artifacts. That's the spirit, for example, in which KlezKamp programs religious material—as an official stance, the approach is ethnographic, although the individual campers' relationship to the material might not necessarily be that detached. In this sense, the revival is a true descendant of the YIVO. Many secular revivalists find an apt metaphor for what they're doing in the fact that old-time klezmorim irreverently but affectionately took liturgical melodies and turned them into upbeat dance tunes. In reality, though, this practice was an expression not of opposition to religion but of total comfort with it and reflects the integration of religion into Jewish life.

I started out by describing how American Jews have been looking for new ways to be more Jewish. I think one can also say, though, that these progressive Jewish movements are the newest expression of a long-standing desire to find specifically Jewish ways to be more American. According to Walter Zev Feldman in his article on the origin of the bulgar (chapter 6 in this volume), the fascination the immigrant generation of American Jews felt at the beginning of this century for Jewish music and culture of Romanian provenance (which, he argues, led to the birth of the music we now call *klezmer*) reflected the notion that Romanian Jewish society, like the mainstream American society the immigrants sought to enter, was a freer, looser, less socially restrictive place than the rest of Jewish Eastern Europe. An identification with Romanian Jewish culture therefore connoted a hipper and more American way of being Jewish (in fact, Feldman argues that this was the real contemporary meaning of the

song "Rumania, Rumania," which today we think of as pure and silly
nostalgia). A few decades later, klezmer music and Yiddish culture in
general went into decline as American Jews became enamored of Israeli
culture, learning modern Hebrew and Israeli folk dancing, and in general making Israel the focal point and major marker of American Jewish
identity. My theory is that Israelism held such appeal for American Jews
partly because Israel, with its frontier ethos, macho sabras, strong military, and statehood, was a kind of Jewish America, more in harmony
with American values than the old eastern European Jewish culture, with
its skinny and unathletic yeshiva boys, its emphasis on the intellect, and
its nationlessness. So identifying with Israel was a way for American
Jews to assimilate and remain Jewish at the same time. In the same way,
fashioning a new Jewish culture in the seventies, eighties, and nineties
that was in harmony with hip and progressive young America can perhaps be seen as yet another Jewish way to be American, complete with
a traditional music scene—klezmer—to mirror its American folk music
counterpart.

One of the most interesting new developments in the Yiddishist movement and the klezmer revival is a move toward a kind of twentysome-
thing, in-your-face radicalism that carries the banner of Yiddish culture
as a symbol of unapologetic Jewish pride à la "Queer Nation." Among
klezmer bands, this approach is represented by the Klezmatics, with our
"out" presentation and our tendency to mine the rich socialist Jewish
past for songs we can relate to (like "Dzhankhoye," whose lyrics include
an admonition to "spit in the anti-Semites' faces"). The wider Yiddishist scene owes this new trend in large part to the growing "Queer Yiddishist" movement, made up of Queer Nation types who also identify
as Yiddishist, and who bring a queer radical sensibility to Yiddishism.
In fact, among progressives of all stripes, gays in particular have found
a home in the new secular Yiddishist environment from the start, surprising each other and everyone else with our unexpectedly large numbers at KlezKamp and the YIVO summer program, and on the staffs of
YIVO and the National Yiddish Book Center. As younger gays started
showing up, they brought queer sensibility, and then Queer Yiddishism,
with them.

A random sampling of Queer Yiddishist cultural production: the
Third Seder, a multimedia Passover extravaganza performed in New
York at La Mama in 1993 and the Jewish Museum in 1995, featuring
radical queer Jewish artists like visual artist Neil Goldberg, playwright
Tony Kushner, author Sarah Shulman, and the explicitly homoerotic

Yiddish love songs of the Klezmatics; the work of Eve Sicular, former YIVO film and photo archivist, who writes and lectures on gay subtext in Yiddish film; the rediscovery of gay Yiddish literature from earlier this century in recent Yiddish "reading circles," and the enactment at a recent YIVO Yiddish summer program graduation of excerpts from Sholem Asch's play about lesbianism, *Got fun nekome;* the work of poet Irena Klepfisz, who has been trying to integrate her Yiddishist and lesbian feminist worlds since long before the advent of the current movement; author Ellen Galford's novel, *The Dyke and the Dybbuk;* and a host of filmmakers and performance artists who are incorporating Yiddish language and music into their gay-themed work. The Queer Yiddishist movement was recently written up for the first time in the *Village Voice* (making it official!).

As Yiddishism and the klezmer revival stretch in these more radical directions, its adherents occasionally run into another movement that is coming from a completely different direction, but ending up in some ways in the same place: downtown N.Y.C. "Radical Jewish Culture." This is a group of people who started out as punks, downtown noise musicians, etc., and have recently decided to come out as Jews in their scenes and celebrate their Jewishness with the same kind of radical pride that they also probably picked up from Queer Nation—although often with little or no knowledge of traditional Jewish culture to draw on, just a feisty newfound sense of Jewish identity. Examples include downtown musicians Marc Ribot and John Zorn, Jewish punk 'zine *Mazel Tov Cocktail,* and rock group God Is My Co-Pilot (who straddle the space between the two movements, performing punk versions of songs from the Workmen's Circle *hagode* [prayerbook for the Passover seder]).

THE MANIFESTO

As an openly Yiddishist klezmer musician, these are the tenets of my faith.

• *No Nostalgia*

Klezmer music is our music, not just the music of our grandparents, to be reproduced in a kind of tourism of the past. When the Klezmatics first formed, I had a job playing at a Greek nightclub in New York and was struck by how identified the young Greek clientele were with Greek traditional and popular music, much more so than they were with American pop music, which they also listened to. I want the same thing for klezmer music—that it will truly become the identity music of Jewish American youth.

• *High Jewish Self-Esteem*

There's an unfortunate tradition of "Uncle Tom-ing" in American Jewish culture—that is, of presenting Yiddish language and music as something funny and cute. This spilled over into the early phases of the klezmer revival, when, encountering the Rorschach blot of available source recordings, many musicians somehow heard goofy and cartoony elements (the chirps and scoops of clarinetist Kramtweiss, the supposedly "drunken" tuba sounds) and chose to reproduce and emphasize them. Tempos were also speeded up, producing an effect reminiscent of cartoons or old movies. When I first heard the recordings of clarinetist Naftule Brandwein, what struck me was the total seriousness and dignity of his music (which, again, reminded me of the Greek music I was involved with). High Jewish self-esteem would mean taking the music completely seriously.

Of course, 1990s revivalists also hear what we want to in that Rorschach blot, like the power chords I heard in Brandwein's "Terkish Bulgarish" that led to the Klezmatics' arrangement of that tune on *Rhythm and Jews*. The Klezmatics also sometimes speed up tempos, but in an emulation of a punk, rather than a cartoon, aesthetic.

• *Our Own Language*

My grandmother's sister, who was a native Yiddish speaker, used to deny Yiddish was really a language, calling it a *zhargon* (jargon). Similarly, journalists and music critics repeatedly emphasize the supposedly hodge-podge nature of klezmer, calling it a mix of everything from polkas to calypso. In fact, neither is true. Yiddish is a language—Yiddish linguist Max Weinreich used to say "a dialect is a language without an army"—and klezmer is an idiom with its own stylistic unity and integrity. Like any musical language, klezmer needs to be studied and absorbed so it can be spoken with a native accent.

Perhaps this tendency of American Jews to deny the legitimacy of our language and music, prevalent among older Jews, is a reflection of low Jewish self-esteem or of a desire to assimilate. Or maybe, like comic "Uncle Tom-ing," it's the strategy a minority culture comes up with to avoid antagonizing the often-hostile majority—in this case, a self-representation that says, "Don't worry, we're just like you; we don't really have our own language and we're not really a group apart."

• No Folk-Fetishism or False Definition of "Authenticity"

A corollary to the idea that this is our music is the notion that, having inherited it, we can now do with it whatever we wish. I want to play authentic Jewish folk music—but not in the sense of reifying a particular slice of Jewish musical history, such as, say, the 1920s. There are defining elements of klezmer style (melodic types, ornamentation) that have remained constant over time, but as a musician, I know that every musical idiom constantly changes and interacts with other musics, and the 1920s were no more "authentic" a period than any other. Rather, I believe in playing "authentically" in the sense of being true to oneself. My hope is that now that we're becoming fluent in our language, we can go beyond simply reciting a received text to speak spontaneously in our own voices.

Sources

PUBLISHED SOURCES

Adler, Israel. "A la recherche du chants perdus—La redécouverte des collections du 'Cabinet' de musique juive de Moisei I. Beregovski." In *Ndroje balendro. Musiques, terrains et disciplines: Textes offerts a Simha Arom,* 247–67. Paris: Peeters, 1995.

Akhmetova, Tat'iana Vasil'evna, comp. *Russkii mat.* Moscow: Kolokol-press, 1997.

Anderson, Benedict R. O'G. *Imagined Communities: Reflections on the Origin and Spread of Nationalism.* Rev. ed. London: Verso, 1991.

Bakhtin, M. M. "Forms of Time and of the Chronotope in the Novel." In *The Dialogic Imagination: Four Essays,* translated by Caryl Emerson and Michael Holquist, edited by Michael Holquist, 41–83. Austin: The University of Texas Press, 1981.

Balaban, Majer. *Zyda Lwowsey na przelomic XVI^{go} XVII^{go} wieku.* Lwow, 1906.

Beregovski, Moshe. *Evreiskaia narodnaia instrumental'naia muzyka.* Edited by Max Goldin. Moscow: Sovetskii kompozitor, 1987.

———. *Jewish Instrumental Folk Music.* Edited and translated by Mark Slobin, Robert Rothstein, and Michael Alpert. Syracuse, N.Y.: Syracuse University Press, 2001.

———. "Yidishe instrumentalishe folksmuzik." In *Old Jewish Folk Music: The Collections and Writings of Moshe Beregovski,* edited and translated by Mark Slobin. Philadelphia: University of Pennsylvania, 1982. Reprinted 2000, Syracuse University Press.

Bern, Alan. "From Klezmer to New Jewish Music: The Musical Evolution of Brave Old World." *Mens en Melodie* 1 (1998): n.p.

Bik, Moshe. *Klezmorim be-Orgeev.* Haifa: Publications of the Haifa Music Museum and Library, 1964.

Bikel, Theodore. *Theo: The Autobiography of Theodore Bikel.* New York: HarperCollins, 1994.

Blacking, John. "Some Problems of Theory and Method in the Study of Musical Change." *Yearbook of the International Folkmusic Council* 9 (1977): 1–26.

Blumenson, Sol. "Revolt of the Reefer Makers." *Commentary* 8, no. 1 (February 1949): 62–70.

———. "Utopia on Columbia Street." *Commentary* 6, no. 4 (October 1948): 358–62.

Bogach, Georgii Fedosievich. *Pushkin i moldavskii fol'klor.* Kishinev: Kartia Moldoveniaske, 1963.

Bohlman, Philip V. *"The Land Where Two Streams Flow": Music in the German-Jewish Community of Israel.* Urbana: University of Illinois Press, 1989.

Borgo, A. "Pharao barna ivadekai es a klezmorim: A cigany es jiddis zenekultura magyarorszagi kapcsolatai." *Muszika* 36, no. 9 (1993): 32–40.

Borokhov, Ber. "Di bibliotek funem yidishn filolog. Fir hundert yor yidisher shprakh-forshung." In *Shprakh-forshung un literatur-geshikhte,* edited by Nachman Mayzel, 76–135. Tel Aviv: Farlag I. L. Peretz, 1966 [1913].

Botkin, B. A. "The Folksong Revival: Cult or Culture?" in *The American Folk Scene: Dimensions of the Folksong Revival,* edited by David A. De Turk and A. Poulin, Jr., 95–100. New York: Dell, 1967.

Brand, Oscar. *The Ballad Mongers: Rise of the Modern Folk Song.* New York: Funk and Wagnalls, 1962.

Braun, Joachim. "The Unpublished Volumes of Moshe Beregovski's Jewish Musical Folklore." *Israel Studies in Musicology* 4 (1987): 133–36.

Brodkin, K. *How Jews Became White Folks.* New Brunswick: Rutgers University Press, 1998.

Burke, Peter. *Popular Culture in Early Modern Europe.* New York: New York University Press, 1978.

Cahan, Abraham. *Bleter fun mayn lebn.* Vol. 3. New York: Forverts, 1926.

———. *The Imported Bridegroom and Other Stories of the New York Ghetto.* Boston: Houghton, Mifflin, 1898.

Cantwell, Robert. "When We Were Good: Class and Culture in the Folk Revival." In *Transforming Tradition: Folk Music Revivals Examined.* Edited by Neil V. Rosenberg. Urbana: University of Illinois Press, 1993.

Caplan, Marc. "Borsht-Belt Badkhonim: Carnival Performance Recordings of Gus Goldstein and Mickey Katz." Unpublished essay, 1997.

Chagall, Bella. *Burning Lights.* Translated by Norman Guterman. New York: Schocken, 1946.

Clark, C.U. *Bessarabia.* New York: Dodd and Mead, 1927.

Commons, John R. *Labor and Administration.* New York: Macmillan, 1913.

Czekanowska, Anna. *Polish Folk Music: Slavonic Heritage, Polish Tradition, Contemporary Trends.* Cambridge: Cambridge University Press, 1990.

Davidow, Ari, comp. "Memories of the Klez Revival and 'The Klezmorim.'" Excerpts from e-mails from Lev Liberman and David Julian Gray. 1999. *http://www.klezmershack.com/articles/klezmorim.hist.html* (January 2001).

De Turk, David A., and A. Poulin, Jr. *The American Folk Scene: Dimensions of the Folksong Revival.* New York: Dell, 1967.

Dion, Lynn. "Klezmer Music in America: Revival and Beyond." *Jewish Folklore and Ethnology Review* 8, no. 1–2 (1986): 2–8.

Druker, Irme. *Klezmer.* Moscow: Sovetskii pisatel', 1976.

Dushkin, Alexander M. "A Statistical Study of the Jewish Population of New York." In *The Jewish Communal Register of New York City, 1917–1918,* 2d ed., 82–90. New York: Kehillah (Jewish Community) of New York City, 1918.

Dushman, Leon. "Fakh-leshones." *Tsaytshrift far yidisher geshikhte, demografye un ekonomik, literatur-forshung, shprakh-visnshaft un etnografye* [Minsk] 2–3 (1928): 875–77.

Elzet, Yehude [Yehude-Leyb Zlotnik]. "Melokhes un bale-melokhes." *Der vunder-oytser fun der yidisher shprakh.* Part 4. Warsaw: Bracia Lewin-Epsztein, 1920.

Epstein, Melech. *Jewish Labor in the U.S.A.* New York: Trade Union Sponsoring Committee, 1950.

Epstein, Shifra. "Drama on a Table: The Bobover Hasidim *Piremshpiyl.*" In *Judaism Viewed from Within and Without: Anthropological Studies,* edited by Harvey Goldberg, 195–217. Albany: State University of New York Press, 1987.

Estreicher, Karol. *Szwargot więzienny.* Cracow: Księgarnia D.E. Friedleina, 1903.

Evreiskaia entsiklopediia. St. Petersburg: Brockhaus-Efron, 1908–13.

Feld, Steven. *From Schizophonia to Schismogenesis: Notes on the Discourses of World Music and World Beat.* Working Papers and Proceedings of the Center for Psychosocial Studies 53, edited by Greg Urban and Benjamin Lee. Chicago: Center for Psychosocial Studies, 1992.

Feldman, Walter Zev. "Bulgărească/Bulgarish/Bulgar: The Transformation of a Klezmer Dance Genre." *Ethnomusicology* 38, no. 1 (1994): 1–35.

———. "Klezmer Music: Eastern Europe." In *The New Grove Dictionary of Music and Musicians,* edited by John Tyrrell and Stanley Sadie. London: In press.

———. "Modulation in Jewish Instrumental Folkmusic." Paper presented at the annual meeting of the Mid-Atlantic Chapter of the Society for Ethnomusicology, Baltimore, Md., 1988.

Findeisen, Nikolai Fedorovich. "Evreiskie tsimbaly i tsimbalisty Lepianskie" (The Jewish Cimbal and the Lepianski Family of Cimbalists). In *Muzykal'naia etnografiia,* edited by N.F. Findeisen, 37–44. Leningrad: Izdatel'stvo Komissii Po Izucheniiu Narodnoi Muzyki Pri Etnograficheskom Otdelenii Russkogo Geograficheskoko Obshchestna, 1926.

Forry, M. "Bečar Music in the Serbian Community of Los Angeles: Evolution and Transformation." *Selected Reports in Ethnomusicology* 3, no. 1 (1978): 173–209.

Friedman, M. *Philadelphia Jewish Life, 1940–1985.* Philadelphia: Seth Press, 1986.

———, ed. *Jewish Life in Philadelphia, 1830–1940.* Philadelphia: Ishi Publications, 1983.

Garfias, R. "Survivals of Turkish Characteristics in Romanian Musica Lăuta-reasca." *Yearbook for Traditional Music* 13 (1981): 97–107.

Garofalo, R. "Whose World, What Beat? The Transnational Music Industry, Identity, and Cultural Imperialism." *World of Music* 35, no. 2 (1993): 16–32.

Geertz, Clifford. "Epilogue." In *The Anthropology of Experience*, edited by Victor W. Turner and Edward M. Bruner, 373–80. Urbana: University of Illinois Press, 1986.

Georgescu, Corneliu Dan. *Melodii de joc din Oltenia.* Bucharest: Editura Muzicala a Uniunii Compozitorilor, 1968.

Goldin, Max. *On Musical Connections between Jews and the Neighboring Peoples of Eastern and Western Europe.* Edited and translated by Robert A. Rothstein. Amherst: University of Massachusetts, 1989.

Gordin, Jacob. *The Kreutzer Sonata.* Adapted by Langdon Mitchell. New York: Harrison Grey and Fiske, 1907.

———. *Yakov Gordin's Dramen.* 2 vols. New York: Soyrkel fun Yakov Gordin's fraynt, 1911.

Gordon, Milton M. *Assimilation in American Life: The Role of Race, Religion, and National Origins.* New York: Oxford University Press, 1964.

Gruber, Ruth Ellen. "Filling the Jewish Space in Europe." *International Perspectives*, no. 35. New York: American Committee, 1996.

Hajdu, André. "Niggun Meron." *Yuval* 2 (1971): 73–113.

Hapgood, Hutchins. *The Spirit of the Ghetto.* New York: Funk and Wagnalls, 1902.

Harkavy, Alexander. *Yidish-english-hebreisher verterbukh / Yiddish-English-Hebrew Dictionary.* 4th ed. New York: Hebrew Publishing, 1928.

Hebdige, D. *Subculture: The Meaning of Style.* New York: Routledge, 1979.

Henry, E. O. "Institutions for the Promotion of Indigenous Music: The Case of Ireland's Comhaltas Ceoltoiri Eireann." *Ethnomusicology* 35, no. 1 (1989): 67–95.

Hentoff, Nat. "Indigenous Music." *Nation* (14 January 1978): 28–29.

———. "The Future of the Folk Renascence." In *The American Folk Scene: Dimensions of the Folksong Revival*, edited by David A. De Turk and A. Poulin, Jr., 326–31. New York: Dell, 1967.

Heschel, Abraham Joshua. *The Earth Is the Lord's: The Inner World of the Jew in Eastern Europe.* New York: Henry Schuman, 1950.

Hillquit, Morris. *Loose Leaves from a Busy Life.* New York: Macmillan, 1934.

Howe, Irving. *World of Our Fathers.* New York: Harcourt Brace Jovanovich, 1976.

Idelsohn, A. Z. "Artistic Endeavors." In *Jewish Music in Its Historical Development.* New York: Henry Holt, 1929; New York: Schocken, 1967; New York: Dover Press, 1993.

International Socialist Congress. *Protokoll des Internationalen Arbeiter-Congresses zu Paris.* Nurnberg: Worlein, 1890.

Joll, James. *The Second International, 1889–1914.* London: Routledge, 1966.

Joselit, Jenna Weissman. *The Wonders of America: Reinventing Jewish Culture, 1880–1950.* New York: Hill and Wang, 1994.

Katz, Mickey, and Hannibal Coons. *Papa, Play for Me: The Hilarious, Heartwarming Autobiography of Comedian and Bandleader Mickey Katz.* New York: Simon and Schuster, 1977.

King, Chris. "Klezmatics to Appear at Washington U." 11 September 1996. http://www.klezmershack.com/articles/king.klezmatics.9609.html (23 January 2000).

Kirshenblatt-Gimblett, Barbara. "Culture Shock and Narrative Creativity." In *Folklore in the Modern World,* edited by Richard M. Dorson, 109–22. The Hague: Mouton, 1978.

———. *Destination Culture: Tourism, Museums, and Heritage.* Berkeley and Los Angeles: University of California Press, 1998.

———. "Performance of Precepts, Precepts of Performance." In *By Means of Performance: Intercultural Studies of Theatre and Ritual,* edited by Richard Schechner and Willa Appel, 109–17. Cambridge: Cambridge University Press, 1990.

———. "Problems in the Early Historiography of Jewish Folkloristics." In *Proceedings of the Tenth World Congress of Jewish Studies,* edited by David Assaf, 21–32. Art, Folklore and Music, Div. D, vol. 2. Jerusalem: World Union of Jewish Studies, 1990.

———. "Sounds of Sensibility." *Judaism: A Quarterly of Jewish Life and Thought* 47, no. 1 (1998): 49–80.

———. "Theorizing Heritage." *Ethnomusicology* 39, no. 3 (1995): 367–80.

Kligman, Mark. "On the Creators and Consumers of Orthodox Popular Music in Brooklyn." *YIVO Annual* 23 (1996): 259–94.

Korchinski, V. *Moldavskie naigryshi i pesni.* Moscow: Muzgiz, 1937.

Korn, Yitshak, ed. *Yahadut Besarabyah.* Vol. 11 of *Entsiklopedyah shel galuyot.* Jerusalem: Hevrat entsiklopedyah shel galuyot, 1971.

Kostakowsky, Wolff N. *International Hebrew Wedding Music.* Brooklyn, N.Y.: Kostakowsky, 1916.

Kotliarov, Boris Iakovlevich. *O skripichnoi kul'ture v Moldavii: kratkii ocherk.* Kishinev: Gos. izd-vo Moldavii, 1955.

Kurka, Antoni. *Słownik mowy złodziejskiej.* 3d ed. Lwów: Antoni Kurka, 1907.

Landau, Alfred. "Zur russisch-jüdischen 'Klesmer'sprache.'" *Mitteilungen der Anthropologischen Gesellschaft in Wien* 43 (1913): 143–49.

Lark's March, The (pseud.). "Klezmorim Interview." Lark in the Morning. http://www.larkinam.com/MenComNet/Business/Retail/LarkNet/ArtKlezmorimInterview (24 January 2001).

Lawrence, Jerome. *Actor: The Life and Times of Paul Muni.* New York: G. P. Putnam's Sons, 1974.

Lenzon, Viktor. "Muzik in Sholem-Aleykhems verk." *Sovetish heymland* 1989, no. 3: 60–67.

Lewis, Joel. "Heavy Shtetl: The New In-Your-Face Jewish Music." *Moment* (August 1995): 46–50.

Liberman, Lev. "Memories of the Klez Revival and 'The Klezmorim.'" http://www.well.com/user/ari/klez/articles/klezmorim.hist.html (30 November 1995).

Lifschutz, E. "Merrymakers and Jesters among Jews." *YIVO Annual of Jewish Social Sciences* 7 (1952): 43–69.

Lifson, David S. *The Yiddish Theatre in America.* New York: Thomas Yoseloff, 1965.

Lipaev, Ivan. "Evreiskie orkestry." Parts 1, 2, 3, and 4. *Russkaia muzykal'naia gazeta* 1904, no. 4: 101–3; no. 5: 133–36; no. 6: 169–72; no. 8: 205–7.

Loeffler, James. "A Gilgul fun a Nigun: Jewish Musicians in New York, 1881–1945." Harvard Judaica Collection Student Research Papers, no. 3. B.A. thesis, Harvard University, 1997.

————. "Di Rusishe Progresiv Muzikal Yunyon No. 1 fun Amerike: The First Klezmer Union in America." *Judaism* 47, no. 1 (1998): 29–39.

Logan, Andy. "Profiles: Five Generations." *New Yorker* (29 October 1949): 32–51.

Mazor, Yaakov. "A Hasidic Ritual Dance—The *Mitsve Tants* in Jerusalemite Weddings." *Yuval* 6 (1994): 164–224.

Mendes-Flohr, Paul. *Divided Passions: Jewish Intellectuals and the Experience of Modernity.* Detroit: Wayne State University Press, 1991.

Mlotek, Chane, and Yosl Mlotek. "Perl fun der yidisher poezye." *Forverts* (22 November 1996): 13.

Moore, Deborah Dash, and Ilan Troen, eds. *Divergent Centers: Shaping Jewish Cultures in Israel and America.* New Haven: Yale University Press, in press.

Mullaney, Steven. "The Rehearsal of Cultures." In *The Place of the Stage: License, Play, and Power in Renaissance England,* 60–87. Ann Arbor: University of Michigan Press, 1995.

Neugroschel, Joachim, trans. and ed. *The Shtetl: A Creative Anthology of Jewish Life in Eastern Europe.* Woodstock, N.Y.: The Overlook Press, 1979.

Nicolescu, Vasile D., and Constantin Gh. Prichici, eds. *Cîntece și jocuri populare din Moldova.* Bucharest: Editura muzicala a Uniunii compozitorilor din R. P. R., 1963.

Nulman, Macy. *Concise Dictionary of Jewish Music.* New York: McGraw-Hill, 1975.

Oring, Elliott. *Jokes and Their Relation.* Lexington: University Press of Kentucky, 1992.

Ottens, Rita, and Joel Rubin. *Klezmer-Musik.* Kassel: Bärenreiter, 1999.

Patten, Charlotte Kimball. "Amusements and Social Life: Philadelphia." In *The Russian Jew in the United States,* edited by Charles S. Bernheimer, 233–48. Philadelphia: John Winston, 1905.

Peña, M. "From Ranchero to Jaiton: Ethnicity and Class in Texas-Mexican Music (Two Styles in the Form of a Pair)." *Ethnomusicology* 29, no. 1 (1985): 29–55.

Perlman, Itzhak. *In the Fiddler's House.* Angel Records A3VE724347782732, 1995.

Prilutski, Noyekh. "Lashon ha-'klezmorim' be-polaniyah." *Reshumot* 1 (1918): 272–91.

Prizament, Shloyme. *Broder zinger.* Buenos Aires: Tsentral-farband fun poylishe yidn in argentine, 1960.

Rischin, Moses. *The Promised City: New York's Jews, 1870–1914.* Cambridge: Harvard University Press, 1962; New York: Corinth, 1964; with a new preface by the author, Cambridge: Harvard University Press, 1977.

Rogovoy, Seth. "Andy Statman's Hasidic Jazz." *Boston Phoenix.* 21 March 1997. http://www.berkshireweb.com/rogovoy/interviews/statman.html (26 January 2001).

———. "David Krakauer's Klezmer Incites, Provokes," *Berkshire Eagle,* 30 August 1996, http://www.berkshireweb.com/rogovoy/concerts/klezmer.html.

———. "Making Old-World Music New." *Berkshire Eagle.* 22 August 1996. http://www.berkshireweb.com/rogovoy/popcorner/pop8-22.html (23 January 2001).

———. *The Essential Klezmer: A Music Lover's Guide to Jewish Soul Music, from the Old World to the Jazz Age to the Downtown Avant-Garde.* Chapel Hill, N.C.: Algonquin Books, 2000.

———. "The Klezmatics: Outing Klezmer." *Boston Phoenix.* 16 May 1997. http://www.berkshireweb.com/rogovoy/interviews/klezmat.html (January 2001).

———. "The Klezmer Revival: Old World Meets New." *Berkshire Eagle.* 31 July 1997. http://www.berkshireweb.com/rogovoy/interviews/klez.html (24 January 2001).

Rosenberg, Neil V., ed. *Transforming Tradition: Folk Music Revivals Examined.* Urbana: University of Illinois Press, 1993.

Rosenblatt, Frank. "Mutual Aid Organizations." In *The Jewish Communal Register of New York City, 1917–1918,* 2d ed., 730–978. New York: Kehillah (Jewish Community) of New York, 1918.

Rothstein, Robert A. "Klezmer-loshn." *Judaism* 47, no. 1 (1998): 23–28.

Rubin, Joel. "Rumenishe Shtiklekh: Klezmer Music among the Hasidim in Contemporary Israel." *Judaism* 47, no. 1 (Winter 1998): 12–23.

Rubin, Ruth. *Voices of a People: The Story of Yiddish Folk Song.* New York: Thomas Yoseloff, 1963.

Salmen, W. *Jüdische Musikanten und Tänzer vom 13. bis 20. Jahrhundert.* Innsbruck: Edition Helbling, 1991.

Samuel, Maurice. *The World of Sholom Aleichem.* New York: Knopf, 1943.

Sandrow, Nahma. *Vagabond Stars: A World History of the Yiddish Theater.* New York: Harper and Row, 1977.

Sapoznik, Henry. "Dave Tarras: Father of Yiddish-American Klezmer Music, 1925–1956." Liner notes for *Dave Tarras: Yiddish-American Klezmer Music, 1925–1956.* Yazoo Records. Yazoo 7001, 1991.

———. *Klezmer!: Jewish Music from Old World to Our World.* New York: Schirmer Books, 1999.

Sapoznik, Henry, and Pete Sokolov. *The Compleat Klezmer.* Cedarhurst, N.Y.: Tara Publications, 1987.

Sarosi, Balint. *Gypsy Music.* Budapest: Corvina Press, 1970.

Schafer, R. Murray. *The Tuning of the World.* New York: Knopf, 1977.

Scherer, Barrymore Laurence. "Country and Eastern." *Wall Street Journal* (28 December 1994), Eastern edition: A11.

Schwartz, Martin. Presentation. Wesleyan Klezmer Research Conference. October 1996.

Secunda, Victoria. *Bei Mir Bist Du Schön: The Life of Sholem Secunda.* New York: Magic Circle Press, 1982.

Sendrey, Alfred. *The Music of the Jews in the Diaspora.* New York: Thomas Yoseloff, 1970.

Shandler, Jeffrey. *While America Watched: The Holocaust on Television.* New York: Oxford University Press, 1999.

Shapiro, Herman S. *The European-Jewish Wedding.* New York: Hebrew Publishing, 1905.

Sharvit, U. "Jewish Musical Culture—Past and Present." *World of Music* 11 (1995): 3–17.

Shelemay, Kay. "Mythologies and Realities in the Study of Jewish Music." *World of Music* 11 (1995): 24–38.

Shitnovitzer, Shelomoh. *Sefer kehilat hotin (Besarabyah).* Tel Aviv: Irgun Yotse Hotin (Besarabyah) be-Yisrael, 1974.

Sholem Aleichem. *Ale verk fun Sholem-Aleykhem.* New York: Sholem-Aleykhem folksfond, 1927.

———. *Di yidishe folksbibliotek.* Vol. 1. Kiev: Sholem Aleichem, 1889.

———. *Oysgeveylte verk.* Vol. 6. Edited by Dawid Sfard. Warsaw: Yidish bukh, 1955.

———. *Sobranie sochinenii v shesti tomakh.* Edited by M. Bazhan, et al. Moscow: Khudozhestvennaia literatura, 1974.

Shvarts, Itsik. "Jewish Musicians in Moldavia." http://www.klezmershack.com/articles/1972.moldavia.shvarts.html (April 28, 2000).

Slobin, Mark. "A Fresh Look at Beregovski's Folk Music Research." *Ethnomusicology* 30, no. 1 (1986): 253–60.

———. *Chosen Voices: The Story of the American Cantorate.* Urbana: University of Illinois Press, 1989.

———. "Fiddler off the Roof: Klezmer as an Ethnic Musical Style." In *The Jews of North America,* edited by Morris Rischin, 95–104. Detroit: Wayne State University Press, 1987.

———. *Fiddler on the Move: Exploring the Klezmer World.* New York: Oxford University Press, 2000.

———. "Klezmer Music: An American Ethnic Genre." *Yearbook for Traditional Music* 16 (1984): 34–41.

———. "Searching for the Klezmer City." *Studies in Contemporary Jewry* 15 (1999): 35–48.

———. "Some Intersections of Jews, Music, and Theater." In *From Hester Street to Hollywood: The Jewish-American Stage and Screen,* edited by Sarah Blacher-Cohen, 29–43. Bloomington: Indiana University Press, 1983.

———. *Subcultural Sounds: Micromusics of the West.* Hanover, N.H.: University Press of New England, 1993.

———. *Tenement Songs: The Popular Music of the Jewish Immigrants.* Urbana: University of Illinois Press, 1982.

———. "Ten Paradoxes and Four Dilemmas of Studying Jewish Music." *World of Music* 11, no. 1 (1995). 18–23.

———. "The Music of the Yiddish Theater: Manuscript Sources at YIVO." *YIVO Annual of Jewish Social Sciences* 18 (1983): 372–90.

Soloveitchik, Haym. "Rupture and Reconstruction: The Transformation of Contemporary Orthodoxy." *Tradition* 28, no. 4 (1994): 64–130.

Soltes, Avraham. "The Hebrew Folk Song Society of Petersburg: The Historical Development." In *The Historic Contribution of Russian Jewry to Jewish Music,* edited by Irene Heskes and Arthur Wolfson, 13–27. New York: National Jewish Music Council, 1967.

Spivak, Yitzkhak, et al. *Orheyov be-vinyanah uve-hurbana.* Tel Aviv: Vaad yotse Orheyov, 1959.

Spottswood, Richard K. *Ethnic Music on Records: A Discography of Ethnic Recordings Produced in the United States, 1893–1942.* Vol. 3, *Eastern Europe.* Urbana: University of Illinois Press, 1990.

Stern, Elizabeth G. *My Mother and I.* New York: Macmillan, 1917.

Stoianov, Petr Fedorovich. *500 melodii de jocuri din Moldova.* Chişinau (Kishinev): Kartia Moldoveniaske, 1972.

Stutchkoff, Nahum. *Der oytser fun der yidisher shprakh.* New York: Yiddish Scientific Institute–YIVO, 1950.

Stutschewsky, Joachim. *Ha-klezmarim: Toldotehem, orah-hayehem vi-yetsirotehem.* Jerusalem: Mosad Bialik, 1959.

Tabak, Robert Phillip. *The Transformation of Jewish Identity: The Philadelphia Experience, 1919–1945.* Ann Arbor: University Microfilms, 1990.

Tcherikower, Elias. *Di geshikhte fun der yidisher arbeter-bavegung in di fareynikte shtatn.* 2 vols. New York: YIVO Institute for Jewish Studies, 1943–45.

Tcherikower, Elias, ed., and Anton Antonovsky, trans. and ed. *The Early Jewish Labor Movement in the United States.* New York: YIVO Institute for Jewish Research, 1961.

Thompson, E. P. *Customs in Common.* New York: The New Press, 1991.

Trivaks, Avrom-Yitskhok. "Di yidishe zhargonen." In *Bay undz yidn,* edited by M. Vanvild (Moyshe-Yoysef Dikshteyn), 159–78. Warsaw: Pinkhes Graubard, 1923.

Weinreich, Max. "Yidish." In *Algemeyne yidishe entsiklopedye,* 2d ed., supplementary vol., *Yidn 2.* New York: CYCO, 1940.

Weinreich, Uriel. *Languages in Contact: Findings and Problems.* The Hague: Mouton, 1968.

———. *Modern English-Yiddish Yiddish-English Dictionary.* New York: YIVO Institute for Jewish Research and McGraw-Hill, 1968.

Weinstein, Bernard. *Idishe yunyons in amerike.* New York: United Hebrew Trades, 1929.

Weissenberg, Samuel. "Die 'Klesmer'sprache." *Mitteilungen der Anthropologischen Gesellschaft in Wien* 43 (1913): 127–42.

Whisnant, David E. *All That Is Native and Fine: The Politics of Culture in an American Region.* Chapel Hill: University of North Carolina Press, 1983.

Williams, Raymond. *Keywords: A Vocabulary of Culture and Society.* Rev. ed. New York: Oxford University Press, 1983.

———. *Marxism and Literature.* New York: Oxford University Press, 1977.

Winchevsky, Morris. "Eliakum Zunser: Jester, Printer and Writer of Yiddish Verses." *New Era* 6, no. 3 (1905): 297–300.

Wischnitzer, Mark. *A History of Jewish Crafts and Guilds.* New York: Jonathan David, 1965.

Wolff, Jeremy. "A 'Cat' from the Bronx Makes His Mark on Klezmer." *Wall Street Journal* (19 September 1991), Eastern edition: A12.

Yablokoff, Herman. *Arum der velt mit idish teater: Oytobiografishe iberlebungen un teater-dertseylungen.* 2 vols. New York: Herman Yablokoff, 1968–69.

Yanovsky, Saul. *Ershte yorn fun yidishn frayhaytlekhn sotsializm.* New York: Fraye Arbayter Shtime, 1948.

Yudelson, Larry. "Dylan: Tangled up in Jews." *Washington Jewish Week.* 7 July 1997. http://www.well.com/user/yudel/Tangled.html (24 January 2001).

Zaagsma, German. "The klezmorim of Prague." http://www.klezmershack.com/articles/zaagsma.prague.html (April 28, 2000).

Zalmanoff, S. *Sefer haniggunim.* Vol. 3. New York: Kvar Chabad, n.d.

Zborowski, Mark, and Elizabeth Herzog. *Life Is with People: The Culture of the Shtetl.* New York: Schocken, 1995.

Zipperstein, Steven J. *The Jews of Odessa: A Cultural History, 1794–1881.* Stanford: Stanford University Press, 1986.

Zunser, Eliakum. *Tsunzers biografye: geshriebn fun im aleyn.* Edited by Abraham Hyman Fromenson. New York: Tsunzer yubileum komite, 1905.

INTERVIEWS

Aaron, Joe. Interview with Hankus Netsky, November 1993.

Block, Bobby (Robert Alan). Interviews with Hankus Netsky, November 1996; 1997; 1999.

Borock, Joe. Interview with Hankus Netsky, 1996.

Davis, Mel. Interviews with Hankus Netsky, October 1997, June 1998.

Drootin, Al. Interview with Hankus Netsky, 8 November 1996.

Epstein, Max. Interview with Hankus Netsky, February 1998.

Feldsher, Samuel. Interview with Hankus Netsky, June 1988.

Hoffman, Morris. Interviews with Hankus Netsky, June 1996, 1 August 1996, October 1996, June 1997.

Katz, Samuel. Interview with Hankus Netsky, June 1981.

Uhr, Bernie. Interview with Hankus Netsky, 1997.

INTERNET RESOURCES

Unless otherwise noted, web sites were most recently accessed during February 2002. Endnotes to individual chapters may list additional web sites that are no longer accessible.

Balkanarama. "Home Page." http://www.troutdream.com/balkanarama/

Davidow, Ari. *Ari Davidow's Klezmer Shack.* http://www.klezmershack.com

German Klezmer Page. http://www.ta-deti.de/klezmer/
Sunday Morning Klezmer & Other Jewish Music. "Home Page." http://www
.angelfire.com/nj/WBZCFMsndymrnngklzmr/
Virtual Klezmer. http://www.klezmer.de/index.html
Vurma. "Home Page." http://hem.passagen.se/vurma/
The Yiddish Voice, WUNR, 1600 AM (Brookline, Massachusetts), http://www
.yiddishvoice.com/

SOUND RECORDINGS

Bernardi, Herschel, Shoshana Damari, Netania Davrath, Leon Lishner, Jan
Peerce, Martha Schlamme, Abraham Ellstein, Gershon Kingsley, Robert
De Cormier, and Vladimir Golschmann. *The Yiddish Dream: A Heritage
of Jewish Song.* 33⅓ sound recording. 2 discs. Vanguard. VSD 715/716,
1971.
Bikel, Theodore. *Folksongs of Israel.* 33⅓ sound recording. Elektra. EKL-32,
1955.
Bikel, Theodore. *Theodore Bikel Sings Jewish Folk Songs.* 33⅓ sound record-
ing. Elektra. EKL-141, 1959.
Brave Old World. *Beyond the Pale.* CD sound recording. Rounder Records.
CD 3135, 1994.
Brave Old World. *Blood Oranges.* Pinorrekk Records. CD sound recording.
PRCD 3405027, 1997.
Brave Old World. *Klezmer Music.* Flying Fish Records. CD sound recording.
FLY 560, 1990.
Feidman, Giora. *Jewish Soul Music.* 33⅓ sound recording. Hed-Arzi Ltd.
BAN 14297, 1972.
Feidman, Giora. *Long Live Giora, His Clarinet and His Soul Music.* 33⅓ sound
recording. Star Record Co. ST AE 76 A/B, 1977.
Feidman, Giora. *Rabbi Chaim's Dance: Traditionals from Israel.* CD sound
recording. RCA International. AAD 71-75, 1996.
Fershko, S., Mort Freeman, Adele Margolin, and Dave Tarras. *Rejoice: Torah in
Song/Wedding in the Old Country.* Dave Tarras. 33⅓ sound recording. Heri-
tage Records. CH501.
Hajdu, André, and Yacov Mazor. *Hassidic Tunes of Dancing and Rejoicing.*
Folkways Records. LPFE 4209, 1976.
Halberstam, Solomon, David Werdyger and Velvel Pasternak. *Cantor David
Werdyger Sings New Bobover Nigunim Composed by the Bobover Rebbe
(Rabbi Solomon Halberstam) Shlita.* Accompanied by The Epstein Brothers
Orchestra and The Bobover Chassidic Choir. 33⅓ sound recording. Aderet
Records. LPW 303, n.d.
Kapelye. *Future & Past.* 33⅓ sound recording. Flying Fish Records. FF 249,
1981.
Kapelye. *Jakie Jazz 'Em Up: Old-Time Klezmer Music, 1912–1926.* 33⅓ sound
recording. Global Village Music. GVM 101, 1984.
Katz, Mickey. *Mickey Katz Plays Music for Weddings, Bar Mitzvahs and Brisses.*
Capitol. T-1021, 1958.

Klezmatics. *Possession.* CD sound recording. Green Linnet Records/Xenophile. XENO 4050, 1997.

Klezmorim, The. *East Side Wedding.* 33⅓ sound recording. Arhoolie Records. 3006, 1977.

Klezmorim, The. *Jazz-Babies of the Ukraine.* 33⅓ sound recording. Flying Fish Records. FF 465, 1987.

Klezmorim, The. *Metropolis.* Flying Fish Records. Sound cassette, FF 90258; 33⅓ sound recording, FF 258. 1981.

Klezmorim, The. *Streets of Gold.* 33⅓ sound recording. Arhoolie Records. 3011, 1978.

Klezmorim, The. *The Klezmorim: First Recordings, 1976–78.* CD sound recording. Arhoolie Records. CD 309, 1989 (re-release).

Levitt, Marty. *Wedding Dances.* 33⅓ sound recording. Tikva Records. T94, [1960s].

Margolin, Adele, et al. *Pages of History.* 33⅓ sound recording. Heritage Records. L.P.DC 477, n.d.

NAMA [Orchestra]. *Best of NAMA.* CD sound recording. NAMA. NAMA 5 CD, 1999.

NAMA Orchestra, and Pearl Rottenberg. *Mazltov!: Yiddish Folk Songs.* 33⅓ sound recording. NAMA. NAMA 3, 1978.

Orchestra "Plaiurile Bistritei" din Bacau. *Jocuri din Moldova.* Electrechord. EPC 10.018, n.d.

Sapoznik, Henry, comp. *Klezmer Pioneers: European and American Recordings, 1905–1952.* CD sound recording. Rounder CD 1089, 1993.

Schwartz, Martin. *Yikhes: Klezmer Recordings from 1907–1939, from the collection of Professor Martin Schwartz.* Trikont LC 4270, 1991.

Schwartz, Martin, ed. *Klezmer Music: Early Yiddish Instrumental Music, The First Recordings: 1908–1927.* CD sound recording. Arhoolie Folklyric CD 7034, 1997.

Sherman, Allan. *Allan Sherman's Mother Presents My Son, the Folk Singer.* 33⅓ sound recording. Warner Bros. WS 1475, 1962.

Andy Statman Quartet. *Between Heaven & Earth: Music of the Jewish Mystics.* CD sound recording. Shanachie Records. 64079, 1997.

Tarras, Dave. *Dave Tarras: Yiddish-American Klezmer Music, 1925–1956.* Yazoo Records. Yazoo 7001, 1991.

Tepel, Rudy. *Chassidic Wedding: Rudy Tepel and His Orchestra Play Dance Melodies of Vizhnitz, Lubavich, Modzitz, Satmar, Skulen, Mea Shearim.* 33⅓ sound recording. Collectors Guild. CGL-623, 1962.

Contributors

Michael Alpert is a founding member of Brave Old World and a researcher of eastern European and Jewish music and dance.

Walter Zev Feldman is the author of works on the literatures of the Middle East and Central Asia and a pioneering scholar and performer in the klezmer "revival" movement.

Marion Jacobson is a doctoral student in musicology at New York University and is completing a dissertation on Yiddish folk choruses.

Barbara Kirshenblatt-Gimblett is professor of performance studies at New York University and the author of numerous works on eastern European Jewish culture.

James Loeffler is a doctoral candidate in Jewish history at Columbia University. He has been a research associate at the Jewish Music Research Centre in Jerusalem.

Frank London is a founding member of The Klezmatics and of Hasidic New Wave and has produced an extensive body of work in live and recorded music and film music in the United States and Europe.

Hankus Netsky is an instructor in jazz and improvisation at the New England Conservatory and is the founder and director of the Klezmer Conservatory Band.

Robert A. Rothstein is professor of Slavic and Judaic studies and of comparative literature at the University of Massachusetts, Amherst, and the author of works on the linguistics, folklore, and popular culture of eastern Europe.

Henry Sapoznik is the head of Living Traditions, which sponsors KlezKamp, which he founded, has authored two books on klezmer, and was a charter member of Kapelye, a pioneering "revival" band.

Mark Slobin is professor of music at Wesleyan University and the author and editor of books on the musics of Central Asia and the eastern European Jews in Europe and the United States.

Alicia Svigals is a founding member of the Klezmatics and of Mikveh, and composes and collaborates in many music and theater projects in the United States and Europe.

Index

Designer:	Ina Clausen
Compositor:	G&S Typesetters, Inc.
Text:	10/13 Sabon
Display:	Sabon
Printer and binder:	Thomson-Shore, Inc.
Indexer:	Andrew Joron